CRITICAL SOCIAL WORK

CRITICAL SOCIAL WORK
AN INTRODUCTION TO THEORIES AND PRACTICES

edited by

JUNE ALLAN, BOB PEASE AND
LINDA BRISKMAN

ALLEN&UNWIN

First published in 2003

Allen & Unwin
83 Alexander Street
Crows Nest NSW 2065 Australia
Phone: (61 2) 8425 0100
Fax: (61 2) 9906 2218
Email: info@allenandunwin.com
Web: www.allenandunwin.com

National Library of Australia
Cataloguing-in-Publication entry:

Critical social work: an introduction to theories and
practices.

   Bibliography.
   Includes index.
   ISBN 1 86508 907 9

   I. Social service. I. Briskman, Linda. II. Pease, Bob.
   III. Allan, June.

361

Set in 10.5/13 pt Garamond Book by Midland Typesetters, Maryborough, Victoria
Printed by South Wind Production

10 9 8 7 6 5 4 3 2 1

CONTENTS

CONTRIBUTORS

June Allan is a Senior Lecturer in the School of Social Science and Planning at RMIT University. She has worked in the tertiary education, family services, health and bereavement sectors, and has coordinated the Bachelor of Social Work and Social Work Field Education programs at RMIT University. She holds a PhD from La Trobe University where she undertook a study of parenting and parenting education from a critical theory perspective, and has a Graduate Certificate in Bereavement Counselling Practice. Her teaching interests include social work practice, loss and grief, and trans-cultural issues. She is currently undertaking research into the provision of counselling services in rural and remote areas, and cultural understandings of grief responses.

Jacques Boulet has spent the largest part of his professional life as a social work educator, development worker and activist across five continents. He has taught and practised in the areas of community development, participatory and action research, intercultural and anti-racist work and international social development. Jacques was formerly an Associate Professor of Social Work at RMIT University and is currently involved in Borderlands Cooperative, a community-based research, consulting and activist organisation. He continues to participate in social work teaching, supervision of postgraduate work and other social work related activities.

Linda Briskman holds a PhD from Monash University, and is Associate Professor of Social Work in the School of Social Science and Planning at RMIT University where she teaches advocacy, research and community development. She has worked as a practitioner in public welfare in rural Victoria, in the fields of child and family welfare and youth and adult corrections. Linda is the co-editor of *Challenging Rural Practice* (Deakin University Press 1999) and has published widely on Indigenous issues, rural policy and practice and social work ethics. She is author of *The Black Grapevine: Aboriginal activism and the stolen generation* (The Federation Press, 2003).

Susie Costello has practised social work for over twenty years, working in diverse fields including child protection, family and women's services, adolescent psychiatry and local government. For the past ten years, Susie has convened and taught the Advanced Family Casework course for social work practitioners and provided training for workers in the field on responses to domestic violence, family therapy and family-sensitive practice. She is currently a lecturer in social work at RMIT University, teaching in Social Work Theory and Practice, Family and Women's Services, Communication Skills and Human Services Planning. She has a Masters in Social Policy, is a member of the management collective of the Domestic Violence and Incest Resource Centre and maintains a small private practice.

Gary Hough is Associate Professor of Public Management in the School of Social Science and Planning at RMIT University. He worked as a practitioner and manager in public welfare for ten years before moving to tertiary teaching. Gary has coordinated the Masters Program in Community Services Management at RMIT and was President of the Australian Association for Social Work Education and Welfare Education during 1993 and 1994. His recently completed PhD was a study of the organisational construction of child protection practice.

Jennifer Martin is a Senior Lecturer in Social Work at RMIT University. She has direct practice experience in hospital, community and psychiatric services and maintains an active research interest in mental health policy and practice, particularly around issues of consumer participation and involvement in planning and delivery of mental health services. Jennifer is author of *Mental Health Needs of Women Prisoners*, published by Forensicare in 1999, and a series of Occasional Papers published by the Ecumenical Migration Centre in 1999 on the mental health needs of Chinese communities. She teaches mental health, conflict resolution and social work theory and practice.

Bob Pease holds a PhD from La Trobe University and is an Associate Professor of Social Work at RMIT University where he teaches courses on Critical Social Work, Self and Society, and Men and Masculinities. He has worked in social work education in Tasmania and Victoria since 1980. Bob has been involved in profeminist masculinity politics for many years and is a founding member of Men Against Sexual Assault. He is author of *Men and Sexual Politics: Towards a Profeminist Practice* (Dulwich 1997), *Recreating Men: Postmodern Masculinity Politics* (Sage 2000) and *Men and Gender Relations* (Tertiary Press 2002), and is co-editor of *Transforming Social Work Practice* (Allen & Unwin 1999), *Working with Men in the Human Services* (Allen & Unwin 2001) and *A Man's World? Changing Men's Practices in a Globalized World* (Zed Books 2001).

Marjorie Quinn is a Senior Lecturer in Social Work at RMIT University, at present on leave and working in Zambia for an indigenous non-government organisation through the partnership of TEAR Australia and Australian Volunteers International. She has extensive experience in family and community work in the north-west of Melbourne. Her teaching and research interests are in critical approaches to family, group and community work, cross-cultural practice and international development. Marjorie is co-editor of the third edition of *Issues Facing Australian Families* (Pearson Education 2000).

Wendy Weeks became involved in the women's movement in Canada, where she lived and worked during the 1970s. Her involvement with women's services and organisations has continued since her return to Australia in 1982. Wendy was previously Head of Social Work at RMIT University and is presently an Associate Professor of Social Work at the University of Melbourne. She has written many articles and research reports on women's services, women's issues and social policy. She is author of *Women Working Together: Lessons From Feminist Women's Services* (Longman 1994), co-author of *Making Social Policy in Australia* (Allen & Unwin 1996) and co-editor of *Issues Facing Australian Families: Human Services Respond* (Addison Wesley 1991, Longman 1995, Pearson Education 2000).

PREFACE

This book arises out of historical and contemporary efforts by staff at RMIT University to develop a critical curriculum in social work education. The origins of these efforts date back to the early 1980s when the then School of Social Work at Phillip Institute of Technology (now RMIT) adopted structural (Moreau 1979), developmental (Benn 1981) and feminist approaches to social work practice.[1] Almost twenty years later, the Social Work Program at RMIT University is still committed to the development of critical approaches to social work

Lecomte (1990: 34) argues that 'the first characteristic of a progressive curriculum is its explicit philosophical orientation in the analysis of social and personal problems'. The educational philosophy of the Social Work Program at RMIT has undergone various revisions over the years. However, the core value commitments remain. The social work staff at RMIT have long held as a basic premise that a central goal of social work practice in the human services industry is social change to redress social inequalities and injustice. The philosophy of the program affirms that both social-structural and personal change can be complementary strategies towards a more equitable and just society. Social workers are considered to have a particular responsibility to work with those groups who are marginalised and discriminated against, to expand their power and resources. They also have a responsibility to contribute to the transformation of the human services to facilitate increased control by disadvantaged groups over their life and work experiences.

The production of this book has involved a level of collaboration and cooperation that runs counter to the more individually based competitive traditions of most academic scholarship. We have tried to mirror some of the collective processes we advocate in our teaching as we grappled with difficult concepts and the implications of these concepts for the book. As Lecomte (1990: 47) comments: 'The development of a [critical social work] program is an ongoing process and it is still a struggle fuelled with conflict, anxieties and ambiguities. It is not a search for a particular true way.' We certainly found that to be so. Thus, we present the book as offering a diversity of constructive ways to understand the possibilities and limitations of critical theories and practices in social work.

We acknowledge that there are many social work educators in Australia and elsewhere who have struggled with the same tensions and contradictions that we have. We hope that this book will resonate with them. The book is also intended to provide an introduction to critical social work for practitioners in the human services who are interested in new theoretical developments to inform their practice.

1

INTRODUCING CRITICAL THEORIES IN SOCIAL WORK

Bob Pease, June Allan and Linda Briskman

When we were in the process of writing this book and discussing the project with academic colleagues and practitioners, we were sometimes asked: Is there still a need to articulate a 'critical' social work? Is not all social work 'critical' in the sense of being committed to social as well as individual transformation? Some contemporary social work writers believe this to be so. Ife (1997: 178), for example, argues that 'social work is, by its very nature, radical' and he stresses the importance of bringing radical social work in from the margins of the profession. He argues that the task is to 'conceptualise social work in such a way that its inherent radicalism is recognised and incorporated into "mainstream" understandings of social work practice' (Ife 1997: 178). More recently, Alston and McKinnon (2001) have argued similarly that professional social work is concerned with human rights, social justice and support for marginalised people. We believe, however, that the notion of social work as a 'radical profession' is as elusive now as it was when Rein (1970) wrote about this possibility over 30 years ago.

We argue (for reasons that will become clear throughout this book) that it is still important to name and promote critical perspectives in social work. Most of these perspectives are informed by some form of critical theory, including Ife's (1997) 'critical practice', Mullaly's (1997) 'structural social work', Thompson's (1997) 'anti-discriminatory' practice and Pease and Fook's (1999) 'postmodern critical perspectives'. Feminist, anti-racist and postcolonial perspectives in social work are also informed by revised versions of critical theory. Thus, it is important to set the scene by examining some of the key debates within critical theory and by exploring some of the criticisms that have been levelled at it.

CRITICAL THEORY AS A FOUNDATION FOR CRITICAL SOCIAL WORK PRACTICE

It should be stated at the outset that the term 'critical theory' does not designate a unified theoretical perspective. It is a term that embraces a variety of different theoretical positions (Alway 1995; Cheek et al. 1996). On a narrow level, it is a school of Western Marxism known as 'the Frankfurt School', encompassing the writings of Herbert Marcuse, Jurgen Habermas, Theodor Adorno, Erich Fromm and Max Horkheimer. These writers attempted to integrate elements of Marxism with an understanding of subjectivity. At a broader level, critical theory has involved a variety of analyses that have endeavoured to link the concern with subjectivity, with the structural focus on the social and political context of people's lives (Thompson 2000). From the point of view of critical theorists, contemporary Marxists neglected the impact of dominant ideologies upon people's consciousness. Unlike structuralist Marxists, who spoke about the inevitability of the structural contradictions of capitalism in bringing about transformation, critical theorists stressed the importance of people's agency, that is, their capacity to be actively involved in the process of social change (Alway 1995).

Most critical theorists are concerned with emancipatory education that enables people to see the links between their experiences and the material conditions and dominant ideologies in society. In this regard Fay (1987) emphasises the capacity of critical theories to explain the sources of oppression in society in such a way as to encourage those affected by oppression to take action to transform it. In the words of Alvesson and Willmott (1996: 13): 'The intent of critical theory is to challenge the legitimacy and counter the development of oppressive institutions and practices.' Critical theory thus places a significant emphasis on reflecting upon how dominant ideologies or ways of thinking, as well as societal institutions, impact on people's lives. Critical theory also questions the place of existing institutions, such as the family, educational establishments and governance, with a view to constructing a more just society.

Critical theory has not been without its critics. Some have argued that critical theory in general, and the Frankfurt School in particular, failed in their attempts to link individual and social consciousness with institutional analysis and political economy (Held 1980). Others suggest that critical theory 'exaggerates the importance of consciousness in the processes of radical social change' (Alvesson and Willmott 1996: 86). Feminist writers also note that critical theory has not adequately engaged with feminist theory and subsequently has been unable to appreciate the significance of gender analysis (Alvesson and Willmott 1996; Cheek et al. 1996).[1] Further, Alway (1995: 73) argues that rather than imposing a particular claim or interpretation, emancipatory politics should be 'expanding the opportunity for groups to determine and live according to their own claims and interpretations'. This development is consistent with some forms of postmodern thinking.

A number of writers have commented that postmodernism shares many of the concerns of critical theory (Cheek et al. 1996). Just as the origins of critical theory came out of a project to reappraise and re-construct Marxist theory in light of changed historical conditions, so critical theory itself may now need to be reappraised for the same reasons. The vision of emancipatory politics in critical theory has thus been rethought by many critical theorists in light of postmodernism (Yeatman 1994; Nicholson and Seidman 1995).

POSTMODERNISM AND ITS INFLUENCE ON CRITICAL THEORY

Just as modernity implies a departure from earlier ways of thinking about the world that incorporated superstition, paganism and traditional forms of authority associated with religion and feudalism, postmodernity has now emerged as a break from modernity. Modernity may be seen as 'the cluster of social, economic and political systems which emerged in the West with the Enlightenment in the late eighteenth century' (Parton and O'Byrne 2000a: 19). The notion of modernity is usually associated with the Enlightenment Project, which has sought to replace fear and superstition with consent and truth, and the establishment of a social order based on reason and natural law (Macey 2000).

Distinguishing features of the age of modernity are the understanding of history as having a definite and progressive direction; the idea that reason can provide a basis for all activities; the attempt to develop universal categories of experience; and the creation of order, boundaries, classifications and certainties through formal reason, laws, typologies, uniformity and universality. Importance is given to the objectivity of knowledge, the universality of values and the progress of science and society, and truth is centred in human reason (Seidman 1994; Parton and O'Byrne 2000a). Modernity's 'grand narrative' (the form of knowledge seen as legitimate) is the emancipation of all people and production of a universal knowledge that speaks for all. Objectivity and politico-economic rationality are the central elements underpinning modernity (Macey 2000; Parton and O'Byrne 2000a).

This fundamental belief in the value of scientific knowledge in the human sciences as a means of public enlightenment and social progress of modernity has been debated and challenged by thinkers as diverse as Jurgen Habermas and Michel Foucault. Scepticism has emerged of the Enlightenment's promise that humanity will be or can be emancipated by rational knowledge. Such scepticism is 'one of the hallmarks of the age of postmodernity' (Macey 2000: 111).

Difficulties surround the meaning and status of postmodernism, a term often used to connote the social transformation of contemporary times, because of its many forms and interpretations. The term will be used here to refer to a cultural phenomenon in contemporary society, characterised by fragmentation brought about by an explosion of information and new technologies, consumer capitalism with its pro-liferation of products and images, political shifts and upheavals, and new experiences of space and time (Best and Kellner 1991; Bordo 1993). Key elements of this social transformation include the increasing pace of change; the growing significance of difference; plurality and the growth of various new political movements and strategies; growing awareness of relativities, the opening up of individual 'choice' and 'freedom'; and the increasing awareness of the socially constructed nature of reality (Parton and O'Byrne 2000a). This last factor concerns a recognition that society 'is a symbolic construct composed of ideas, meanings and language which is all the time changing through human action [choice and creativity] and imposing constraints and possibilities on human actors themselves' (Parton and O'Byrne 2000a: 16).

What are the implications of these postmodern changes, and the associated debates, for our ways of experiencing and making sense of the world, and for critical social work? Three aspects in particular have brought about a significant reorientation of thought in the wake of postmodernism. These are an emphasis on difference and diversity; attention to language and discourse; and a rethinking of the notions of power and knowledge. Each will now be considered.

The development of identity politics, increasingly important from the 1970s onwards, contributed to questioning the universalist values of the Enlightenment and modernity. Identity politics is based upon the idea that all members of the same oppressed group share a common identity defined by criteria of ethnicity, religion, gender or sexual orientation. Development of these new social movements created new subjects of knowledge (for example, blacks, gays, women, lesbians) and new knowledges, previously ignored, contesting the social scientific paradigm of modernity (Seidman 1994). 'Identity politics usually takes the form of a demand for the right to be different, and for that difference to be recognised as legitimate' (Macey 2000: 196).

The challenge to objective universal knowledge and certainty opens the door to knowledges that are partial and viewed from multiple social and political perspectives along the axes of class, race, nationality, sexuality, gender and body-abledness (Seidman 1994). Such emphasis on difference and diversity has led to a constant and growing questioning of modern approaches, which are not seen as necessarily humanitarian or emancipatory because of their failure to recognise difference. Claiming that 'the views, experiences and interests of white, middle-class, able-bodied males have invariably been embedded in ideas, theories and approaches but presented as if they were universal, objective and neutral', Parton and O'Byrne (2000a: 21) point out that the nature and implications of relying on totalising belief systems such as capitalism, patriarchy, ablism or colonialism have been overlooked.

A growing awareness of lack of sameness between individuals within collectivities has led to further recognition of the significance of difference. This has been illustrated, for example, through the recognition of the diversity of experiences among women, in particular because of their social class and ethnicity (Parton and O'Byrne 2000a). Black feminists such as Carby (1982), hooks (1984) and Bhavnani and Coulson (1986), for instance, have challenged the perspectives of white Western women such as Barrett and McIntosh (1982) who saw the family as the key to women's oppression. These black feminists have argued that the family is to some extent a force of solidarity for black women, arguments which have also been raised in Australia about traditional forms of Aboriginal society compared with postcolonial Australian forms (Pettman 1992).

Also questioned in the 'postmodern' is the core assumption that there is a close association between the way something is represented through symbols—usually language—and its underlying reality. Meaning is related by complex systems of representation, the symbols having a life of their own and taking on meaning on the basis of the context in which they are being used rather than on the basis of what reality they are meant to represent. As Parton and O'Byrne (2000a: 55) claim, 'the meaning of a word is greatly, if not totally, determined by the *use* we make of it'.

Thus an understanding of language and discourse is of fundamental importance to postmodern approaches. The notion of 'discourse' has particular significance in postmodernity. Drawing on the work of Benveniste (1966), Macey defines discourse in the broadest sense as any utterance involving a speaker and a hearer, and an intention on the part of the speaker to influence the hearer. Language is the 'instrument of communication, with discourse as its form of expression' (Macey 2000: 100). Discourse is viewed as an intersubjective phenomenon, playing a role in producing symbolic systems that shape our existence (Macey 2000). How we talk about concepts such as 'family', 'sexuality' or 'poverty', for example, shapes the meaning these concepts come to hold in a given culture, and the dominant stories that people develop about their lives. As reality is embedded in interpretation, 'truth' is a product of language rather than reality—'reality' emerges from the language of people. According to this postmodern perspective, understanding the role of language in the formation of individual thought and subjectivity is crucial (Parton and O'Byrne 2000a). Because of its suspicion of all claims to knowledge and truth, a postmodern culture assumes that all discourses are involved in the making of ourselves and our societies. Because they contain values and social interests, these discourses are always contestable (Seidman 1994).

Through the influence of the French poststructuralists, especially Foucault, and the feminist and other social movements stemming from social conflict around issues of race, gender and sexuality, there is a rethinking in postmodern thought on the workings of power. Foucault, for example, in discussing the notions of power and social control, sees power as woven into the texture of everyday life and embedded in technologies of control. These technologies of control include incarceration, rehabilitation and surveillance in institutions such as prisons, factories, schools and hospitals, and 'expert' medical–scientific discourses maintained by judges, psychiatrists, social workers, prison officers and others (Foucault 1967, 1969, 1977, 1979, 1980). As Seidman (1994) states, in his discussion of Foucault's ideas, dominant discourses that define the social world as natural and normal conceal particular social interests and power relations.

For Foucault, social conflict and resistance cannot be centralised, for power does not just comprise the state and its structures but involves more subtle 'multiple and mobile power relations' (Foucault 1978: 98), employed on all levels and in many forms. This power is located within the everyday and the local. In understanding power and how it penetrates and controls, Foucault emphasises the need to analyse the most immediate power relations at a particular historical time and place, as well as how power relations make possible the discourses taking place and, in turn, how the discourses are used to support the power relations (1978).

From this perspective, resistance and oppositional practices thus need to be local, diverse, and specific to the field of concern, whether it be schools, prisons or sexuality. Foucault regards power as a productive force rather than one only of repression or domination, arguing that power does not

> only weigh on us as a force that says no, but that it traverses and produces things, it induces pleasure, forms, knowledge, produces discourse. It needs to be seen as a productive network which runs through the whole social body, much more than as a negative instance whose function is repression (Foucault, in Gordon 1980: 119).

Hence postmodernism emphasises attention to difference rather than sameness, and awareness of the importance of language and the part played by discourses in the construction of social reality. It also recognises that power is operating in many ways, creating opportunities for the individual to resist and to be other than a victim of 'an oppressive and monolithic social order' (Leonard 1984: 5). Rather than modernity's vision of a society free of domination and control, the focus in postmodernity is on expanding possibilities for developing just and democratic ways of life that allow for choice, individuality and tolerance (Seidman 1994). Such factors have had a significant influence on the theorising of critical social work practice, as will be seen in later chapters of this book.

However, postmodernism has come under considerable criticism from radical critics. As Seidman asks, if there is no objective or universal standpoint from which to generate explanations because of multiple and specific social interests and values, 'how are knowledge and social criticism possible?' (1994: 277). Many have argued that postmodernism represents 'either a threat to or a flight from the real world of politics and struggle' (Giroux 1990: 11). Hancock and Taylor (2001: 74) say that 'the postmodern fascination with the realm of micro social relations and localised politics . . . is unable to envision the larger structural forces that underpin relations of organisational power and control'. Similarly, Taylor-Gooby (1993) argues that the emphasis on difference and diversity ignores the actual existence of some universally valid themes. There is thus a concern among many critical theorists that postmodern perspectives can obscure the material reality of oppression in which people have unequal access to resources (Healy 2000).

Certainly, some applications of postmodernism to social work ignore the broader structures that generate oppression (see, for example, Parton and O'Byrne 2000a), similar to the (modernist) clinical social work practice of the 1960s. It does seem that some forms of postmodernism are incompatible with social justice. Here we argue against any postmodern principles that would undermine the process of social change. However, we reject the view by some writers that postmodernism *per se* is incompatible with human rights and social justice. O'Brien and Penna (1998a: 57) argue that 'it is disingenuous to suggest that postmodernism delegitimises political struggles and sweeps away the possibility of radical action to counter oppression, exploitation and domination'. Along with Fraser and Nicholson (1990), we argue that some forms of postmodern theory can retain large historical narratives and an analysis of societal structures such as sexism, racism and class domination.

Postmodern theory encompasses contradictory radical, apolitical and conservative perspectives. Giroux (1990), for example, differentiates between 'progressive' and 'reactionary' orientations, while Rosenau (1992) distinguishes between 'affirmative' and 'sceptical' postmodernisms. Whereas sceptical postmodernists offer a pessimistic view of contemporary times characterised by fragmentation, meaninglessness and unsurpassable uncertainty, leaving no place for commitment to social, political or practical projects, affirmative postmodernists offer a more optimistic view in which, because of their positive orientation towards the importance of process, there is a place for practical actions and for building practical and political coalitions and collaboration (Parton and O'Byrne 2000a).

Many critics of postmodernism fail to acknowledge this diversity of perspectives. The editors of this book and many of the contributors would argue that we should not reject all forms of postmodernism. However, even those who are interested in the intersection between critical theory and progressive postmodern thinking disagree on the implications for critical practice in social work. Pease and Fook (1999), for example, brought together fifteen social work academics from across Australia who were struggling with these linkages. While the editors advanced a 'postmodern critical' perspective on practice, the contributors emphasised quite different theoretical trends in their explorations. This relationship between postmodernism and critical theory continues to be explored.

Many critical social work theorists argue that we need to draw upon both modernist and postmodern appropriations of critical theory (for example, Ife 1997; Mullaly 1997; Pease and Fook 1999; Fook 2000b; Healy 2000). However, the tensions and contradictions in adopting this dual perspective are often evident when the implications for practice are explored. We do not want to suggest that we have 'the answers' in this book. We do not consider that any one version of critical theory has a monopoly on the truth. There is more than one critical stance within social work, and we agree with Pozzuto (2000), who argues that each of these perspectives has something important to offer the project of critical social work. Along with O'Brien and Penna (1998a: 53) we reject the view that 'one true theory will overturn the system of false ideas and lead to the elimination of exploitation, oppression, and domination'. If, as Pozzuto (2000) suggests, no singular answer to what is critical social work is necessary or even possible, it may be more appropriate to follow Hekman's (1999: 22) exhortation to develop 'an epistemology of truths rather that the Truth'. This will enable us to avoid both a new form of universalism and 'an "anything goes" relativism'. Leonard (1997) refers to these multiple critical views as 'radical pluralism'. Such perspectives would draw upon Marxism, critical theory—modernist and postmodern—feminism, postcolonialism and anti-racism among others. We encourage linkages between these perspectives without attempting to develop an integrative theoretical framework.

We also need not assume that postmodernity necessarily marks a complete break from modernity. For example, Zygmunt Bauman, who became Professor of Sociology at the University of Leeds and has developed a postmodern sociology shaped by French post-structuralism and the Frankfurt School of critical theory, views postmodernity as the development of aspects of modernity such as the values of choice, diversity, criticalness, reflexivity and agency (Seidman 1994). The stance of the editors of this book is that postmodernity has not (yet) superseded modernity. Despite cultural and technological developments that emphasise heterogeneity, fragmentation and difference, many basic institutions and structures of society concerning gender, class, race and sexual orientation, for example, appear not to have changed dramatically, continuing to be strongly normalising factors within our culture. Hence we take the view that heterogeneity of experience, the local and the particular, as well as ongoing structures, are necessary considerations in theories and practices for critical social work.

As we are opposed to the very idea of a single model of critical social work, we encourage the reading of this book alongside other recent attempts to construct a critical social work practice (Ife 1997; Leonard 1997; Mullaly 1997; Thompson 1998; Pease and Fook 1999; Healy 2000). We encourage readers to extend their understanding of the contribution that each has to make to the development of critical practices in social work. Perhaps, as Leonard (1997: 143) says, 'if our own political beliefs and commitments are to be seen not as absolute Truth but as insurgent critical discourses, bearing the indelible traces of their historical and cultural origins, then we may be more open to communication with political others'. We offer this book as a contribution to that necessary dialogue.

OVERVIEW OF THE BOOK

The book is divided into three parts. Part I provides an introduction to historical and contemporary debates about critical social work theories and practices. Part II surveys the implications of critical theories for developing critical practices in relation to different sites of domination and oppression. Part III outlines the challenges facing critical social work in the future.

Part I begins with a chapter by Jennifer Martin tracing the origins of the critical tradition in social work in the United Kingdom, North America and Australia. She explores the implications of the radical critique of social work in the 1970s and the early attempts to develop a radical practice informed by Marxism and critical theory. Structural social work in Canada, the developmental model in Australia, the feminist critique of social work and anti-discriminatory practice models in the United Kingdom are examined as forerunners to more contemporary frameworks of practice informed by postmodern critical theories.

In Chapter 2 June Allan reviews contemporary structural and postmodern theoretical approaches to critical social work practice. While she notes that both approaches seek the transformation of social structures and institutions, she illustrates how they place different emphases on the various systems of oppression and underline different ways for achieving change. Structural approaches to practice focus on addressing material issues primarily through politicisation and collec-tivisation of social problems. Postmodern approaches affirm diversity between people, locating them in their historical and cultural contexts, and seek to bring about change by resisting and challenging dominant discourses at local sites. She argues that the approaches chosen by the critical social worker are best determined by the cultural context, the historical moment and the needs of the particular situation.

In Chapter 4, a follow-up to the previous chapter, June Allan considers the implications of structural and postmodern critical social work per-spectives for practice in social work. She discusses practice issues central to these perspectives and emphasises the importance of integrating 'the personal and the political' within the various levels of intervention. The use of socio-political analysis and discourse analysis are fundamental to critical social work practice, as are the relationships between practi-tioners and the people they work with. June discusses the implications of these issues for bringing about changes in people's consciousness and in their material conditions.

In the first chapter in Part II, Marjorie Quinn argues that cultural awareness and cross-cultural capacity have become major requirements in social work practice in contemporary Australia. In her view, critical theory approaches to social work provide the most useful frameworks for working with racial and cultural diversity in policy development and in personal, family and community work. Drawing on practice examples concerning recently arrived immigrants, refugees and asylum seekers, she explores the theme of white privilege in Australia, and ways in which that shapes policy and practice. She emphasises the importance of racial and cultural self-knowledge for workers in engaging with other people's cultural frameworks and in developing anti-racist and cul-turally affirming practice.

Continuing the theme of race and culture, in Chapter 6 Linda Briskman examines the complex relationship between social work and Indigenous peoples in Australia. Drawing specifically on the area of child welfare policy and practice, she explores the role of social work in past practices, and the challenges social workers face in changing their approaches in tackling the racism and white privilege inherent in social work. Linda uses the constructs of citizenship, postcolonial theory and 'whiteness' to interrogate past and present relationships between social work and Indigenous Australians and to suggest ways forward for social work.

In Chapter 7, Wendy Weeks reviews key features of feminist practice, as described by Western feminist social workers. In the absence of systematic research on the practice by social workers identifying as 'feminist', she turns to research on feminist women's services to further explore feminist practice. The research studied a wide range of aspects of the operation of Australian women's services, and she reports in her chapter on their stated philosophies and activities. She concludes by identifying future challenges for women's services and feminist practice.

The chapter by Bob Pease explores the implications of profeminist principles for working with men in the human services. He argues that the implications of profeminism for understanding men's lives are that we must locate men in the context of patriarchy and the divisions of class, race, sexuality and other forms of social inequality, while at the same time exploring the ways in which patriarchal belief systems become embedded in men's psyches. He identifies six main arenas of men's practices where patriarchy is either reproduced or resisted: sexuality; intimacy and emotional expressiveness; health and well-being; family and care of others; paid work; and violence against women. He concludes by outlining the practice implications of a profeminist approach to men in the areas of one's own gender privilege, and in working with men as individuals, in men's groups and in working for structural change at the community and societal levels.

Susie Costello's chapter focuses on working with families from a critical theoretical perspective. She observes that the concept of the traditional family prevails in Australia in spite of the diversity of family forms. She argues that this has oppressive implications for the lived experience of family life. Susie offers a critique of traditional ways of conceptualising families and considers the limitation of conventional social work responses to the family. Raising awareness and challenging the impact of social inequalities resulting from racism, sexism, classism, homophobia and familism, she argues, can contribute to new forms of social accountability. Against this background, she explores ways of working with families that address the need for progressive policies, and for associated practices that empower families and respect cultural diversity and sexual preference.

Jennifer Martin, in Chapter 10, discusses women and mental health from a feminist perspective. Drawing upon feminist theory and anti-oppressive practice, she explores the challenges of working with women in a mental health context. She argues that a shift in practice in mental health is required that moves away from individual pathologising of women's lives to the acceptance and recognition of the social and political factors that impact on individual women's levels of health and well-being.

In the final chapter in this section, June Allan illustrates ways of understanding and responding to loss and grief from critical social work perspectives. She argues that loss and grief are social experiences and that working with people to live constructively with their grief can only be understood through the knowledge that the personal, political and cultural are intimately bound together. June explores contemporary understandings of grief in the context of social, political and cultural influences. Drawing on narrative approaches, discourse analysis and meaning reconstruction, she demonstrates how social workers can assist grieving people in their journey of healing by supporting them to question disabling dominant discourses and to develop communities of support for themselves.

In the first chapter in Part III, Bob Pease examines the social work claim that the relationship between the individual and society is the primary focus for intervention. He argues that it is the ability to conceptualise more adequately the relationship between subjective experience and the societal context of people's lives that distinguishes critical approaches to social work from mainstream professional models. After identifying the limitations of the 'person-in-environment' configuration for critical social work, he explores attempts within the critical tradition to theorise the relationship between self and society, with a particular emphasis on the concepts of oppression and domination, and on agency and resistance in the context of the material and discursive constraints on critical practice.

In Chapter 13, Gary Hough and Linda Briskman examine the changes in public policy in Australia which have privileged economic interests over social goals and entrenched inequality, alienation, social exclusion and violence. They demonstrate how responses to social difference and inequality are severely compromised by cutbacks in community services, increased privatisation, competitive tendering and increased reliance on packaged programs of services. They acknowledge that restructuring of human services within the current ideological and economic climate has made some aspects of critical social work more difficult to practise, but stress the importance of assisting people to make the links between private troubles and public issues.

Gary Hough in Chapter 14 focuses on the contemporary terrain of public welfare and the new boundaries within which a critical social work practice must be enacted. He notes that the policy and organisational context has always been a prime determinant of the parameters of practice in public welfare. Gary argues that while there have been significant discontinuities in the history of public welfare policies, there are continuities too, mostly relating to the actual practice, which have been resistant to the policy and management prescriptions that have sought to re-engineer the public welfare practice systems. In this context, he argues, the practice realm continues to provide points of leverage for a critical practice.

In the final chapter, Jacques Boulet critically examines the relevance of the emerging global and international context within which social work theory, practice and education are enmeshed. After some brief reflections on the violent events in New York and Washington DC on 11 September 2001, he provides an overview of the last 40 years of international solidarity work and its changing context. He analyses what is referred to as the 'Western development syndrome' and outlines six philosophical principles that underpin the development bias in Western thinking, and concludes by reflecting on the relevance of human rights for social work practice in a global but diverse context.

The dilemmas and contradictions arising from our attempts to construct critical practices in social work open up new questions that provide the basis for further theoretical investigations. We have drawn from our own experiences of critical practice in specific sites, but are also mindful that many sites of domination and oppression have been neglected here. Experiences of disability, later life, sexual oppression, homelessness, unemployment and rural poverty, to name just a few, have not been addressed. We hope that this book will provide the impetus for others to address the new questions that arise and relate the emerging frameworks of critical social work practice to other sites where people struggle to resist dominance and overcome oppression.

PART I

Critical social work:
Theories and practices

2

HISTORICAL DEVELOPMENT OF CRITICAL SOCIAL WORK PRACTICE

Jennifer Martin

The aim of this chapter is to trace the origins of critical social work in the United Kingdom, North America and Australia. The chapter begins by providing some snapshots of critical practice in the early years of social work. It then explores the implications of the Marxist critique of social work in the 1970s and the attempts to develop a radical practice informed by Marxism and critical theory. Structural social work in Canada, the developmental model in Australia, the feminist critique of social work and anti-discriminatory practice models in the United Kingdom are examined as forerunners to more contemporary frameworks of practice informed by postmodern critical theories.

THE ORIGINS OF CRITICAL PRACTICE IN SOCIAL WORK

From its beginning there has been a critical orientation in social work. Social work has always struggled with a tension between its focus on the individual and its concern about socio-economic and political forces in society. Dominelli (1998: 154) refers to this as a struggle between 'the social activists' and 'the individual interventionists'. Mullaly (1997) argues that these two traditions in social work can be traced back to the nineteenth century, where the tension was represented by the settlement houses movement and the Charity Organisation Society (COS). While the COS was concerned with distributing charitable funds and distinguishing between the so-called 'deserving' and 'underserving' poor, those in the settlement movements believed that the poor 'were victims of an unjust social order' (Mullaly 1997: 24).

The settlement house movement had its origins in England in 1884 with Canon Barnett establishing Toynbee Hall in London's East End slums (Wilson 1977). The main principle behind the settlements was that middle- and upper-class men and women would relinquish their economic privileges by living and working in working-class communities. The first settlement house in the United States was founded by Jane Addams in 1889 in Chicago (Brieland 1990). Known as Hull House, it became the most famous settlement in the United States and was considered in its time to be a 'hot bed of radicalism' (Specht and Courtney 1994: 84).

Gil (1998) argues that the residents of the settlements were the 'pioneers' of critical social work, involved as they were in community organising, women's suffrage and trade union struggles. While contemporary critical social workers may not all agree that the settlement movement represented a radical approach to the problems of poverty and slum housing, we can see the beginnings of an attempt to develop a structural analysis of social inequality during this time.

From this time onwards, social work would fluctuate between a focus on individual adjustment and a concern with social justice and social change. This conflict remains an unresolved dilemma today (Haynes 1998). While Gil (1998) notes that throughout history social workers have been involved in practices to challenge unjust and oppressive social institutions, Dominelli (1997) argues that professional social work has been dominated by the focus on individual adjustment. It appears that critical social work has been strongest in periods of economic crisis and social unrest, and that 'when the crisis ends social workers return to psychotherapeutic modes of work' (Dominelli 1997: 163).

It has been well documented how social work embraced Freudian psychology as a theoretical framework for social work practice during the 1920s and 1930s in the United States and in the United Kingdom (Yellowly 1990). Woodroofe (1974) has referred to this period in social work as the 'psychiatric deluge'. From the point of view of many social workers at this time, social work was seen as coming of age 'when its focus shifted from the environment to the psyche of individuals' (Wharf 1990a: 17). Changing oppressive social conditions was not seen as being either as scientific or as professional as therapy.

The dominance of psychiatric social work during this time was not without challenge, however. In the 1930s in the United States a rank-and-file movement in social work unions developed in response to the poverty and despair caused by the Depression (Wagner 1989). One of the main activists of this new movement was Bertha Capen Reynolds, a social worker, teacher, writer, social activist and unionist. Reynolds (1963) believed that social workers should align themselves with clients and workers in order to fight for social justice. She was forced to resign from the Smith College School of Social Work in 1938 because of her social and union activism (Reynolds 1963). Cullen (n.d), writing in the Australian context, regards Reynolds's heritage as an inspiration for contemporary critical social workers. It is interesting to note that in 1985 a new organisation of progressive social workers in the United States was named the Bertha Capen Reynolds Society (BCR Society 1990).

These historical snapshots of course do not do justice to the history of critical social work in the United States and England, and an historical account of developments in Australia has yet to be mapped. Nevertheless, they do challenge the notion that critical social work began during the social unrest of the 1960s and 1970s. Because this latter period marks the beginning of contemporary critical social work, it warrants closer attention.

THE CRISIS IN SOCIAL WORK

Social work in the 1970s was described as going through a period of 'crisis'. The crisis commenced in Britain and North America in the early 1970s, with Australia following the trend in the late 1970s. The beginnings of this crisis arose out of the Marxist critique of the welfare state in North America (Mandell 1975) and the United Kingdom (Gough 1979), and led to a questioning of the role of social work as an apparatus of social control by the state. Social workers themselves were also expressing considerable doubt, disillusionment and cynicism about the work they were doing. Many were disenchanted with the traditional theories of social work and techniques, particularly therapeutic casework.

Prior to the 1970s social work was dominated by therapeutic models of intervention, influenced by psychodynamic theory and systems perspectives. Psychodynamic theories were used to explain and understand individual behaviour, with a focus on personality and interpersonal relationships. The influence of psychodynamic theories has been to emphasise feelings and unconscious processes, as opposed to locating 'personal troubles' within social structures.

From the 1960s, systems theory was used in therapeutic social work to identify patterns of interaction and relationships in families, and transactions between individuals and their social environment. The family was divided into the marital, parental and sibling sub-systems, and the focus was on boundaries and transactional patterns between the three sub-systems. The idea of reciprocity was important in that if change occurs in one sub-system, change is likely to occur in another as a flow-on effect.

These therapeutic and systemic approaches were criticised by radical social work theorists for not including broader social, political and economic structures that acknowledge issues of power and subsequent disadvantage. Critiques of these early writings on psychodynamic theory and systems perspectives were that they were generally from a white middle-class perspective, and couched in language that was disrespectful and disempowering.

In response to the limitations of these approaches, attempts were made by Corrigan and Leonard (1978) to develop a Marxist theory of the welfare state, as well as a Marxist theory of social work. This analysis held that the welfare state was in a condition of 'profound crisis', and that other theories and ideologies had failed to adequately explain the continued poverty, exploitation and deprivation that were evidence of this crisis.

Rapid changes were occurring in the employment practices of social workers in Australia in the late 1970s, following trends in Britain and the United States at that time. The first half of the 1970s in Australia witnessed a period of growth in the number of social work positions under the federal Labor government led by Gough Whitlam (1972 to 1975). Social welfare was a major concern of the Whitlam government, as reflected by the introduction of the Australian Assistance Plan in 1973. This saw increased expansion and expenditure in the welfare sector with local community participation and control. Universal programs of community health, community mental health and universal health insurance were introduced during this period. There was growth in the number of social work positions and career opportunities.

The second half of the 1970s, however, was characterised by economic recession with severe unemployment and cutbacks in welfare expenditure, along with the dismissal of prime minister Whitlam and the termination of the mandate of the Labor government late in 1975.

During the 1970s, social workers were increasingly organised as part of the welfare apparatus of the state rather than on an independent professional basis. Social work roles and practices as a result, were becoming prescribed and circumscribed by bureaucratic and statutory requirements that were frustrating for those social workers interested in social change. The feasibility of psychotherapeutic casework was also challenged within this new bureaucratic environment, as organisations were not providing social workers with sufficient time and resources to use such methods effectively. Social workers were becoming increasingly frustrated in their efforts to integrate theory and practice, in a context of demands for greater productivity. Efforts to bring about significant social change in the conditions of people's lives were also increasingly difficult.

THE EMERGENCE OF RADICAL SOCIAL WORK

An attempted solution to the 'crisis' of social work in the 1970s was the search by some for a radical social work practice. Marxist critics such as Corrigan and Leonard (1978) and Ginsburg (1979) in Britain, Galper (1975) in the United States and Throssell (1975), Pemberton and Locke (1975) in Australia, argued that the crisis was linked with the contemporary crisis in capitalist society at the political, economic and ideological levels. A Marxist analysis highlighted the contradictions inherent in the welfare state and the functions of social work within it, seeing the welfare state as a tool of capitalism to appease the poor, ease the conscience of the wealthy classes and ward off possible rebellion. According to this analysis, the primary function of the welfare state was social control. An understanding of the contradictory nature of the state, and particularly the welfare state, was seen as essential for the development of a radical social work (Pemberton and Locke 1975).

The welfare state, in this view, was an essential tool of capitalism to contain individual and collective pressure for change, especially by rationing services and benefits to those deemed deserving. Galper (1975) criticised it for being geared toward the needs of capital and its labour force rather than the needs of the working class. Capitalism demanded a mobile and autonomous labour supply with relationships based on the selling of individual labour power. One of the costs of capitalism was thus the alienation and privatisation of the individual, with individualism replacing reciprocal social relationships. The privatised individual was necessary for both production and consumption. Increased alienation, separation from others and loneliness increased the importance of compensatory consumption of material goods, a basic requirement of capitalism (Bailey and Brake 1975).

Ginsburg (1979) focused on the 'value of labour' and drew attention to the role of unpaid domestic labour, mostly performed by women, and the provision of state welfare supports to ensure a capitalist labour supply. Bailey and Brake (1975) argued that there was nothing about the welfare state and welfare legislation that was socialist; rather, the welfare state was seen as having developed in direct response to the continuing plight of the working classes while restricting their input into the development of policy and administration.

Social workers engaged, uncomfortably at times, with critical theories in the social sciences. This was particularly evident in the sociology of deviance literature that attacked social work as a form of social control under the guise of humanitarian caring (Goffman 1961; Foucault 1967; Scheff 1968). Writing on mental health, Scheff (1968) and Goffman (1961) were critical of professionals in psychiatric settings for representing forms of exploitation as forms of benevolence. Scheff (1968) criticised the professional–client relationship and the perceived superior status assumed by the social worker in knowledge, attitude and influence. According to this view, the social worker was defining 'pathology' against norms of 'health' derived from white middle-class values. He argued that the emphasis on the professional relationship, stressing neutrality and emotional distance, had disastrous effects at both the personal and political level. At the personal level, social workers were seen as aloof and uncaring. At the political level, neutrality could imply that the social worker was aligned with the dominant social institutions and forces of oppression. The pathologising and fragmenting of people's lives thus served the interests of capitalist society and was counterproductive to notions of a collective class experience or response.

Social workers were seen as double agents, legitimating and ameliorating the existing social order. Galper (1975) asserted that, while claiming to be working on behalf of the client, social workers in reality were exercising socio-political control by reinforcing and interpreting political, social and moral rules to bolster the existing social order. He claimed that traditional social work concepts did not adequately account for the social, economic and political constraints and conflicts of everyday practice. Social work theories and practices, it was held, individualised what were seen to be essentially societal troubles. Critics argued that the individual casework focus of social work functioned as a direct form of social control of its 'clients'. Indirectly, the activities of social workers were seen to reinforce an ideology that concealed the true nature of inequality within a capitalist society (Bailey and Brake 1975; Galper 1975; Clarke 1979).

Pemberton and Locke (1975) argued that social workers were politically naïve and preoccupied with the frustrations and stressors of micro-level casework activity, unable therefore to see the broader parameters and collective experiences of people's lives. Applying Marx's concept of 'demystification', Pemberton and Locke (1975) argued that social workers must acknowledge their contribution to reinforcing inequality and the status quo before 'enlightenment' could occur.

Throssell (1975) was critical of the dichotomy between the situation of the poor and those deemed to be helping them, with social workers having gained increases in status, income and influence. He condemned social workers for 'the official dedication to overcoming human misery, and yet the failure to do much more than achieve professional advancement' (Throssell 1975: 17). Pemberton and Locke (1975: 33) were also critical of what they referred to as the paradox of social work and its alienation from the practice context due to the emphasis on professionalism. Radical social workers argued that professional interests had become paramount, superseding the welfare of the people social workers were supposed to serve (Laursen 1975; Pemberton and Locke 1975; Throssell 1975; Corrigan and Leonard 1978).

RECONCEPTUALISING SOCIAL WORK IN THE 1970s

The reconceptualisation of social work advocated by radical social workers in the 1970s focused on changes in social values and a redistribution of wealth. The importance of nurturing and fostering the 'community', and sharing supports and resources, was central to this approach. Society needed to change to meet the human needs of its members with fewer social welfare services, and people caring for each other in more natural and communal ways. This would involve a sharing of monetary resources as well as knowledge and information. Radical changes were required, as it could not be assumed that the minority who controlled wealth and power were likely to relinquish these voluntarily. This was particularly the case for large multinational companies outside the control of elected governments and yet wielding considerable influence over their political decisions. A radical social work could only be built on collective action with strong links between Marxist theory, day-to-day practices of social workers and politics. Because it was necessary for the working class to become conscious of its experience as a class to overcome its exploitation, it was essential for both social workers and welfare clients to engage together in this collective practice (Bailey and Brake 1975; Galper 1975; Pemberton and Locke 1975; Throssell 1975; Corrigan and Leonard 1978).

Social workers were thus called upon to have a far greater social and political awareness. At the same time, they were considered well positioned for involvement in political processes that encouraged and supported movements of people endeavouring to improve their own lives (Pemberton and Locke 1975; Throssell 1975; Corrigan and Leonard 1978). However, while more social workers were presenting themselves as radical, they were still in the minority.

Statham (1978), however, argued that the term 'radical social work' was a contradiction because of the location of social work activity in state institutions within a capitalist society. She maintained that the main base for radicals seeking an alternative society must be in movements operating outside social work rather than from within. Clarke (1979) asserted that radical social work failed to integrate theory and practice, describing the theory itself as 'academic, sterile criticism' focused on abstract structures and functions without sufficient emphasis on the processes, struggles and contradictions inherent in the everyday practice of social work. He warned against the danger of 'making the assumption that the creation of radical social work is necessarily the only, or final solution to the problem' (Clarke 1979: 138). Structural social work was a beginning attempt to address these contextual issues.

THE STRUCTURAL APPROACH TO SOCIAL WORK

The structural approach to social work practice was developed in the late 1970s and early 1980s by Maurice Moreau in the School of Social Work at Carleton University in Canada. Moreau (1979) asserted that traditional approaches to social work were based upon a medical and disease model that tended to place people in a dependent or passive position, with the focus of attention on the individual rather than their situation. Structural social work was an attempt to move away from dichotomising the person and situation by focusing on interactions between people and specific social, economic and political circumstances. Power, both personal and political, was a main feature of structural social work. Of central concern to structural social workers were the ways in which the rich and powerful within society constrain and define the less powerful. A major focus was concern for people in poverty who were obvious victims of economic inequality. The concern extended to other groups who, although not experiencing economic hardship, also suffered due to ideologies that supported, legitimated or maintained the existing social order. This included the ways in which men define women, hetero-sexuals define homosexuals, white people define black and Indigenous people, so-called normal people define deviants, adults define children and the young define the aged (Moreau 1979).

The central goal of structural social work was to help people develop a social praxis. In other words, the aim was to assist the person to critically reflect on the personal, social, economic and political situation they were in by looking at who benefits and who suffers because of the labelling of behaviours, values, ideas or feelings as undesirable. The key task of a structural approach was analysis of how the dominant institutions define and interpret specific situations. For example, counselling women involves examining the relationship between what are presented as personal problems, and a capitalist social structure that perpetuates the sexist, ideological and economic oppression of women (Moreau 1979).

A main intervention of a structural approach is what Moreau referred to as 'immediate tension relief'. This involves providing or linking people with required material resources while at the same time identifying assumptions underlying relationships to these resources. Analysis is required of the power relations between the person, worker and agency. Is the relationship between the person and the worker, as agency representative, one of service provision as a right, privilege or regulation? A second objective of a structural intervention is to assist people to develop countersystems both within and outside of existing systems in an endeavour to bring about social change. Group intake processes are advocated in place of individualistic casework practices. This is so that, as much as possible, people in similar situations are brought together to share the connections they perceive between the similar contradictions they experience as individuals. This strategy provides support by normalising problems and experiences and providing for a collective response to institutionalised problems.

Structural social workers need to perceive and understand the contradictions inherent within the agencies in which they work. The next step is to strategically highlight and document these contradictions, and to use them collectively to advocate for change. In recognition of the structural limitations of effecting desired changes within agencies while also keeping their jobs, structural social workers are encouraged to form alliances with social movements outside their organisation that are tackling similar issues.

Structural social workers focus on the power dimensions in relationships. A dialogical relationship is formed that does not involve the imposition of power by social workers over those with whom they work. This is particularly challenging, and in some situations impossible, given the increasing role of social workers in statutory settings, such as mental health and child protection and the resultant enforcement of legislation and regulation. It also requires willingness by social workers to give up positions of power and privilege. What is required is self-awareness combined with political awareness, and insight into the ways social workers deal with power and powerlessness in their daily lives and in their work contexts.

The critique of power developed within radical and structural social work also occurred in the developmental model in Australia in the 1970s.

THE DEVELOPMENTAL MODEL

The developmental model's focus is exemplified in the work of the Brotherhood of St Laurence in Melbourne. In 1972 the Brotherhood dismantled its social work service and youth and family services, and in its place established an anti-poverty program in the Family Centre Project. The aim of the Family Centre Project was to demonstrate, with a small group of families in poverty, that structural change was necessary to eliminate poverty. During the first three years of the project the emphasis was on tackling poverty through the redistribution of resources and power within the program. The program had a number of unique features including the provision of an income supplement to project participants. Conventional social work, or therapeutic case-work, was replaced with a multidisciplinary approach employing a developmental model of social work practice. In this model social workers were one of a range of resources available to families. Program participants managed the program, with professional staff gradually replaced by members of the project. There was a commitment to the de-professionalisation of the working relationship between social workers and their 'clients'. The emphasis was on self-help, welfare rights and social action (Liffman 1978; Benn 1981).

Throughout the project, numerous instances of structural disadvantage became evident in the lives of the families, manifested in limited education and employment opportunities, inadequate incomes, discrimination and exploitation (Benn 1976). The findings of the project highlighted the complexity of the relationship between poverty and broader social structures, questioning simplistic models of cause and effect, and highlighting the interplay between structural and individual factors. While for some families addressing the material aspects of poverty clearly resulted in overall improvements in their situation, for others this was not the case. Of increased importance were processes that developed self-confidence, social and practical skills, an understanding of social and welfare rights and an individual sense of purpose, alongside addressing broader structural concerns (Benn 1981).

In discussing the project, Liffman (1978) asserts that the common tendency to attribute poverty to structural causes only, where the structural factors are immediate and visible, is often inhumane and false and not helpful in attempts to address poverty. He warns of the dangers of the potential misuse of such an approach, with it being used to justify models of 'deserving' and 'undeserving' poor. This could result in those who can be readily identified as disadvantaged because of structural constraints receiving assistance, and those who cannot be so identified being denied services and viewed harshly by society. This highlights the importance of an awareness of the complex dynamic of structural constraints and individual behaviour that may not be immediately apparent. A more sensitive understanding of the numerous ways social structures can create or maintain poverty is a prerequisite for more humane and responsive social policies.

Ultimately, the conclusions of the project were that addressing structural issues and concerns was both essential and effective in creating conditions conducive to overcoming individual poverty. However, individual factors including awareness, motives, values, strengths and weaknesses were also seen as important (Liffman 1978). Effective social work practice drawing on a developmental model requires an imaginative and flexible response that integrates a broader structural approach with the actual lived experiences of people. Reliable theoretical and empirical information on poverty is required, including its origins, nature and effects, and how people understand it and cope, and in some instances overcome it. Structural factors that contribute to poverty need to be identified and remedied. This includes sensitivity and responsiveness to structural factors that are immediately apparent, as well as those that are less apparent, yet nonetheless significant.

In a developmental approach, while the primary focus is on social structures and work directed at social change, there is also a role for interpersonal work.

In a similar way, feminist influences on social work highlighted the connection between the personal and the political.

FEMINIST SOCIAL WORK IN THE 1980s

In the 1980s gender was recognised as having great significance for social work practice. Feminist social work is based on the premise that people's material and emotional well-being can only be enhanced if gender is taken into account, applying equally to women, men and children. Gender-based inequality was viewed as 'permeating social relations in a profound way' (Dominelli and McLeod 1989: 173). As a result of powerful vested interests, progress is likely to be slow and faltering, yet this is not to be used as an excuse for inaction. Feminist social work rejects any approach which asserts that women are by nature subordinate to men.

Social work drew upon four broad approaches to feminist theory in the 1980s: liberal feminism, Marxist feminism, radical feminism and socialist feminism. Liberal feminists seek opportunities for the education and professional advancement of women, equal to men, within the existing social structures. In contrast to this view, Marxist feminists assert that the oppression of women is inextricably linked to capitalism and the class system. For Marxist feminists, liberation will occur only when a classless society is achieved. The focus of radical feminism is on the social construction of gender as the source of women's oppression, rather than the economic system. Drawing upon both Marxist and radical feminist constructs, socialist feminists argue that capitalism and sexism reinforce each other. For socialist feminists, class and gender oppression are both inseparable and fundamental to a feminist critique (Wearing 1986).

Dominelli and McLeod (1989) have identified five main areas where feminist social workers have focused their efforts. These are the manner in which social problems are defined, the development of feminist campaigns and networks, social work in statutory settings, counselling and therapy, and feminist working relations.

In feminist social work, personal problems are defined as political, thereby focusing on social justice campaigns to increase the allocation of resources to gender-specific programs. Gender-related issues for women include violence, rape, incest, women's emotional welfare and women's labour. Feminist social work intervention involves organising campaigns and networks and developing collectivist organisational structures to manage subsequent funding and resourcing of programs.

Feminist counselling and therapy focuses on the expression and acknowledgment of women's emotions as legitimate, alongside activities to promote and develop self-confidence, with women supporting each other in promoting anti-sexist practices. Individual work with women contributes to and informs action on a broader political level. Feminist social work in statutory settings aims to channel resources into tackling issues of gender and social injustice, with advocacy for the development of female-specific services.

Feminist social work identifies and confronts issues of gender inequality and discrimination in the workplace that impact both upon female social workers and women using their services. While the majority of social workers are female, they hold a minority of senior management positions in human services (Orme 1998). Feminist social work challenges this inequality and questions the impact it has on both the female workers and those who use social work services.

Black feminists in the United Kingdom have provided a major contribution to feminist social work by providing a perspective that places issues of inequality within a theoretical analysis of power, powerlessness and discrimination. This has led to an increased knowledge and understanding of inequality and oppression that has attracted allegiance from other groups in the community who face oppression and discrimination (Burke and Harrison 1998).

ANTI-OPPRESSIVE AND ANTI-DISCRIMINATORY PRACTICES

Anti-oppressive social work practice was a response from social work practitioners and academics in the United Kingdom to the development of social movements in the late 1980s led by women and black people. These new social movements were developed and led by oppressed people to challenge the inadequacies of the prevailing system (Dominelli 1998).

Key features of anti-oppressive practice are a commitment to social justice and a challenge to existing social relations. A main tenet is to highlight social injustice, particularly forms of injustice that are reproduced within and by social work practice (Dominelli 1998). The aim of anti-oppressive practice is social change focused on ameliorating social injustices. A focus is on progressive practices by social workers, aligning themselves with those who have been subjugated by structural inequalities. Anti-oppressive practice sees a causal and interconnected relationship between discrimination and oppression; according to this analysis it is necessary to deal with discrimination before oppression can be challenged. As in the structural approach, this includes discrimination and oppression based on factors of class, race, gender, age, disability and sexual preference (Thompson 1998).

Contemporary anti-oppressive practices are occurring within the context of globalisation, economic rationalism, the privatisation of the welfare state and an increasing gap between the rich and poor in Western industrialised nations. An anti-oppressive approach assists people to engage with these oppressive forces.

Anti-oppressive practice challenges notions of professionalism, focusing on power-sharing and egalitarian relationships based on shared values (Dalrymple and Burke 1995). An alliance is required between those who provide and those who use social work services. Empowerment can be achieved through equal power relationships, with professional relationships modelling anti-oppressive practices. Dominelli (1998) argues that the future of anti-oppressive practice requires social workers to form stronger alliances with other professional groups which advocate anti-oppressive practice, and with activists involved in the social movements.

CONCLUSION

Critical social work practice in the 1970s was originally informed by Marxist theory. It has been further developed by structural social work, the developmental model, feminist social work and anti-discriminatory and anti-oppressive approaches to social work.

A Marxist analysis highlights the contradictions inherent in the welfare state and the functions within it. Structural change is advocated by radical social workers, with social workers called upon to have a far greater social and political awareness. The goal of structural social work is critical reflection on the interplay between personal, social, economic and political processes. Of central concern to structural social workers are the ways in which the rich and powerful within society constrain and define the less powerful. Structural social workers focus on issues of class, gender, race and ethnicity, ability, age and sexual preference. In a developmental approach, the primary focus of social work is addressing structural inequalities while recognising the importance of interpersonal work.

Feminist social work stresses the importance of issues of gender inequality and the connection between the personal and political. The focus of developments in anti-discriminatory and anti-oppressive practices on issues of inequality has further enriched critical social work. A central theme common to all these approaches has been the concern of social work with issues of social justice.

3

THEORISING CRITICAL SOCIAL WORK

June Allan

This chapter examines conceptualisations of critical social work theory developed within a modernist framework, followed by a discussion of critical approaches to practice that incorporate postmodern perspectives. Recent debates (for example, Young 1990; Fook 1999; Pozzuto 2000) suggest that the dichotomisation of modernist and postmodern perspectives is problematic. I propose that the principles and strategies of either approach are best drawn on according to the cultural context and historical moment, the needs of the situation and the opportunities for dialogue and contestation. Regardless of the particular situation encountered by social workers, paramount to practice is an overall commitment to social justice and equality, and actions that are consistent with such a commitment.

STRUCTURAL APPROACHES

Chapter 2 has shown how some of the first attempts to develop a critical social work practice shaped by the modernist critical tradition, and developing out of the radical social work movement, emerged among scholars who developed practice frameworks focusing on the materialist dimension. Among these scholars are Moreau (1977, 1979; Moreau and Leonard 1989) and Mullaly (1993, 1997), who developed structural approach to practice. Middleman and Goldberg (1974) first used the term 'structural social work' in 1974, but their framework was based on a conservative view of the social environment as the location of social problems that left the fabric of society unchallenged and unchanged.

Conceptualisations of the approach that followed Middleman and Goldberg were based on a contemporary Marxist analysis. Emphasising solidarity among oppressed peoples and collective action, a structural approach to practice links the personal with the political, making it possible for people to consider their personal experience of oppression within a broader political understanding (Mullaly 1997). An assumption in this approach is that prevailing ideology, policies, practices and procedures of most social organisations maintain the power of workers and reduce the power of the users of their services (Moreau and Leonard 1989).

Moreau did not view the structural approach to social work practice as new because it incorporated tasks that social workers had always undertaken as part of their professional commitment and responsibility. In this problem-focused approach, what was new was the way in which social problems were conceptualised and objectives formulated. The new approach moved from dichotomising person and situation, directing 'attention to the transactions between people and specific social, political and economic situations' (Moreau 1979: 78). In particular, Moreau states, 'The central concern of structural social work is power, both personal and political. The key assessment question is the relationship between a client's "personal" problems, dominant ideology and his [sic] material conditions in the class structure' (1979: 78).[1]

According to Moreau (1979: 79), the concern of structural social work is with groups in society who are marginalised by 'an ideology that supports, maintains and legitimates the present social order'. Because of the focus on power, intervention works towards a more equal power relationship between social worker and client to overcome the usual sanctioning in professional relationships between workers and clients, of emotional, physical and social distancing.

Moreau's (1979) work highlighted the need in practice to account for the structural oppression of individuals. However, even at this early stage in the development of a critical approach, he saw the importance of considering the individual because of the interconnection between personal aspects of a problem and the institutional/political elements. He warns against blaming all social problems on social structures and of working only with the environment.

Moreau and, after his death in 1990, his colleagues continued the evolution of this approach. A follow-up study (Moreau and Leonard 1989) on the application of the structural approach by over a hundred practitioners who had been educated in the approach in Canada, was published in 1989. The study, which focuses on the contribution of a structural approach to social change and democratisation, shows that in the face of constraints, social workers are able to engage in practice that works toward such change. Practitioners reported that all of the practices on which the study focused were considered to be useful to clients, and frequent use was made of strategies for building a dialogical relationship. However, collectivisation practices for creating resources or bringing about change were found to be quite difficult if they required the central involvement of clients. The approach was easier to apply where it was congruent with the worker's personal philosophy and where peer support was available.

Noting the resistance from practitioners and the organisations within which they worked to many of the practices of the structural approach, the authors conclude that social workers committed to social change must continue to act where the contradictions are greatest and have the most potential for change. This could occur in both conventional and alternative settings. One of the key implications of the study was the need for improved theorising regarding the dynamics of internalised oppression and on how to help clients reverse destructive feelings and behaviours.

A further study, completed by Moreau's colleagues after his death (Moreau et al. 1993), explored the meaning of the structural approach for workers using the approach, and its implementation in direct service with individuals. Workers confirmed the importance of a critical social analysis incorporating feminism. They also agreed on the value of defending clients against institutions, of the materialisation and collectivisation of problems and solutions, and of increasing clients' power in the working relationship and enhancing their power by assisting them to change thoughts, feelings and behaviours. Workers were questioning oppressive ideologies and using techniques identified in the radical social work literature, but needed support in implementing the approach.

Others writing in Canada at the time developed this critical analysis and advocated an alternative form of social work practice. Carniol (1990), for example, challenging the conventional social work of the time and questioning institutions for their lack of accountability to the public, argued for a social work theory more useful for the realities of practice.

Consistent with and supportive of the structural approach, Carniol stressed the importance of action underpinned by a personal and political awareness of the root causes of social inequalities. He emphasised the importance of both radical counselling, and collective action through social networks and social change movements, to increase pressure on established institutions.

However, it was Mullaly (1993, 1997) who in the 1990s further developed a structural perspective based on an analysis of the welfare state in Canada, the United States and the United Kingdom. Mullaly (1997: 133–4) identifies the elements constituting the theoretical basis and framework for structural social work as being a socialist ideology, a radical social heritage, a critical social theory base, a conflict perspective, a dialectical analysis and inclusion of all forms of oppression. Underpinning this framework is the belief that particular groups defined along lines of class, gender, race, culture, sexuality, age, ability and geographical region experience inequality, a self-perpetuating and inherent part of capitalism. These groups are excluded from opportunities and meaningful participation in society.

Focusing on oppression as the central factor in the social problems that people experience, Mullaly's emphasis is on people's awareness of how capitalist society shapes, limits and dominates their experiences, thus alienating them from society, each other and themselves. Mullaly challenges social workers to change the oppressive relational contexts of institutionalised structures, rather than the individual, the family or the subculture adversely affected by social problems. According to this perspective there are two goals. The first involves alleviating the effects on people of exploitative and alienating practices. The second involves bringing about change in the conditions and social structures that cause these negative effects (Mullaly 1997). Similarly to Moreau, Mullaly (1997: 134) states that the change process involves 'immediate relief or tension-reduction on one level accompanied by longer-term institutional and structural change'.

Like Moreau, Mullaly (1997) views the various forms of oppression as intersecting with each other to create a total system of oppression. He claims that the structural approach is a generalist model of practice, as it does not only focus on social institutions but requires knowledge and skills for working with individuals, groups, families and communities. Despite this claim, Mullaly's approach focuses primarily on the broad structural aspects. Although Mullaly (1997) engages with postmodern ideas in the second edition of his book, he pays less attention to the human, communicative and relationship faces of social problems as they are often presented. Similarly to Moreau, he does not develop ways of engaging effectively with the multiple realities of people's lives and the differences to which he refers, whether geographic, ethnic, local or other.

Mullaly's approach is valuable for its focus on addressing the root causes of oppression through social transformative practices. But the question remains as to how to understand the impact of social structures on different groups of oppressed and marginalised groups, and how to respond in a way that is meaningful to them. How do practitioners engage effectively with such groups and involve them in social action when day-to-day survival is their main concern? Further developments need to be explored to address these issues.

CRITIQUE OF STRUCTURAL APPROACHES

The approaches influenced by the modernist critical tradition dominated the critical social work literature from the late 1970s through to the 1990s. However, the contemporary context highlights the growing phenomena of fragmentation, uncertainty and localisation, all of which are seen as characterising a postmodern world. Indeed, 'there has been a turn to postmodern thinking, as a way of understanding current changing and uncertain contexts' (Fook 2000a: 129). These changing contexts have made it difficult for structural approaches to remain relevant, and critiques of these approaches have developed, influenced by the emergent French tradition, central to which was Michel Foucault. A growing body of practice literature has questioned the truth status of modernist critical social work perspectives and the usefulness of a structural approach in local policy and practice contexts (Healy 2001). For example, both Fook (2000b) and Ife (1997) have argued that because a structural perspective relies on an analysis at a general and abstract level, based on universal discourses of structural oppression that transcend different cultures, it does not adequately allow for the consideration of difference, within and across cultures. This denies the experience of many groups in society.

Healy (2000, 2001) challenges critical social work theory in the modernist tradition. In particular, she raises concerns about, firstly, its failure to engage with institutional and personal levels of critical practice. Secondly, she challenges the rationalist assumption that people can change the way they live through rational thought and action, noting a range of reasons that (modernist) critical practice theorists have attributed to the disparity between working with a critical vision and actual practice in the contemporary context. These include the limited commitment to radical change among social workers and their lack of political sophistication; the social control functions which social workers are often required to fulfil; and the limited change aspirations of service users. Healy (2000) asserts that the critical approach itself, in its modern form, has marginalised aspects of activist social work by silencing dissension and critiques from within critical social work. In that respect, the approach has suffered from being overly prescriptive and has silenced local features of practice. She suggests that the challenges from within critical social work also arise from practice, from the changing environment of public administration contexts and from postmodern analyses.

Other critiques of a modernist critical social work have addressed theoretical dimensions of the approach. Fook (2000a: 130), for example, draws attention to the ways in which traditional critical perspectives have privileged theory over practice in a way that is problematic for practitioners and students. She also asserts that they have dichotomised 'macro' and 'micro' perspectives. This has resulted in difficulties in applying a structural analysis to direct practice, so that disempowering practices continue at the interpersonal level. Similarly, I believe that there is a risk that practice at the macro level can become disengaged from individual subjectivity and embodiment, such that policies and programs may be unhelpful or disempowering to the people whose conditions they purport to improve. Thus, as Fook (2000b: 130) claims, 'the practice does not fit the theory'. She challenges us to consider whether attempts at generating universal knowledge are meaningful for social work in a postmodern and changing context. How can professional knowledge be 'more directly meaningful and relevant to diverse groups and in diverse contexts?' (Fook 2000b: 108).

There is also continuing debate and ambivalence about the place of postmodern perspectives in critical social work theory (for example, Rees 1991; Dixon 1993). Postmodern theories are treated sceptically because they are regarded as retreating from universal notions of social justice, equity and structural change, and adopting a politics that privileges difference and locality (Fook 2000a; Healy 2000). Writers such as Walby (1992), for example, are reluctant to embrace the notion of fragmented and multiple identities when structures such as class, gender and race remain virulent social divisions because of their historical tenacity and material longevity. Postmodern critical theories are also perceived as offering little in the way of alternatives to address social injustices (Leonard 1995, cited in Healy 2001).

FURTHER DEVELOPMENTS

Some writers from within a modernist critical tradition have drawn on ideas from postmodern theory. These include Ife (1997) and Thompson (1998). How do their approaches inform a critical social work theory for practice?

Writing in the mid-1990s in Australia out of a concern about the impact on social work practice of economic rationalism and associated managerialist and competency approaches, Ife (1997) assumes a universalist position that stresses social justice and social inclusion by focusing on human rights. However, Ife views human rights as a context within which to address the diversity of human needs in culturally appropriate ways. In developing his theoretical framework he draws on humanist, postmodern and feminist perspectives. He views postmodernism as allowing for alternative discourses and realities, acknowledging different forms of experience, and accepting ambiguity and uncertainty. Feminism draws attention not only to the oppression of patriarchy but, more broadly, to structural oppression. However, he regards both postmodernism and feminism as limited, and is also critical of an exclusive reliance on a humanist discourse because of its divisiveness grounded as it is in Western tradition with a lack of internationalist and ecological perspectives. Ife (1997: 98) argues that 'a critical humanist vision of social work . . . requires a perspective that unites and transcends the differences of race, gender, class, age or whatever, in a common vision of humanity'.

To achieve this vision, Ife (1997) argues for a structural analysis, and an understanding of oppression that can lead to action and change, to be combined with an interpretive understanding that allows for multiple and diverse realities. He claims to bring these competing discourses together by allowing a focus on social justice through universal understandings of human rights in support of a better world, while affirming an empowerment-based model that allows for a diversity of voices to be heard. He acknowledges the tension in the position he takes through its competing narratives of unity and difference.

Ife attempts to deal with this tension by negating the dichotomy between structural and post-structural, arguing that radical practice must incorporate both. He argues that although universalist accounts such as humanism can readily incorporate a vision of social justice, they can reinforce marginalisation by ignoring the voices of difference. On the other hand, by rejecting the dominance of a single explanation, relativist discourses such as postmodernism run the risk of removing themselves from a universal commitment to social justice. Ife warns that without a structural analysis, humanism can merely reinforce existing relationships of power and oppression. He considers a structural analysis to be necessary in order to identify the causes of people's oppression or disadvantage within a wider context. This view is based on the belief that the felt needs of people may result from forces of which they have no understanding or knowledge. A structural analysis provides an overall perspective within which individuals construct meanings and take action.

Thus, for Ife, a critical approach incorporates both structures and discourses. His approach is built on the belief that power is defined within changing discourses and is also present in structures of domination such as class, race and gender. Ife's framework for practice is valuable for its explanation of mutually empowering, educative processes. The framework includes changing the nature of discourses, linking the personal and political through a dialogical consciousness-raising approach, integrating policy and practice in work with individuals and communities, becoming involved in policy at the professional level and in the public arena, allowing the voices of the marginalised to be heard, developing and supporting an oppositional politics, relocating social work within 'community', holding an internationalist orientation and developing alliances.

However, Ife's practice framework raises further questions. Although he argues that postmodern thought on its own does not provide a sufficient theoretical base because it provides no vision or direction for a better society, he discusses postmodernism as a homogeneous set of ideas that rejects universal narratives. The postmodern theory he draws on rejects overarching principles such as social justice and liberation. As we shall see in the next section of this chapter, later postmodern approaches to critical social work have concerned themselves with the emancipatory potential of postmodern thought.

In addition, just how Ife takes account of the interplay between structures and discourses in practice is not entirely clear. Recognising that policies can reinforce structural disadvantage unless relevant structural issues are addressed, he calls for practices such as consciousness-raising, education and community action. But he does not pay detailed attention to how power actually becomes entrenched in structures; nor—like Moreau and Mullaly—to how this power in turn impacts on the thoughts and actions of individuals. Issues of identity and subjectivity are not addressed. Left unanswered is how to understand individuals as historical, embodied, traditional and embedded beings (Fay 1987: 206-9). Just as our identities, actions and judgments can never be final and determinate, we cannot be considered separate from our bodily constitutions and the perceptions and feelings deeply rooted in our bodies. Further, our identities cannot be separated from our cultural traditions, and we are part of an entire network of relationships. These factors, Fay (1987) suggests, can act as barriers for individuals to achieve self-clarity and empowerment, and require more than consciousness-raising and educational strategies. Finally, Ife's framework does not provide specific strategies for understanding and analysing clients' material conditions. These are important dimensions to be addressed in a critical social work theory for practice.

Thompson (1998) has also explicitly drawn upon postmodern theory in his work on anti-discriminatory and anti-oppressive practice in the human services in the United Kingdom, developing a perspective that defines oppression as operating at three separate but interrelated levels: personal, cultural and structural. The personal level includes discrimination in the form of prejudice. The cultural level includes 'the way in which members of a particular cultural group become so immersed in its patterns, assumptions and values that they do not even notice they are there'. The structural level 'comprises the macro-level influences and constraints of the various social, political, and economic aspects of the contemporary social order' (Thompson 1998: 15-6). Thus Thompson demonstrates the multiple and interrelated ways in which oppression is maintained.

Thompson (1998: 24) argues that existing power relations are 'maintained and reinforced by certain ideas operating ideologically' and discursively. He believes that the concepts of ideology and discourse have much in common but that 'discourse is more closely focused on language' (1998: 22). He also believes that an analysis of power is central to challenging oppression, recognising that both structuralist and post-structuralist approaches to power are important. Thompson draws upon Foucault to emphasise:

> the role of human service workers in the maintenance of power rela-
> tions in so far that human service work can be seen to involve an

element of surveillance; [the way that] individuals contribute to their own oppression through the internalization of disciplinary practices [and how] those who wield power . . . are also subject to disciplinary practices (1998: 53).

Drawing on the Foucauldian notion that individuals or groups can resist power through struggle against domination, Thompson portrays power in a positive light. However, he has a guarded view of postmodernism. In particular, he comments on the 'fatalism and nihilism [of post-modernism] . . . the mood of pessimism in relation to possibilities of emancipation and social progress' (1998: 62). He argues that postmodernism has 'a tendency to encourage a disempowering and pessimistic outlook' (1998: 64), a view also articulated in Rosenau's (1995) reference to 'sceptical postmodernism'. Thompson believes that in order to challenge oppression, it is necessary to fight discrimination and to view the different forms of oppression as being parts of a complex matrix of multiple and interacting oppressions rather than existing in isolation. To promote equality he proposes a series of specific strategies including empowerment; partnership and participation; conscientisation and politicisation (the process of helping to make people aware of the broader context of the situations they face); collaboration between like-minded workers; critically reflective practice (a process of integrating theory and practice through a process of 'reflection-in-action'); elegant challenging (in which the actions and attitudes of others are challenged where they can be seen to be discriminatory or oppressive); openness and demystification; using the law; professionalism; staff care; and humility (1998: 210–27).

Although there is much to be supported in Thompson's work in terms of its orientation to practice, he draws eclectically from a range of critical theories that are often in contradiction with each other. While he acknowledges the tension between developing practices that challenge the dynamics of oppression faced by particular groups on the one hand, and developing a more holistic framework for challenging the diversity of oppressions, he does not adequately address this issue. Although he argues against a hierarchy of oppressions, some forms of oppression seem to be given more prominence than others. But if we say there is no hierarchy of oppressions, does that mean that we ignore the specific dynamics of how oppressions operate in particular historical and cultural contexts?

There are contradictions and gaps in the work of those who have drawn on postmodern concepts within a material framework. What do those who have drawn more exclusively on postmodern theories contribute to an understanding of critical social work theory for practice? And how do they propose to deal with material inequality?

POSTMODERN APPROACHES

Postmodern approaches to critical social work have appeared in the literature over the last few years (for example, Pease and Fook 1999; Fawcett et al. 2000; Fook 2000a, 2000b; Healy 2000, 2001; Leonard 2001). Common to these approaches are that they are concerned with social transformation, with multiple and diverse social realities which are constructed by factors both internal and external to the individual with the importance of local contexts of practice and with the role of discourse in maintaining power. They also challenge the dichotomies of modern critical theory and engage positively with the complexities of power, identity and change (Healy 2001).

Postmodern perspectives challenge the grand narratives of modernism, especially their attempts to explain and change the social whole. For example, Sung Sil Lee Songh (1998) questions the domination of elites through their control not only of material production, but also of the means of producing knowledge. She asserts that people must continuously struggle for the emancipation of oppressed populations in diverse ways, so that they develop their own ways to raise consciousness and generate knowledge. Postmodern perspectives also identify multiple systems of oppression such as class, race and gender, without privileging one over another. Rather than follow a grand vision of transformation and change, postmodern approaches aim towards the creation of conditions for ongoing dialogue and contestation. This means celebrating minor and local victories for those who are marginalised (Healy 2000).

Postmodern approaches challenge assumptions about power, identity and change central to critical social work approaches. Drawing particularly on the work of Foucault (for example, 1977, 1980), these approaches consider that the power people have available to them arises out of their historical and contextual location in society, not just their material location. In addition, postmodern theories challenge the negative view of power, as it is regarded as being both productive and coercive. It can be used not only to oppress people but also in positive ways. For example, social workers use their professional power and authority to gain needed resources for oppressed and marginalised people, or to provide people with necessary knowledge and information.

Consistent with Foucault's writings (1969, 1980), the postmodern perspective emphasises that power is everywhere. However, as Healy (2000) points out, the focus is less on identifying what or who the oppressors/oppressed are and more on understanding how power is exercised and locally sustained. For example, is it organisational policy that is disadvantaging the client? How is this maintained? How might it be changed? Whose interests does it protect? The postmodern perspective highlights the importance of recognising that power is present in all relationships and of using that knowledge to foster just and humane practices: through respect, sharing information, openness and clear communication, instead of pretending rapport in an equal relationship (Healy 2000: 127-8). These insights about power can enable critical social work theories to engage productively with the diverse range of practice settings in which social workers are located.

Postmodern critical social work values both the lived experience of service users and the knowledge of the professional, through ongoing scrutiny of the knowledge that both bring to the relationship (Healy 2000). The expertise of practitioners is characterised by an ability to work in complex situations of competing interests, and to prioritise factors in ways that allow clear action. The theory of the practitioner is a resource, and their reflections in practice are 'vital sites for knowledge building and action' (Healy 2001: 6). In this way, practitioners are open to change and uncertainty, can create the theory and knowledge needed to practise relevantly in differing contexts, and can locate themselves squarely in these contexts as responsible actors (Fook 2000a).

Healy (2001: 7-10) also draws attention to the importance of analysing how organisational discourses shape practice and to the need for critical social work to engage critically with the new imperatives for human service workers, such as the changing environment of public administration. She claims that elements of modernist critical practice theory, such as the promotion of participant involvement, sharing of power and collective social action, are difficult in contexts where practitioners are constrained by policy and organisational obligations, such as large statutory organisations or organisations dependent on government contracts. Drawing on the work of Yeatman (1998), she asserts that such a focus also renders invisible other forms of effective activist work such as can be found among some government bureaucrats (Healy 2001: 9-10).

The notions of identity and subjectivity have been scrutinised by

postmodern theorists, as discussed in Chapter 2. A postmodern understanding recognises the diverse nature of subjectivities. The construction
of identities has shifted from being ascriptive and natural in the pre-
modern era, socially acquired and quasi-natural in the modern era, to
chosen and socially negotiated in the postmodern (Parton and O'Byrne
2000a: 14). In this view, as language and reality are inextricably linked,
individuals can create their own destinies, because through the exercise
of will they can invent reality (Parton and O'Byrne 2000a). Healy (2000)
proposes that in the postmodern era it is still possible for individuals to
identify as a collective category/group (for example, gay males, women),
but in order not to suppress differences, ongoing negotiation of difference is necessary.

Postmodern practice theorists question the modernist critical theorists' claim that people can change the way they live through rational
thought and action, and advocate approaches to social change that are
anti-dogmatic, flexible, pragmatic and sensitive to the person's context
(Pease and Fook 1999; Fawcett et al. 2000; Fook 2000b; Healy 2001). To
effectively implement such approaches, workers need to be critically
self-reflexive, reflecting on their values, feelings and actions in the work
they undertake (Fook 1999; Healy 2000). In order not to be oppressive,
consciousness-raising needs to be used in a way that recognises the
many different ways of knowing (Healy 2000). In recognition that individuals are irrational, embodied and influenced by tradition, there is an
acknowledgment that consciousness-raising does not always translate
easily into action.

Healy (2000) does not distinguish between the progressive and
more conservative versions of postmodern theories. The French poststructuralists upon whom she draws, such as Cixous (1994), Gatens
(1992) and Grosz (1994), are less oriented to social justice and material perspectives. However, Healy does not turn her back entirely on
lessons from the modern. She argues the necessity of activists drawing
on critical social science's material emphasis on class, gender and race
for analysing and responding strategically to disadvantage. She warns,
for example, that the post-structural emphasis on language and the
symbolic may obscure both the material realities of disadvantage, and
forms of power that are entrenched and dominant, such as acts of
serious violence embedded in patriarchy and culture. Healy (2000) also
acknowledges the political costs of embracing difference and uncertainty given that certainty provides a powerful base from which to
challenge the truths of dominant groups. In the final analysis, she

accepts that both modernist and postmodern theoretical approaches are required.

Healy acknowledges the continuing importance of macro-analysis, but believes that postmodernism enables the interpersonal and institutional dimensions of practices to be revalued 'as more than microcosms of larger structures' (2001: 12). But questions remain. What are the implications of acknowledging structural oppression? What are the implications of not choosing between the two different versions of critical theory?

Before addressing these questions, I will outline the recent work of Parton and O'Byrne (2000a, 2000b), who have developed a model of social work practice strongly influenced by postmodern ideas; they have developed the concept of 'constructive social work' as a way of acknowledging the importance of language and narrative. They do not claim to draw on critical theory, but note the influence of postmodern thought on the development of their ideas. Their approach is of some interest here, because it draws on narrative, strengths and solution-focused perspectives that are compatible with postmodern ways of working. In particular, they provide concrete ways of working with people that respect difference, an aspect missing from other theories for practice that have been discussed.

In developing their theory, Parton and O'Byrne (2000b) were responding to developments in the United Kingdom where the focus of social workers has in recent times been on the mechanistic process of assessing needs and determining categories of risk and vulnerability in functional, proceduralised and bureaucratic ways. They deplore the lack of an adequate theory for practice that includes creativity and skill in dealing with human relationships. Focusing in particular on the face-to-face encounters required of practitioners, Parton and O'Byrne favour a client-centred approach that acknowledges the understanding that 'clients seek to control the meaning of their own experience and the meanings that others give to that experience' (Howe 1993, cited in Parton and O'Byrne 2000a: 5). Drawing on constructionist perspectives in sociology, psychology and other related areas of intellectual life, they acknowledge that the ideas underpinning constructionism have been advanced by the concerns of postmodernity and the centrality of language.

Rosenau (1995) refers to 'affirmative postmodernism', as being concerned with aspects such as the importance of process, deconstruction and reconstruction. Drawing on this orientation, Parton and O'Byrne develop a constructive approach to practice that prioritises receptivity, dialogue, listening to and talking with the other. It 'reveals paradox, myth and story, and persuades by questions, hints, metaphors, and invitations to the possible rather than by relying on science and trying to approximate truth' (2000a: 14). This approach has opened the way for the acceptance of solutions-focused interventions (de Shazer 1985), strengths-focused interventions (Saleebey 1997) and narrative interventions (White and Epston 1990) in social work practice. The social constructionist approach requires a critical stance to our taken-for-granted ways of understanding the world and ourselves. Categories and concepts are regarded as historically and culturally specific, varying over time and place. Because our knowledge of the world is developed between people in our daily interactions, there is a central concern with the social processes that bring this about and that can be changed, and the negotiated understandings and different kinds of actions that result from these processes.

Parton and O'Byrne's (2000b) approach to practice revalues the daily interactions between people, and provides some valuable ways of understanding and theorising practice in a fragmented world that demands attention to uncertainty and diversity. However, despite a professed commitment to social justice and empowerment, their emphasis is entirely on personal agency and personal empowerment to the neglect of social transformation and empowerment (for example, see 2000b: 59–60). Missing from their text is a discussion of structural issues and implications for social transformation.

SIMILARITIES AND DIFFERENCES BETWEEN MODERNIST AND POSTMODERN APPROACHES

Discussion throughout the chapter reveals commonalities and differences between modernist and postmodern approaches to critical theories for social work practice. In particular, several principles underpinning these approaches are common to both. Central to these key principles, shown in Table 3.1, is a commitment to work towards greater social justice and equality for those who are oppressed and marginalised within society.

Table 3.2 identifies in summary form the major similarities and differences between the two approaches. This highlights that although both approaches seek the transformation of social structures and institutions with attention to power relations in society, they place different emphases on the various systems of oppression and underline different ways of achieving change. Modernist approaches focus on

Table 3.1: Principles common to modernist and postmodern approaches to critical social work theory and practice

1. A commitment to the transformation of processes and structures that perpetuate domination and exploitation.
2. A commitment to working alongside oppressed and marginalised populations.
3. Consequently, an orientation towards emancipatory personal and social change, social justice and social equality.
4. A dialogical relationship between social workers and the people with, or on behalf of whom they work.

addressing material issues through politicisation and collectivisation of social problems. Postmodern approaches affirm difference and locate people in their historical and cultural contexts, seeking to bring about change through locating possibilities for resisting and challenging dominant discourses at local sites.

Table 3.2: Similarities and differences between modernist and postmodern approaches in the critical tradition

Modernist approaches emphasise:	Postmodern approaches emphasise:
• The shaping of individual experience and social relations through prevailing social, economic and poliical systems. Although modernist approaches claim to recognise the active agency of individuals and their capacity to create change, this aspect has not been developed extensively in theory and practice.	• The shaping of individual experience and social relations through prevailing social, economic and political systems, at the same time recognising the active agency of individuals and their capacity to create change.
• For meaningful social change to occur, the transformation of social structures and institutions is required to address inequitable material arrangements.	• The transformation of social structures and institutions is required to address inequitable arrangements. But multiple systems of oppression (e.g. gender, class, race) are identified, without privileging one over another.

Modernist approaches emphasise:	Postmodern approaches emphasise:
• Changing the social whole.	• Change at the local level, rather than attempting to explain and change the social whole. The meaning of emancipatory personal and social change, social justice and social equality needs to be understood at the local level, and is associated with the notion that there is more than one way towards achieving social transformation.
• The need to analyse power relations, regarded as fundamentally conflictual, between individuals and society.	• The need to analyse power relations in terms of how they are maintained through discourses (constructed ways of thinking as well as related structures and institutions); consideration of how power is exercised and locally sustained.
	• Power is linked to people's historical and contextual location in society.
• Power is linked to people's material location in society.	• Locating emancipatory possibilities in the sites at which dominant discourses can be resisted, challenged and changed.
• Power is coercive, and is usually exercised top-down.	• Use of the notion that power is present in all relationships to develop just and humane practices. Power is both productive and coercive, and can be used in productive ways by practitioners in their relationship with service users.
• Use of egalitarian processes in practice, with an emphasis on processes of communication and dialogue, including shared information and public debate.	• Valuing the lived experience of service users and the knowledge/ skills of the professional, through ongoing scrutiny of what both bring to the relationship.

Modernist approaches emphasise:	Postmodern approaches emphasise:
• Participation by oppressed groups in the process of change, through the processes of rational self-consciousness and collective action.	• The creation of conditions for on-going dialogue and contestation
• Individual and group practice methods used in non-pathologising ways to assist oppressed groups, focusing on alleviation of distress through provision and creation of needed resources, individual and group support, and collectivisation of problems.	• Understanding how individuals' social realities are constructed internally and externally. • Deconstruction and reconstruction of discourses.
• Long-term actions (social action and advocacy, links with social movements, etc.) aimed at eliminating oppression.	• The importance of difference, diversity and process, and the value of narrative through the telling of the story and the meanings attached to it.
• The practitioner assumes certainty of knowledge.	• The practitioner is self-reflective and open to change and uncertainty, creating theory and knowledge to practise in relevant ways in differing contexts.

IMPLICATIONS FOR THEORIES OF CRITICAL SOCIAL WORK PRACTICE

So where does this leave us? Modernist critical approaches have disputed conventional social work practice. They provide a lens for challenging social injustice and social inequality through social transformation. They emphasise the need to consider injustice and inequality at all levels of intervention—whether working at macro or micro levels—and provide ways for analysing and strategising responses to disadvantage. However, because of their universalist assumptions, they provide little guidance on understanding and dealing with difference within and between oppressed groups. For example, what does Thompson's (1998) analysis of race in the United Kingdom have to offer an analysis of race in Australia? They also say little about practice at the interactional, relational level.

Postmodern approaches, on the other hand, run the risk of over-looking or obscuring the material realities of disadvantage and injustice. They challenge the 'truth' of a modernist approach, highlighting multiple oppressions, difference and the multiple sources and sites of power within a particular historical moment and cultural context. Typically, they focus little on practice at the macro level although there are exceptions to this, such as the work of Iris Young (1990).

Social work theorists such as Ife (1997), Mullaly (1997) and Healy (2000) have drawn on both modernist and postmodern perspectives, even while they favour one over the other. Yet it remains unclear what drawing on both means in practice. A recent suggestion is that we should not dichotomise the two orientations. As Fook (1999: 205) points out, modernist/postmodernist is itself a dichotomy, and 'to place too much importance on the differences between modernist and post-modern thinking may be to miss the bigger picture'. Fook notes the similarities in approach between the modernist and postmodern critical theory traditions, in that they are 'non-dogmatic, open to revision, reflexive and self-critical' (1999: 205–6). Young (1990) perhaps bridges the dichotomy, for although she challenges modernist notions of social justice and equality, urging affirmation of, and attention to, difference between social groups, she nevertheless holds firmly to a universal principle of social justice. For Young, the traditional notion of distributive justice, with its focus typically on the possession of material goods and social positions, obscures the issues of domination and oppression. To avoid this problem, she argues that justice needs to be conceptualised not only in terms of distribution but also in terms of processes and relationships, particularly decision-making processes, culture and the social division of labour. Young argues for group-differentiated policies and practices that strive for social equality through the inclusion and participation of all groups in public life.

The issue here is how to hold together the two approaches and so practise in a way that pays attention to inequitable material arrangements and their impact on individuals and communities, at the same time heeding difference and diversity while maintaining an open, reflexive and self-critical stance. It is the view of the editors of this book that critical social work theories and practices should maintain the tension between the modernist and postmodern, and that it is necessary to work with the contradictions, debates and uncertainties that emerge from taking this position. In his reflections on a possible critical social work, Pozzuto (2000) notes the various critical perspectives in social work, each of which offers its own solutions to the quest for empowering the oppressed and vulnerable. He concludes that perhaps no singular or static answer is necessary or even possible. To have a fixed answer would be to close off possibilities for the future, or to perpetuate the present into the future rather than supporting many alternate futures.

CONCLUSION

Clearly social workers will draw on the principles and strategies relevant to the needs and analysis of a given situation. However, only if they hold firmly to a world-view shaped by socio-political analysis and a commitment to social justice will they be able to work with individuals and groups in appropriate ways to enhance human well-being and address the needs of oppressed and marginalised people. This requires social workers to practise self-reflexively, to constantly reflect on the interplay between their own knowledge and values and the situations they encounter. As Pozzuto suggests, questions and possible solutions are not static—'the task of critical social work is to lift the veil of the present to see the possibilities of the future' (2000: 2). How this might be done will be explored in the next chapter.

4

PRACTISING CRITICAL SOCIAL WORK

June Allan

Different positions have been taken on whether there are practice skills or techniques specific to critical social work approaches. Although Moreau shifted his opinion on the issue (Moreau and Leonard 1989), he expressed the belief in his earliest conceptualisations of a structural approach that techniques specific to the approach were not required (Moreau 1977). Ife (1997: 180) has also argued that the skills of radical practice are those of mainstream social work and therefore new skills do not need to be learned. I maintain that there are particular clusters of knowledge and skills, used within a social justice framework, which enhance the achievement of goals in critical social work practice. Modernist approaches to critical social work draw attention to the importance of a socio-political analysis and the need for methods of 'intervention' that follow from such an analysis. Politicisation of problems, fostering of solidarity among individuals and education to promote change are all emphasised. Postmodern approaches, by contrast, focus on discourse analysis and discursive processes.

This chapter considers the place of such ways of working within an understanding of the operation of power. Core practice issues are addressed, and some particular practices, integral to the implementation of critical social work approaches, are discussed. These practices concern actions for bringing about changes in consciousness, aspects of which were underdeveloped in the early critical social work approaches, and actions for fostering changes in people's material conditions.

CORE PRACTICE ISSUES

There are four issues that I believe are central to critical social work practice. These are, firstly, particular value positions that underpin and guide practice; secondly, dialectical approaches that pay attention to integrating the personal and the political across the so-called 'levels of intervention'; thirdly, the analysis of how socio-political factors and discourses impact on situations in which social workers are involved, and, finally, the notion of empowerment.

Values and ethics to guide practice

The belief in human dignity and worth is a value underpinning all social work practice. Central to this belief is the notion that human beings have a right to be respected, that social workers should not discriminate against people on the basis of race, ethnicity, socio-economic status, gender, sexuality or ability, and that all people should have equal opportunities to meet their basic human needs (Reamer 1987, cited in Miley et al. 1998: 6).

A commitment to social justice, discussed in earlier chapters, is also centrally important to critical social work practice, and the values, processes and skills underlying critical social work need to be consistent with this moral position. A moral concept that was once commonly regarded as having universal acceptance and applicability, social justice is now seen to be highly problematic, neither timeless nor absolute (Camilleri 1999; Ife 1999). Similar to Ife's (2001) position on the notion of human rights, I believe there is an inevitable tension between the attempt to hold to a universal value such as social justice while valuing diversity and giving voice to the oppressed and marginalised populations with whom social workers engage. The challenge for practitioners in the human services is to work with and negotiate these contradictions and tensions.

Such a tension is clearly demonstrated in the quest for a relevant code of ethics or moral framework for practice discussed by Briskman and Noble (1999), who, in their exploration of the possibilities for a progressive code of ethics, alert us to the complexities of universal codes that fail to represent the multiplicity of voices in pluralist societies. However, they also note that an emphasis on different voices can result in intense individualism and a lack of solidarity between people who may share similarities in their differences. They recognise that a social justice framework is necessary to provide direction for change, but acknowledge that there are different concepts of social justice. In order to reflect the interests of all groups in society, they recommend a process of negotiated compromise between the different groups within society to prevent any one privileged position from emerging as dominant.

Dialectical approaches to practice

Within the critical social work paradigm, there has been some debate as to whether to first address the personal or the political in an attempt to tackle social inequalities and bring about change. Conventional social work practices have separated 'intervention' into different 'levels' or methods of practice: individual or family casework, group work, organisational and program planning and development, community development, social policy and social research, with practitioners tending to work primarily within one of these methods. Typically, the emphasis has been on personal change and adjustment within a problem-solving framework, with individual and family casework often being the preferred method. Casework has focused on finding solutions for a psychosocial cause, enabling the client to eventually achieve self-actualisation,[1] both the worker and the skills used have been seen as objective and neutral, facilitating the process. Larger socio-political issues have been left to the minority of practitioners working in community development and social policy, thus weakening the link between the personal and the political (Mullaly 1997; Jessup and Rogerson 1999).

The term 'intervention' is now a contested concept. Conventional social work practices have used the term to refer to the work undertaken by a social worker to bring about change in something of which they are not part. Ife (2001) expresses the belief that the use of the term is problematic for two main reasons. Firstly, it perpetuates the image of the social worker as an outside expert rather than a partner in an action process. Secondly, it reinforces a notion of disadvantaged people being the passive recipients of expert help; of the social worker alone being responsible for affecting change. For these reasons, the notion of 'intervention' is considered to be incompatible with critical social work approaches and is replaced here with alternatives emphasising a greater degree of mutuality, such as 'work with' or 'work carried out' between practitioners and others towards achievement of a goal.

Structural approaches to practice do not favour one particular way of working over another. Because of a dialectical view that the personal and political are fundamentally connected, working with individuals, families, groups, organisations and communities are all regarded as containing possibilities for practice (Moreau et al. 1993). Mullaly expresses the view that no level of structural social work practice is 'inherently more progressive and liberatory than another' (1997: 164). But how might practice at these different levels be integrated? For Moreau, the goal in working from a structural social work perspective is to identify individual and institutional targets for intervention, since the oppressive practices of mediating institutions contribute to a client's personally experienced problem (1979). To achieve this goal, the primary objectives of practice are 'immediate tension relief' and 'group tension relief', carried out within the bounds of the organisation, and working 'towards elimination of oppression' outside the organisational context. This is summarised in Table 4.1.

Table 4.1: Objectives in a structural approach to practice

Working toward immediate tension relief

This involves shorter-term work to help clients cope with their immediate situation:

- By working with a client in relation to other individuals, groups or organisations, through brokerage (linking people with resources), mediation (mediating conflicts when there are common interests) and advocacy (obtaining resources through the use of pressure);
- By action with a client on personal aspects of their situation, through re-definition of problems with the client to clarify personal, institutional and political dimensions; through helping the client cope in the immediate term; and through helping the client change, by identifying and challenging destructive ideas they have learnt and their connection with social structures (Moreau 1977: 27, 29–35).

Working toward group tension relief

This involves longer-term work based on the collective interests of those involved, to change parts of the social, political and economic context:

- By consciousness-raising with the group about the relationship between personal problems and the social, political and economic structure;
- By developing solidarity among group members and supporters;

- By working to change oppressive rules and myths and oppressive conditions and the institutions that support them (Moreau 1977: 27, 36–8).

Working toward the elimination of oppression

This involves work to be carried out outside the bounds of human service organisations:

- By linking individual/collective work with people to the wider struggles of oppressed groups, for example, the labour movement;
- By linking with a political party which represents the working class (if one exists);
- By fighting for the unionisation of workers and the democratisation of work-places (Moreau 1977: 39).

Although the language naming the three processes is not what we might use today, the model nevertheless draws attention to the range of issues that a social worker needs to keep in mind. It also highlights the need to understand and act on the interconnection between peoples' material needs such as financial security, housing and safety, and their social, cultural and political context. The connection can be made, for example, between the despair and exhaustion experienced by a young mother in paid work, and the type of provisions and level of support for working parents in our society, as well as the beliefs and practices surrounding responsibility for domestic labour. The approach encourages problems to be considered as much as possible within group contexts rather than individual terms, assisting people to understand and address their problems within the broader socio-political and cultural context. These actions cannot be considered without working toward structural change, with or on behalf of individuals and groups. However, as mentioned in the previous chapter, Moreau's model did not develop a sufficient understanding of how to work with people to overcome their internalised oppression, as Moreau and Leonard (1989) themselves found from their study of social work graduates' implementation of the structural approach in their practice.

Others who have also made a clear case for practice to concern itself with the personal and the political (for example, Ife 1997; Mullaly 1997), have illustrated particular ways in which this might be done. For Ife (1997), the caseworker is expected to understand the 'client' in terms of her/his community and cultural context, and to seek solutions and supports at the community level. Similarly, community workers would be expected to use interpersonal skills that are designed to build trust and rapport with those with whom they need to work. Ife (1997) argues for a clear link between policy and practice, noting the organisational constraints to policy involvement for social workers whose work in 'direct service' has often made it more difficult to engage in policy issues. Ife suggests several ways in which links might be made. These include the ways in which problems are discussed with individuals, the terms used, the ways in which solutions are sought, and linking people with others in similar circumstances. Assisting people to develop organisational skills, such as advocating for themselves or making representations in meetings, is another way. More recent developments around the notions of dialogical relationships, consciousness-raising and critical questioning have assisted the process of linking the personal and political, and will be discussed later in this chapter.

A postmodern stance also rejects dichotomies and dualisms such as structural/local or community work/casework. However, postmodern critical social work approaches have tended to focus less on targeting change at the broader political/structural level, a point also made by Ife (1999). For example, in her discussion of critical practices, Healy (2000) argues that the dichotomy between structural and local forms of change needs to be dismantled to allow the local concerns and goals of individuals and groups to be seen as part of a continuum of social change. Small-scale localised activities are valued for their radical potential. Because pragmatic and localised approaches to activism are valued, the emphasis is more on social workers engaging in social change activities through the local networks of which they are part (Healy 2000). Workers might band together with their local community, for example, to establish a drop-in centre to provide information and referral services and recreational activities, to help build social cohesion and combat isolation or fear of cultural differences.

Where large-scale political action is considered, ongoing negotiation of the differences between those involved is urged (Yeatman 1993, in Healy 2000: 139). Although not arguing from a social work perspective, Young (1990) calls for policy-making to be taken out of the province of experts by opening it up to explicit public discussion in order not to deny differences between people and thereby reinforce oppression of particular social groups. Young (1990) defines such public discussion by the openness with which it takes place rather than by its unitary nature. It might occur, for example, not in a single assembly but among a proliferation of groups and forums with diverse perspectives, over months or years, involving geographically separated people who may never meet each other.

Common to the dialectical stance within modernist and postmodern critical approaches to change-oriented ways of working is attention to the socio-political and cultural contexts in which people or issues are situated, and to the workings of power through ideologies or discourses. The differences in emphasis between the structural and postmodern approaches on where social workers should focus their attention and actions to bring about change illustrate the tension between diversity and solidarity, or mutual interdependence. These differences cannot be overcome but must be in balance to avoid cultural exclusiveness or intense individualism on the one hand, or domination and homogenisation on the other (Leonard 1997). These are always in tension, and practitioners must learn to work with the contradictions that this phenomenon can create.

Analysis of situations

I now turn to the issue of analysis of situations with which social workers engage. Structural approaches' focus on the importance of socio-political analysis—analysing the relationship between personal problems, dominant ideology and material conditions—requires an analysis of power relationships at all levels. This involves identifying the social, political and economic barriers impinging on individuals, families, communities and organisations (Moreau and Leonard 1989). All forms of oppression and marginalisation based on sexism, racism, colonialism, imperialism, classism, agism, disablism (physical and mental), heterosexism and others need to be considered (Mullaly 1997). This means that practitioners need a sound understanding of political mechanisms and the workings of power. How is a socio-political analysis carried out? Perhaps Moreau's work provides the clearest account of a means for analysing personal/political dimensions. Individuals can be helped to develop social praxis, that is, assisted to critically reflect on their personal/political situation and to develop plans of action that address both aspects of the situation. To do this, Moreau proposes three dimensions.

The first dimension focuses on the contributions of the social, political and economic structure to the formation of social problems, incorporating the material conditions in which people live and the dominant ideology legitimating these arrangements. The second addresses the contributions of significant others. Here, the extent to which people significant to the oppressed individual or group follow the dominant societal rules of relationship is scrutinised. Finally, the extent to which the individual or group is free to participate in or reject the oppression they are experiencing is examined (Moreau 1977). Table 4.2 summarises the questions Moreau believes need to be addressed in analysing a problem situation. Because he is attempting to redress the problems he sees in conventional social work's non-political focus in individual casework, Moreau's focus is primarily on working with individuals. Although he does not develop specific guidelines for analysis at broader levels, he and his colleagues (Moreau and Leonard 1989; Moreau et al. 1993) identify practices such as organisational change and advocacy, for use within mainstream welfare organisations to benefit individuals.[2]

Table 4.2: Analysing a problem situation

(i)   What is the presenting problem and the client's ideology regarding it?

(ii) Who is the identified client? In particular, what are the objective circumstances and material conditions s/he lives in?

(iii) What is the dominant ideology in society regarding who the client is and the presenting problem s/he is facing? To what extent does the client go along with this?

(iv) In contracting with the individual/s, who are the clients? What work needs to be engaged in by whom, to help the client and others like him/her in a more permanent way?

Source: Moreau 1977: 15–26

Approaches from a postmodern perspective, on the other hand, emphasise discourse analysis. Language constructs multiple cultural meanings so that there is a shift from causal and linear thinking to a lateral critique, uncovering the different layers of meaning or deconstructing ideas and practices. The emphasis is educational rather than therapeutic. From this perspective, language is seen to be central in constituting social reality, the assumption being that we can only know 'reality' through language. Experiences in the social world, such as poverty or racism, are shaped by the discourses about them; because of the capacity of discourses to generate new meanings for different experiences, they facilitate understanding of and action towards the experiences. Thus discourses are the sites of 'analysis and struggle'

(Healy 1999: 118). They expand the possible ways of understanding and of actions available to people. Language cannot be regarded as producing the experience of poverty or racism, but the experience, Healy argues, can only be understood through language (Healy 2000).

The understanding of violence within families provides a useful illustration of the power of discourse. The use of the term 'domestic violence' was challenged by feminists for the ways it shaped understanding of and action on the issue of violence against women. The term came into common usage in Australia during the 1970s to distinguish violence in the home from interpersonal violence generally, giving recognition to the violence by a male towards his female partner. This terminology excluded violence towards children, violence towards partners of the same sex, and located violence within the home, reinforcing the notion that it was a private matter that did not warrant outside involvement. It also excluded violence against people in institutional settings, which for all intents and purposes were their 'homes'. The term 'family violence' appeared in response to the narrow understanding engendered by the language of 'domestic violence' (for example, in the state of Victoria's *Crimes (Family Violence) Act 1987* and the federal *Family Law Reform Act 1995*). This broadened the focus of concern to include violence between, or perpetrated on, any family members, such as siblings and children. However, it is a gender-neutral term, belying the evidence that the majority of perpetrators are adult males. Another term that has been adopted is 'violence against women', used in the National Strategy for Violence Against Women, 1993, for its capacity to link the often artificially separated notions of family violence and sexual assault. Again, this term leaves outside the frame of reference children and victims of violence used by some women against others within the family (McDonald 1998: 3–4). Different language and terminology shape the very definition of people's experiences and the actions taken, but are also used strategically for different settings or audiences.

The language of dominant discourses can be analysed for its potential to marginalise individuals and groups and prevent their rights and needs from being met. This analysis can disclose ideas, beliefs and behaviours that reproduce prevailing power structures around race, class, gender, sexuality and so on, and can therefore open up possibilities for them and their outcomes to be altered (Jessup and Rogerson 1999). Several theories and approaches are useful in discourse analysis when working with individuals. These include narrative-focused practices

(White 1992), strengths-focused practices (Saleebey 1997) and solutions-focused practices (de Shazer 1985), and the skill of critical questioning (Jessup and Rogerson 1999), discussed later in this chapter.

Empowerment

'Empowerment' is a contested concept. From a non-critical modernist perspective, it has often been regarded as social workers giving power *to* the people with whom they work, the professionals being seen as central to the process. A more common understanding of empowerment now appears to revolve around the notion that the social worker's role is to bring about personal and social empowerment by helping people empower themselves. Social workers are committed to the empowerment of people and are willing to share their knowledge in ways that help people to 'realise their own power, take control of their own lives, and solve their own problems' (Saleebey 1997: 62). More recent postmodern conceptions of empowerment recognise the centrality of discourse in this process. Parker et al. (1999), for example, argue that a postmodern process of empowerment means being open to alternative interpretations of situations and an understanding of how power relationships both produce and are produced by discourses.

Writers influenced by a postmodern perspective also challenge the image of power as negative, instead acknowledging that there are differences in power between practitioners and clients because of the role and professional knowledge held by the practitioner. There is recognition that the relationship cannot be equal and that it is unrealistic to pretend that power differentials do not exist (for example, Rees 1991; Healy 2000). Rather than trying to dissipate the power of the practitioner, writers acknowledge that the power of professionals is not necessarily a threat and can be used in positive ways to bring about change. More important is how these differences in power are acknowledged and managed (Healy 2000). However, it is questionable to assume that workers always have power. Healy (2000) points out, for example, that female workers who are Indigenous or disabled may have little power in particular situations.

Saleebey's (1997) notion that social workers help people to realise their own power alerts us to one of the more contested issues in empowerment practice—namely, the tendency in non-critical approaches to regard any social work practice with oppressed and marginalised populations as empowering. There is an assumption that power can be generated in the process of empowerment (Dalrymple and Burke 1995; Gutiérrez et al. 1998). Rather than being seen only as a scarce and exploitative resource, personal and interpersonal power can be generated through social interaction (Gutiérrez et al. 1998). However, Rees (1991) warns of the dangers of practitioners claiming they are empowering their clients without taking account of the political nature of empowerment and the interdependence between policy and practice. He challenges the view that social work with oppressed groups and communities is in and of itself a form of empowerment. Processes that involve an improvement in people's image of themselves, access to needed money, shelter or information and the creation of support networks are insufficient (Rees 1991). Structural and post-modern accounts of power highlight the necessity of taking into account both structural disadvantage and dominant discourses (Healy 2000; Ife 2001).

Empowerment has been defined as having three different dimensions, variously labelled as personal, interpersonal/social/cultural and structural/political (Gutiérrez et al. 1998; Thompson 1998). A critical perspective recognises the importance of all three. At the personal level, the emphasis is on assisting individuals to gain greater control over their lives, for example by enhanced confidence and self-esteem. At a cultural level, discriminatory assumptions and stereotypes that perpetuate the oppressive values and attitudes of dominant groups are challenged. At the structural or political level, power relations rooted in the structure of society must be challenged (Thompson 1998).

Is 'personal empowerment' a legitimate concept in the practices of critical social work? A numbers of writers believe that personal empowerment is necessary if structural empowerment is to be achieved. Dalrymple and Burke (1995), for example, assert that changes at the feeling level among those who feel powerless will affect their sense of control and their ability to act, and will facilitate in them the development of new language. This can enable a mobilisation of resources at the level of action, which can in turn affect an individual's feelings because change has occurred. This issue relates to internalised oppression, discussed later in this chapter. To avoid the traps of dualisms, practitioners need to work with people on all dimensions of empowerment—and this can be done simultaneously. For example, as Gutiérrez et al. (1998) suggest, a worker and an individual who have come together around issues of family violence may discuss advocacy organisations or attend a social action event together.

Empowerment practices

Empowerment is both a process and a goal, and is largely educative (Dalrymple and Burke 1995). The components commonly understood to be involved in empowerment are feelings and beliefs regarding self-efficacy; ideas or knowledge and skills for critical thinking and action; development of action strategies, and cultivation of the resources, knowledge and skills needed to influence internal and external structures, including the process of reflection, learning and rethinking (Dalrymple and Burke 1995; Gutiérrez et al. 1998). The process is not linear, and one area is not regarded as more important than another (Gutiérrez et al. 1998). It applies just as much to the development of a community project or implementation of a social policy as it does to work with individuals and groups. Hence there is a broad range of strategies that could be drawn on to facilitate empowerment.

Parsons et al.'s (1998) framework for empowerment practice acknowledges that existing systems approaches are not adequate in taking account of structural influences such as race, class and gender. The worker is required to carry the roles of educator, resource consultant, awareness raiser and group leader, teaching clients the knowledge and skills to perform the agreed upon actions required for themselves and others. The framework focuses on the different levels of action but does not see these as mutually exclusive, linear or sequential. It consists of four sets of empowerment practices that account for relevant personal, interpersonal and political aspects of a problem situation:

1. Establishment of a relationship between workers and individuals. As many problem situations present to workers through individuals, the worker needs to establish a relationship with the individual to address the person's immediate needs and goals, link the person to existing services and entitlements and assist them to engage in learning how to find/request resources. Possibilities for consciousness-raising about the broader political aspects of the situation may be limited at this stage by immediate needs (Parsons et al. 1998: 15–16).
2. Education, skill development and self-help. Individuals are assisted to develop the knowledge and skills they need, such as advocacy and mediation, use of groups to address common issues and solutions, self help and skills in problem-solving. This can be done through workshops, small group formats, newspapers and videos. Such methods can lead to the formation of support networks, self-help and collective action (Parsons et al. 1998: 16–17).

63

3. Development of organisational competence. People are assisted to develop their knowledge about resources and organisations, and skills for communicating with professionals and organisations. Developing organisational and community-change skills and participating in decision-making bodies can be part of this (Parsons et al. 1998: 15, 17).

4. Social action and political change at local, state, national and/or international levels. Individuals are assisted to develop knowledge about issues at the different levels, to develop skills for addressing these issues, to work with organisations, articulating the political nature of personal problems, and to use methods such as letter writing, campaigning, negotiating, mediating, lobbying and picketing (Parsons et al. 1998: 15, 17–18).

Thompson (1998) asserts that although those in the human services cannot expect to make major structural changes on their own, they can at least play a part in undermining inequality at the structural level. It is for these reasons that links between workers and broader social movements such as unions or feminist groups are highlighted in structural approaches to practice, or, from postmodern perspectives, links with local activist groups of resistance.

The information presented so far suggests ways of working with people that emphasise the interconnection between individual experience and socio-political contexts, the impact of language, and empowerment practices. Some particular practices, already alluded to, warrant further discussion. These are practices that appear consistently in the critical social work literature, from structural to postmodern, and are especially important in changing consciousness and material conditions. To be discussed under the first group are the establishment of dialogical relationships; the skills of consciousness-raising, critical questioning, deconstruction and reconstruction; practices for dealing with internalised oppression and internalised domination; and self-reflexive practice. Particular practices to be addressed for altering people's material conditions are advocacy and collective action.

PRACTICES FOR CHANGING CONSCIOUSNESS

Dialogical relationships

A 'dialogical' or egalitarian relationship between practitioners and those with whom they are working, and who are expected to benefit from the work done, is one in which power is shared as much as possible between the parties concerned. Underlying this is the attitude that each party is regarded as having equivalent wisdom and expertise, and worker and client engage in knowledge and theory-building and action together. Professional knowledge is not privileged over knowledge gained through the life experience of clients (Ife 2001). A study by the Brotherhood of St Laurence in Melbourne (Taylor 1990) reveals the significance an equal relationship can have for those with whom social workers have contact. For the women service-users in the study, an equal relationship meant being treated 'on the same level' and 'not being looked down on' (1990: 66). Someone with time to listen, who showed willingness to help, who was friendly, who was understanding and who acted 'human' were also important factors (1990: 39). From a structural perspective, the dialogical relationship is one in which 'perceptions of the social world are shared in order to conscientise clients to the structural aspects of their problem' (Fook 1993: 104, drawing on the work of Freire 1972 and Leonard 1975).

Consciousness-raising

Conscientisation, or consciousness-raising, can occur through linking the personal and the political so that 'people become more aware of the structures and the discourses that define and perpetuate their situations of oppression' (Ife 2001: 151). This increased awareness opens up possibilities for action. But consciousness-raising can be oppressive and patronising if it is based on the assumption that the practitioner's consciousness is superior and is to be imposed on the people with whom s/he is working. This has been illustrated in efforts of workers to 'elevate' Indigenous people to state 'standards' (Grimshaw et al. 1994).

The consciousness-raising process needs to be a mutual one, based on respect and a genuine desire on the part of the practitioner to work together with people, whether individuals, families, groups, organisations or communities, or at national and global levels. This involves shared expertise, mutual learning in which professional knowledge and life experiences are equally valued, and joint action. An attitude of respect towards those with whom the practitioner is working, along with sound active listening skills, provide important foundations for such practice (Ife 2001). From a postmodern perspective, this means that workers need to listen for and negotiate the multiple meanings attached to dialogues, recognise the many different ways of knowing, and even take on board ways of knowing that challenge professional expertise.

Critical questioning, deconstruction and reconstruction

Critical questioning, a strategy derived from the thinking of both Freire (for example, Freire and Faundez 1990) and Foucault (1977, cited in Jessup and Rogerson 1999: 165), has been used in critical social work practices to expose the role of external factors in determining life experience. It is needed because people continue to hold cultural meanings about the ways their lives ought to be, even when they are living in an oppressed situation. Critical questioning has the effect of opening up ways of perceiving a given situation other than in taken-for granted or stereotypical terms, and is used as a way of deconstructing unhelpful ideas and beliefs. Deconstruction can be understood as the pulling apart of a phenomenon 'to understand its meaning within a particular context or discourse, for a particular person or group, at a particular time' (Ife 1997: 87–8).

The use of critical questioning provides the opportunity for a person to explore their expectations and how they feel they have to act (Fook 1993). In a dialogical process, it allows for the exploration of alternative constructions of circumstances or ways of perceiving a situation. As a form of deconstruction, critical questioning acts as an invitation to another person to engage in a dialogue around reconstruction of new ideas and beliefs.

Jessup and Rogerson (1999) provide excellent examples of the ways in which the skill of empathy has been understood and used, showing how different sets of questions can result in different analytical discourses for individuals. Structural empathy elicits hitherto over-looked political understandings of a situation. For example, working with a woman who is likely to have abused alcohol and prescription drugs and is now separated from her partner and children following a violent, disruptive relationship with the partner, a social worker might ask, 'Can you tell me what rights you believe you have as a mother, wife and individual?' and 'What resources do you need to get your children back?' (Jessup and Rogerson 1999: 173). Building on this, a post-structural empathy—'the practice of discourse analysis in the interpersonal context, produced through critical questioning' (Jessup and Rogerson 1999: 172)—clarifies the discourses through which a person constructs their power positions, meanings and behaviours. Questions that might be asked in a dialogue with the woman include, 'Tell me what you think the role of mother and partner should be', 'Where do these expectations come from?' and 'How do you differ from these?' (Jessup and Rogerson 1999: 174).

Internalised oppression and internalised domination

It is important for critical social workers to understand the phenomena of internalised oppression and internalised domination. They create divisions between people, but also occur intrapsychically within an individual (Pheterson 1986). Internalised oppression refers to 'the incorporation and acceptance by individuals within an oppressed group of the prejudices against them within the dominant society' (Pheterson 1986: 148). It includes feelings like self-hatred, fear of violence, inferiority, isolation and powerlessness, and is the mechanism by which domination is perpetuated in oppressive situations. In contrast, internalised domination, such as sexism in men and racism in whites, is 'the incorporation and acceptance by individuals within a dominant group of prejudices against others' (Pheterson 1986: 148). It consists of feelings such as superiority, normalcy, self-righteousness, distortion of reality, guilt, fear, alienation from one's body and from nature, and restricts the individual's capacity to empathise, love and trust. It isolates people from one another and prevents solidarity, binding people together through their power to dominate others rather than on the basis of respect for others (Pheterson 1986).

Internalised domination can be countered by valuing difference, self-reflection and building alliances. Pheterson (1986), for example, describes a Dutch project designed to study the processes of internalised domination and oppression that divide women from each other. She concludes that building alliances with others helps counter the feelings of guilt and confusion that arise from being in social positions of dominance. Recognising and discussing internalised oppression and domination can support people to move from antagonism toward alliance.

The early structural approaches' lack of attention to how to work with people's internalised oppression (Moreau and Leonard 1989) meant the effect of people's own history, health, beliefs and feelings that might prevent them from being able to take action for themselves, or on behalf of others, was overlooked. The shift from problem-solving, therapeutic and reformative types of approaches for working with individuals and families, to educational and discursive approaches compatible with a critical discourse, has been promising in addressing this issue. Narrative and strengths approaches, for example, value the uniqueness of the individual experience and focus on the individual making meaning of that experience (White 1992; Saleebey 1997). Helping the individual to identify the influence of dominant discourses on their individual perceptions and experiences achieves this. White's (1992) narrative approach externalises difficulties experienced by individuals, and focuses on developing different 'stories' from the one they have constructed. The exceptions to the initial story allow for a different conceptualisation of and response to the difficulties (cited in Jessup and Rogerson 1999: 169). A narrative approach provides a means of including people in challenging the status quo or dominant discourse through the exploration of alternative discourses. Saleebey's (1997) strengths perspective focuses on the development of potential 'rather than the magnifying of limitations produced by concentrating on deficits' (Jessup and Rogerson 1999: 170) and opens up ways of building on existing strengths and personal change strategies with action informed by alternative ideas. Similarly, solutions-focused approaches emphasise people's strengths and their capacity to act on their world, through an understanding that solutions can be constructed, invented and discovered, and the assumption that problems exist within interactions between people, rather than within the person (de Shazer 1985; Jessup and Rogerson 1999).

These approaches emphasise cognitive strategies, externalisation and discourse analysis through the use of critical questioning and narratives (Jessup and Rogerson 1999). In contrast to the pessimism of 'sceptical postmodernism' (Rosenau 1995), they offer hope and optimism to people. However, they must not be used in isolation from a material and structural analysis of the person's situation, and the process of internalised domination should be considered as well as internalised oppression.

Self-reflexive practice

Self-reflexive practice is part of the dialogical process between workers and clients, crucial to the avoidance of processes of domination (Healy 2000). A concept originating with Argyris and Schon (1976), it is referred to in the literature by various terms: self-reflexivity, critical reflection, critical reflectivity and critically reflective practice. In essence, practitioners integrate theory and practice through a process of 'reflection-in-action', questioning their knowledge claims in an ongoing way. Self-reflexive practice involves 'the ability to locate oneself in a situation through the recognition of how actions and interpretations, social and cultural background and personal history, emotional aspects of experience, and personally held assumptions and values influence the situation' (Fook 1999: 199). The practitioner reflects on his/her knowledge development and integrates this awareness into further knowledge-building and action (Healy 2000). Its use prevents taking things for granted and encourages practitioners to re-analyse situations in ways that provide for new actions and changes in power relations (Fook 1999).

As a way of knowing, critical reflection allows marginalised aspects of experience, such as emotions and personal history, to be valued. As a process, it focuses attention on the practitioner's influence on the situation and how this might have affected power relations or perpetuated existing structures and beliefs (Fook 1999). It requires awareness of the influence of self in determining and changing a situation. It also requires the recognition of the role of personally held assumptions in influencing a situation, and an appreciation of how individuals can act to influence a situation. Analysis is woven with action, and the use of uncertainty as a catalyst for active change emanates from the process of critical reflection (Fook 1999).

PRACTICES FOR CHANGING MATERIAL CONDITIONS

Advocacy

Advocacy involves acting, mediating and interceding for another, in an attempt to influence the behaviour of decision-makers. It aims to improve the responsiveness of social arrangements to people's needs (Fook 1993; O'Connor et al. 1995). It is a service that argues people's views and needs, a set of skills for achieving this, and the interpretation of the powerless to the powerful (Payne 1997). Traditionally, advocacy has been divided into two types, case advocacy and class or cause advocacy, seen as a service provided by professionals to clients. Case advocacy involves 'the process of working with, or on behalf of, another or a small group, to obtain services to which an individual is entitled, or to influence a decision which affects the individual' (O'Connor et al. 1995: 212). This might occur, for example, when an individual is refused a service or benefit to which they are entitled, when an individual needs benefits or services urgently as a result of a crisis, or when a person is denied their legal rights or unable to act on their own behalf (O'Connor et al. 1995). Class or cause advocacy refers to 'activity directed at changing policy, practices and laws' affecting a class of individuals (O'Connor et al. 1995: 212), and/or promoting social change for the benefits of social groups. This is required, for example, when organisational or government policies affect people adversely, or when groups of people are discriminated against (O'Connor 1995; Payne 1997).

Skills for effective advocacy, decided between the worker and the individual or group, include letter writing, personal lobbying, sit-ins, submission writing, providing people with information about their entitlements, finding loopholes in bureaucratic rules, bending rules, developing familiarity with formal and informal agency rules and procedures, skills in handling conflict, negotiating and bargaining skills and acting as consultant to the individual (Fook 1993; O'Connor et al. 1995). At a broader level, advocacy involves being able to make moral arguments and generating recognition of common values, useful, for example, when forming an inter-agency coalition. Other strategies involve bargaining and negotiation, when decision-makers have a neutral view about the advocacy effort, or coercive strategies, involving the use of conflict and complaint, where there is no shared understanding between parties (O'Connor et al. 1995).

Since the 1980s, new forms of advocacy have emerged—details of these can be found in Payne (1997: 270–1). They are based on a belief in people managing their own lives, as advocacy can be potentially disempowering. For, as Ife (2001) asserts, speaking on behalf of a person may represent profoundly conservative rather than empowering practice. Self-advocacy (helping people speak for themselves), citizen advocacy (involving volunteers in developing relationships with isolated individuals) and peer advocacy (involving people recovering from difficulties in their lives to work together to represent individual needs) are newer forms of advocacy.

Collective action, alliances and citizen participation

Collective action, through groups of people coming together, provides opportunities for consciousness-raising, developing solidarity, lobbying to change opinions on oppressive rules, conditions and institutions, and developing alliances. This calls for educational, support and social change-oriented groups, either facilitated by practitioners or set up as self-help groups. Joining a group can help shift people from individual views towards the development of collective views. Initiating, supporting or facilitating a group from a critical perspective means that personal issues will be discussed in their political context. Group solidarity among participants can develop as people share their individual and common experiences of frustration, anger and oppression, and ideas about what might be needed to make their situations different. Full discussion on group work to help promote social change can be found in Brown (1992), Brown and Mistry (1994) and Benjamin et al. (1997). Mullender and Ward's (1991) work on self-directed groups also provides useful insights on a form of group work based specifically on conflict theory and empowerment practices.

Factors that act as barriers to people's participation in society need to be addressed through institutional change and reform, policy advocacy and social activism (Ife 2001). This involves changing the nature of discourses (Ife 2001; Thompson 1998), using the law and developing alliances and oppositional (alternative) politics (Ife 1997). With the last two terms, Ife is referring to the need for social workers to develop alliances with other groups working for social and political change, such as social justice and human rights groups, trade unions and protest groups. Another strategy is 'elegant challenging'—a concept used by Thompson (1998) to refer to questioning the actions and attitudes of others in tactful and constructive ways that allow people to save face and that avoid unnecessary hostilities and tensions. It needs to occur in a genuine spirit of commitment to social justice rather than one of taking the moral high ground. Collaboration between workers and others with like interests, and understanding the policy process and influencing the policy agenda, are other useful strategies (Thompson 1998).

CONCLUSION

A common and binding theme for practising from a critical social work perspective is the requirement to work in ways that link the personal and the political to ensure that people's immediate material needs are addressed and that also consider the need for longer-term social change. The focus on postmodern narrative work and discourse analysis opens up opportunities for people to be helped to deal with their internalised oppression and thus become actively engaged in actions aimed at social change. Many tensions and contradictions arise in the course of the work undertaken by social workers with or on behalf of individuals and groups. One of the central tensions to be confronted is that of whether to focus activist energies on changes at the structural level, focus more specifically on small-scale resistances at the local level, or to put effort into changing the language and power of discourses. Consistent with a dialectical analysis, social workers engaged in critical social work should consider all of these possibilities in addressing the rights and needs of those individuals and groups with whom they work. It is important for social workers not only to acknowledge and negotiate the contradictions that are inevitable when dealing with uncertainty and difference, but also to educate those with whom they are working to do the same.

PART II

Confronting domination and oppression

5

IMMIGRANTS AND REFUGEES: TOWARDS ANTI-RACIST AND CULTURALLY AFFIRMING PRACTICES

Marjorie Quinn

Social work theory and practice is shaped by theories of both the social and personal worlds. Critical social theories are particularly useful, as they grapple with understandings of social and personal power, and bring a commitment to seeking more just social, economic and political relations. They point to the strength of social structures, and people's location within them, in both shaping their life opportunities, such as access to adequate shelter and housing, health and health care, education, food and water, and decision-making, and in shaping personal subjectivity and psychological processes. At the same time, critical theorists' views of the social world, informed by postmodern ideas, embrace the understanding that people have some power and agency, even within oppressive social structures, to shape their own lives and their own personal consciousness. Personal subjectivity involves the making and remaking of personal meaning structures or narratives, while culture and language are fundamental to these processes.

Such understandings of critical theory are discussed in earlier chapters, and this particular chapter seeks to develop them further in relation to racial, cultural and language diversity. In this context critical postmodern theory directs us to consider the assigning and operations of power within this diversity, and also to working with the cultural frameworks which are central to the creation of people's personal and collective meaning-structures and agency. Following an introductory discussion of these concepts, this chapter explores some directions for the further development of social work theories and practices towards 'just' practice that is both anti-racist and culturally affirming. It challenges us as practitioners and students to continue a journey of learning about ourselves in relation to race relations and culture, and of learning about other cultural meanings and contexts.

CONTEXTS

This chapter is written from Zambia in central southern Africa where I have been living and working since 2000. Zambia is a long way from well-stocked libraries with relevant books, and from conversations about critical perspectives and theories of social work. Communication technologies, which might facilitate such dialogue, are more a promise than an everyday reality. However, in other ways this is a very rich and immediate context in which to reflect on critical perspectives in social work across differences of race, culture and language, issues and concepts with which I must grapple daily. These issues and concepts are important right across the world because of today's significant movements of people, goods, information and values, and because of the conflict and tragedy related, at least in part, to racial and cultural difference, and to lack of understanding and unjust relationships between people(s).

They are important matters within Australia too, where the history of movements of people to the country has shaped development since colonial invasion more than 200 years ago. The history of colonisation has left the families, communities, culture and languages of Indigenous Australians fragmented and disenfranchised, and social indicators such as levels of income, employment rates, education and health status show that they remain the most disadvantaged group of Australians. These indicators, of course, capture only one aspect of the effects of colonisation on Indigenous Australians and do not portray the way history has shaped personal and collective subjectivity and suffering. The contemporary context of race relations and cultural diversity in Australia is also very much shaped by the extraordinary rate of immigration and refugee movement into the country in the second half of the twentieth century, with its various distinctive historical waves and countries of origin. People who have come as immigrants, refugees and asylum seekers, and their children, form a higher proportion of the total population here than almost anywhere else in the world, and are among the most diverse in terms of countries of origin.

The building of a socially just, cooperative and cohesive society which embraces difference and diversity is a big challenge to Australia, and to its social workers pursuing these aspirations. In order to help bring about greater justice and healing, social workers will need to develop the intertwined knowledge and skills required to both challenge racism and nurture emancipation from its operations, and to work effectively with cultural and language difference. It is also increasingly likely that Australian social workers will draw on such knowledge, skills and capacities as they work and live in other countries across the world.

RACE AND RACISM

For the purposes of this chapter I am choosing to use the contentious language of 'race' and 'racism' despite the controversy and the range of strong feelings the terms engender in our community. By race and racism I mean the processes involved in categorising and valuing people on the basis of differences which include physical attributes, particularly colour, and cultural and language differences. The meanings of these terms are complex, and shift and change over time and place. Race was a very powerful descriptor during the historical period of the Enlightenment and colonial expansion in the eighteenth and nineteenth centuries, when there was thought to be a scientific basis to the categorising and valuing of people according to physical characteristics. Certain attributes and deficits, virtues and vices, were ascribed according to physical types or 'races', and the belief in the superiority of white and the inferiority of black was strong. These ideas were increasingly challenged during the first half of the twentieth century by developments in biology and genetics, the growth in social sciences and the decline of Western colonialism. As a result, the concept of race, and terms such as 'pure race', 'full blood' or 'half caste', no longer have scientific support as a way of describing and valuing differences between people.

Nevertheless, despite its lack of validity in this way, race remains today as a very powerful means of categorising people. It is an important concept therefore, 'not because it is real biologically, but because people believe it is real and therefore make it real in its consequences' (Chambers and Pettman 1986: 5). The categorisation and valuing of people on the bases of physical attributes, and cultural and language difference, is still a part of our social structure. The concept of race is now recognised as one which is socially constructed, rather than one which is inherently meaningful. It still, however, has immense power to generate hatred, oppression and violence, and to produce intense emotions in people, whether they are the perpetrators or the victims of racism (Frankenberg 1993; Vasta and Castles 1996).

Power and prejudice (literally 'pre-judging') are key ingredients in racism. Racism includes not only obvious, overt acts of exploitation and oppression, but also a whole range of personal actions and institutional structures and practices in society which serve to exclude or devalue people on the basis of factors such as appearance, culture and language. The term 'institutional racism' refers to the way in which major institutions and structures in society operate to the advantage of one or some racial groups, and to the disadvantage of others. A further element of racism, which interacts with personal and institutional racisms, can be described as cultural racism. Here, the values, beliefs, meanings and practices from the dominant culture become not only central, but also the benchmark. Other values and meanings are perceived as different and become constructed as inferior, deviant or pathological.

These expressions of racism serve to assign power and privilege in society. 'White' usually ensures power and privilege through processes of withholding, exclusion and denial of opportunity (Fine et al. 1997). Typically, racism is thought of as an issue more for those people marginalised and oppressed by its operations than for those privileged by it. Everyone, though, has a place in the relations of race, and Katz (cited in Carter 1997: 205) considers that racism is in fact 'a white problem in that its development and perpetuation rests with white people'. Carter goes on to say that victims of oppression can fight against it, protect themselves and act in spite of it, but they cannot stop something they are not creating. White people, therefore, must acknowledge their position of race privilege, and resist and challenge racism at all levels if a more just society and world is to be achieved.

Despite the usefulness of this language of race, of 'white' and 'black', in highlighting not only difference and diversity but also power relations, there are significant dangers and problems attached to its use. These categories quickly and easily become reified as fixed, separate and monolithic categories of experience and identity, rather than being seen as socially constructed, blurred and changing. The reality is much more complex than these dualistic terms imply. My current situation exemplifies this complexity well. I am part of a small minority of white people in Zambia, constituting less than one per cent of the total population. Contemporary race relations are very much shaped by the history of exploitation through colonialism, and the struggle for independence. Subsequent experiences of a particular form of socialism, where consumption more than production was subsidised through the raising of an enormous overseas debt, were followed by a very difficult decade through the 1990s of economic restructuring driven by the Western world which has resulted in increased poverty and inequality. These stories are part of the complexity of race relations in this country. In addition, perceptions of Western culture and values are fed daily through the media, especially television. 'White' means wealth and power, health, education, cleanliness, honesty and choices in life. It evokes resentment together with a kind of respect at the same time. Within and between the categories of 'black' and 'white' there are, of course, significant variations which become masked by stereotypical categorisation and perceptions. For example, although many of the white residents and expatriates here have wealth and receive very large salaries, not all white people are in this situation. Some like me are working for local wages and so have little ready cash, and others are retired citizens of long standing with little wealth or power. In addition to this, and despite the fact that most Zambians live in grinding poverty, there are growing numbers of very wealthy and powerful black Zambians.

A further dimension is added to the analysis through the consideration of gender. Traditionally, women's roles and positions are culturally tied to and defined by the men in their lives—husbands, fathers, sons, employers and bosses—and women are poorly protected by law or by social convention from abuse, violence, exploitation, sexual assault, invisibility, exclusion and poverty. As a white woman in Zambia I am not immune from some of this. Another aspect of race relations concerns language diversity, and my lack of facility with local languages is a factor which limits my participation and social power.

The implications of each of these and other issues in relation to social and personal power need to be teased out much further than space here will allow. Such an analysis would demonstrate something of the complexity and particularity of race relations, and also their connectedness to other dimensions of oppression. This is the kind of analysis which critical postmodern theory invites. It encourages our attempts to understand in each situation the complex and particular structures and operations of power and dominance, and subjugation and oppression, and of personal meaning. It rejects monolithic and dualistic categorisation. Many threads of my social story carry with them privilege and power; others carry less privilege and power, and even some vulnerability. If we are seeking to live and work in ways which affirm difference and promote understanding and equality, we must explore, and manage ourselves through, such complexities. At the same time as engaging with these particularities and differences, we must not be blind to the fact that overall very real privileges accrue in our world from being white.

ETHNICITY

Ethnicity is a widely used term in social life and it is often preferred over the language of race. It too, is a complex concept, and to some extent the two have overlapping meanings. Ethnicity refers to belonging and commonality in relation to factors such as national origin, historical experience, shared culture or physical type (Ely and Denny 1987; Cox 1989; Hartley 1995). It emphasises the social and historical determinants more than the physical. The term usually does not invoke the same political/power implications and judgments as the concept of race, but instead the sense of difference and belonging. Writing about race relations in the United States, Frankenberg (1993) considers that it is part of the language of difference which tends to shroud the existence of structural, material and power inequalities, and oppression, that are based on physical, cultural, national and historical differences. The adoption of such race-neutral terminology thus operates to mask and protect race privilege and power. There are however, differences of opinion about the use of this language within social science and social work literature, Devore and Schlesinger, for example, in *Ethnic-Sensitive Social Work Practice* (1996), take a different point of view to the one taken in this chapter. Their stance is to adopt the terminology of ethnicity and ethno-sensitive practice because they say (as I have noted earlier in this chapter) the concept of race lacks scientific basis, and because they feel that in many contexts its use is 'pejorative and divisive' (1996: 25, 28).

Social work literature, theories and practices are frequently critiqued for their ethnocentricity. This important concept refers to the tendency to hold 'a view of the world in which oneself or one's group is at the centre of things: a failure to take into account the perceptions of others'

(Cashmore and Troyne, cited in Ely and Denny 1987: 17). The concept is similar in meaning to cultural racism. Giddens (1983: 23) argues that 'ethno-centrism is deeply entrenched in Western culture though it is also found in many (if not most) other countries as well'.

CULTURE

Like ethnicity, culture is a term frequently used in contemporary society, and has a range of meanings both over time and in current use. An early meaning of 'tending crops' (agriculture, horticulture) was extended by the early sixteenth century to more abstract things, particularly the culture of the mind. This soon took on notions of elitism and 'high' culture, and became associated with only certain groups of people, such as artists or intellectuals. This meaning has been extended further so we now talk of 'popular culture', the culture of 'ordinary people' and the 'cultures of institutions'—their daily practices, norms and beliefs. Another meaning comes from the Enlightenment period around the eighteenth century, when writers used it to refer to the general process of secular social development taking place within Europe. The Eurocentric, colonising imagination of that time thought that this was a linear process of development through which all societies would pass, following the superior leadership of Europe. These conceptions of culture soon involved a clear understanding of what marked the West off from the non-West. The West was seen to be rational, historical, progressive and devotional, and the non-West superstitious, static, archaic and magical (Geertz 1995).

The anthropological tradition of defining culture evolved following colonial expansion and development of Western social sciences. In this tradition, the term has come to mean the distinctive ways of life and shared values, beliefs and meanings common to groups of people. With developments in anthropology and other social sciences, the emphasis is placed on processes of signification—on what culture does, rather than on what it is. So culture can be understood as the 'set of practices by which meanings are produced and exchanged within a group' (Bocock 1992: 233). Culture is often described as a complex web of meanings which underlie everyday life and behaviour, the understandings and expectations which guide actions and interactions with others. These are the meanings relevant to this chapter.

This latter understanding of the concept of culture has implications for how we learn about it. Geertz (1973: 5) suggests that the 'analysis of culture then is not an experimental science in search of law but an interpretive one in search of meaning.' He proposes that these understandings are grounded in language and other symbolic communication practices such as rites and rituals. Things and events occur, but of themselves they do not necessarily have intrinsic meaning. Meaning is given by language, through which comes the construction and exchange of understandings. These matters will be explored further later in the chapter.

Cultures are dynamic, and continually evolving and changing over time in response to all sorts of factors in the economic, political, ideological and social worlds. The boundaries of cultural groups, where they begin and end, are blurred and changing. And they are not internally homogeneous. Within any cultural group there will always be diversity according to differences such as class, education, gender, sexuality, rural/urban, religion, personal and family factors. Also, for a wide range of reasons people will be drawing on more than one set of cultural meanings.

THE AUSTRALIAN CONTEXT—UNEQUAL RELATIONS

Beliefs and attitudes about race and culture have significantly shaped Australia's development since 1788, and race relations have been the seat of tensions, struggle, violence and inequality (Pettman 1992; Butler 1993; Vasta and Castles 1996). The story is about diversity, and also about injustice, privilege and oppression. At some levels, Australia claims success in meeting the challenge of building a socially-just, cooperative and cohesive society. Overtly racist laws and policies towards Indigenous people and immigrants were abolished in the 1960s and 1970s (Vasta and Castles 1996: 1), but the actual experience of members of minority groups, especially those who are visibly different, does not fit this picture. There is ample evidence from social indicators that Aboriginal people and Torres Strait Islanders are severely oppressed, and that overall great inequality exists for immigrants and refugees, although their experiences vary widely. The inequality, privilege and oppression of the present time are likely to be exacerbated by the current trends in the political, economic and social environment involving the ascendance of ideologies of liberalism, economic rationalism, deregulation and small government.

TOWARDS THEORIES AND PRACTICES WHICH ARE ANTI-RACIST AND CULTURALLY AFFIRMING

If social workers and other human service workers are to be committed to social change towards justice, inclusion, diversity and participation, we must be seeking to develop theories and practices which place social, political and economic power relations, as well as cultural relevance, firmly in the foreground. Structural approaches (Moreau and Leonard 1989; Mullaly 1997), anti-oppressive social work (Dalrymple and Burke 1995; Dominelli 1998), radical approaches (Fook 1993), critical approaches (Ife 1997) and postmodern approaches (Leonard 1997; Pease and Fook 1999) have all provided helpful frameworks for anti-racist practice because they hold analyses of power relations central to thinking and acting. (Some of the detail of the similarities and differences in their conceptions of social and personal power are discussed earlier in this book, especially in Chapter 4.) However, the theoretical development of these approaches has been mainly grounded in analyses of class inequality and oppression and contemporary Marxism, significantly influenced by feminism (Moreau and Leonard 1989). An expanded understanding of racial and cultural oppression is also necessary if the latter are not to be subsumed into the narratives of other dimensions of oppression. These are not sufficient, as we saw earlier in this chapter, because of the very particular and historical operations of racism, and because of the central place of culture in personal and collective subjectivity and meaning-making.

Of the many texts on social work and cognate disciplines which focus particularly on racism and cultural diversity, most are written from British and North American contexts (for example, Dominelli 1988; Herberg 1993; Devore and Schlesinger 1996). They include a range of different approaches, some giving more emphasis to the broad socio-political context and power relations, and others to more individualistic, psychologically oriented understandings. Some engage with the particularities of race oppression as experienced historically and locally, and with intersecting dimensions of oppression such as poverty and gender relations. These texts emphasise the racial and cultural power embedded in social policies, professional theories and practices, social work roles, agencies and organisations, and in teaching institutions. They affirm the necessity for workers to recognise their own racism and ethnocentricity.

Critical postmodern approaches to social work direct attention to all spheres of action: to legislation and policy formation, to organisational practice, to professional education and development, and to community, group, family and individual work. In each of these situations scrutiny and attention will be given to material, ideological and discursive aspects, and to the connectedness between the broad social, economic and political conditions and the personal.

Issues which I find are not sufficiently emphasised in available literature include: the importance of cultural knowledge—of self, of the cultural bases of theories and practices, and of other culturally based pathways for practice; understandings of race relations, especially of white privilege and power; and how these understandings are most effectively learned.

THE PLACE OF CULTURAL KNOWLEDGE IN ANTI-RACIST PRACTICE

Substantial and particular cultural knowledge, and understanding of one's cultural self, are critical to all aspects of anti-racist practice. Cultural ignorance and ethnocentricity of people within the dominant cultural and racial group perpetuate cultural and racial oppression. Ignorance results in the cultural meanings, values, beliefs and ways which are at the centre of the lives of people within dominated cultural groups being marginalised, not recognised, valued or accepted in the process. Cultural domination results whether it is intended or not. Although very important, good will, good intentions and fine skills of empathy are not sufficient on their own.

Informed and sensitive cultural knowledge is essential to processes of healing and recovery from the devastating community, family and personal effects of race-related oppression, and therefore to anti-racist practice. Waldegrave and colleagues from the Family Centre in New Zealand have made a significant contribution to this area of theory development and practice (for example, see *Dulwich Centre Newsletter* 1990, No. 1). Their family and community work involves carefully listening to people's stories for the articulation of meanings and hopes, and assisting in various ways with the weaving of new and liberating meanings and opportunities. It is probably the cultural context more than any other factor, which determines underlying meaning systems, so an informed and particular cultural knowledge is essential for 'just' and healing practice. They consider that these understandings have been given too little emphasis in literature, conferences and teaching.

Wahiri Campbell, a Maori therapist/community worker from the

Family Centre, illustrates these points in the following story (from personal conversations with the author, 1993). The Centre was asked to work with a young Maori family to help them decide on custody and care arrangements for their children, who had been in state care and were now to be returned to their family. The parents had separated, and the mother was unable to assume care for them at the time because of illness. They were seeking cooperatively to make a decision. A Pakeha (white) worker saw the family, and together they considered at least two possibilities, including the father caring for the children, and the maternal grandmother. After much discussion, the worker and the family were tentatively in the process of agreeing that the father take custody of the children. Wahiri, the cultural consultant on this occasion, intervened: 'In our culture the closest family relationship is between grandparents and *mokopuna* (grandchildren); these mokopuna should be with their grandmother.' When this possibility was put to the family, they immediately recognised it as the right way for them, and so made their decision accordingly. Wahiri went on to explain that if the former course had been adopted, deep sensibilities of a number of people would have been fractured. Relationships within the extended family would have been weakened further, the *mana* (status or position) of the family in the community lowered, and therefore, the usual supports for the care of the children would have been seriously eroded. Clinical knowledge based in Western understandings would have supported a decision for the father to assume care, but Maori culture indicated another way, which was immediately recognised by the family as the right way for them. This experience was a critical one for the Family Centre in forming the principle that 'cultural knowledge must take precedence over (Western) clinical knowledge'.

Cultures give rise to particular understandings and patterns of relationship which are not simply different configurations of the same component parts. They are not readily or automatically recognisable from one culture to another. These relationships provide a very significant context for the development and maintenance of the sense of identity, of belonging and of well-being, and they will be threatened rather than affirmed by workers operating from different and sometimes contradictory cultural values. Theories and practices need to be congruent with the particular cultural understandings of the people concerned and to take account of their culturally based pathways to healing and growth. This does not imply that all cultural understandings and ways are liberating or just, but it respects the principle that change must evolve from within, rather than being imposed from outside.

Theories and practices most commonly adopted in Australia come from Western European and North American cultures, and reflect their underlying values, meanings and arrangements. They involve an emphasis on individualism and nuclear families; particular gender arrangements, and patterns of marriage and child-rearing; higher esteem for youth than for eldership; democratic processes of participation and authority; and secular approaches to life. Individual self-worth is often regarded as a primary goal. However, people from communal and extended family cultures do not relate easily to such concepts, finding them confusing and alienating. Personal identity in such cultures is expressed through the extended family and places of belonging, not in individualistic concepts.

Spirituality is another dimension of personal, family and cultural life where particular knowledge and understanding is critical to affirming and working with people's meaning systems. In many non-European Indigenous cultures, spirituality is a fundamental value integrated into every aspect of life. An integrated spirituality is centred on the essential quality of relationship and connectedness—between people, between people and their ancestors and descendants, between people and the land and environment, between people and the creator spirit. These understandings will be profoundly relevant to the ways in which people see their identity and belonging, their relationships, and cultural processes of recovery, healing and change. The denigration of spirituality by much of Western scientific, clinical and technical knowledge, the dualistic separation of spiritual and physical, linear and logical ways of thinking, and values of materialism and consumerism, all mean that workers socialised within these Western meanings struggle to understand this more central and integrated spirituality. Such failure to understand can lead to disrespectful and dismissive responses where the meanings of life that other peoples bring, and their issues and pathways to healing, are not recognised. This results in a form of cultural racism, and social work practice becomes another forum for domination.

Cultural knowledge is therefore central knowledge. There are many contentious questions concerning how human services respond to this assertion. Sometimes, for example, it is considered important that the worker (or the organisation/agency) hold similar cultural understandings to the family or group concerned. This may be particularly important for Indigenous peoples because human service work can so easily become a further site for domination. Language, and fluency in English, might be another consideration supporting such responses. However, workers in the mainstream also need to take up the challenge of this assertion that cultural knowledge is central knowledge, and find ways of developing sufficient cultural knowledge to facilitate healing, growth and change. This is a big challenge. Waldegrave (1990) sounds a warning against what he terms 'cultural tourism'; that is, the tendency for workers 'to move around culture' with about as much sensitivity and cultural understanding as a tourist. He suggests that inadequate knowledge unknowingly involves those workers in cross-cultural collisions, and finally causes a retreat back to the known, in the belief that the approach will not work, and that people are 'resistant' or closed to help. My experience supports this observation.

It follows then that the place of cultural knowledge requires more emphasis than it gets in social work and anti-racist literature. It also follows that workers, particularly from the standpoint of the dominant racial and cultural context, need more resources and direction for developing the necessary knowledge and skills than are readily available. This knowledge-seeking will involve: identification of the cultural base of theories and practices currently in use, and critiquing them for their claims to be international and intercultural; development of principles for culturally based practice by and with people from marginalised cultural communities; and more direction for learning about culture and about self-awareness within the relations of race and culture.

LEARNING ABOUT CULTURE

So how do we go about seeking this important knowledge and understanding? Many of the texts focusing on cultural knowledge, cross-cultural practice and work with immigrants, while helpful in some ways are problematic at two levels. The first is that many either do not acknowledge, or do not integrate, the understanding that in working with race and culture we are not just dealing with diversity, but with social processes of racism, of domination and subjugation, privilege and oppression, at both institutional and personal levels. The second concerns the approaches they take to understanding and learning about cultural difference. In this context two broad approaches are commonly referred to in the literature, the 'etic' and the 'emic' (Cox 1987; Locke 1992). Etic approaches study culture from the outside in the light of categories and concepts external to the culture but universally applied. Emic approaches are those in which learning is undertaken from within and where understandings generated are understood as specific to that culture. These latter approaches are congruent with critical postmodern perspectives in their search for the particularities of each situation.

Some of the etic approaches to learning cultural frameworks for social work are simplistic, others are difficult to grasp at a meaningful level without substantial existing cultural knowledge. They are easily reduced to mechanistic conceptual constructs, even though they are sometimes presented in contexts which emphasise the dynamic and changing nature of culture, and the human processes of respect and listening required for learning. For example, the Asia Partnership for Human Development (APHD) project report (1991), which offers an elaborate conceptual framework for examining cultures, states that

> it will not suffice to train social workers in the use of this tool; more important will be to develop his or her art of listening and looking, an ability to see or to have an intuition of what happens. This cannot be achieved without a process of knowledge and transformation of self . . . [Further], to learn to know a people is not like going 'hunting' for data . . . this type of knowledge turns people into objects. Rather than understanding, it is better to 'stand under'. This framework can help if it is just seen as a modest reminder within a larger process of human encounter (1991: 24).

While many texts on cultural practice rely heavily on cognitive processes of learning and understanding culture, and on etic frameworks, other literature and my own experience suggest that effective cultural practice may not be learned most effectively this way. Geertz (1995) advises students to immerse themselves in observation and reading, weaving from the particular through the general narratives (the larger social contexts) and back. He is critical of etic approaches as he considers that it is not helpful to conceive of culture as a massive causal force shaping belief and behaviour to an abstractable pattern, that we are not faced with a set of abstractable themes which can be summarised and somehow put together. In considering gender relations, for example, he says, one cannot simply identify dimensions such as sex, status, boldness or modesty, and configure them together. Cultures are more complex and contradictory fields of action than this, involving as they do the interplay of the local and the broad, the figure and the ground, the particular and the general narrative. He considers emic approaches to be more propositional and dynamic, and more constructive approaches to learning culture.

Learning about cultural meanings and ways, and race privilege from 'within' (the emic approach) often involves personally confronting experiences, and moving away from familiar places of belonging, position and culture in order to provide an opportunity for viewing oneself with something of an outsider's view. I have found that in the course of this learning it is very important to accept the position of learner, which involves deep respect and humility. It is important to 'stand under' more than to understand. This is a stance which involves giving up the power of dominance, together with a preparedness to relinquish one's own cultural ways of making meaning, and to learn and value new ones. It involves acceptance of, and engaging with, uncertainty and discomfort. The approach of observer/inquirer is often preferable to that of questioner/inquirer, and skills of empathy are important. The learning process is not simply about learning facts or frameworks, but about gaining a deeper awareness of diverse culturally based meanings of life, relationships and communication. I have learned that, for me, the deepest enlightenment and learning come not from books, nor etic analytic tools, but from exposure to, and immersion in, a particular cultural context.

LEARNING ABOUT RACE RELATIONS AND 'WHITE' PRIVILEGE

Closely interconnected with learning about culture and culturally based theories and practices, and learning about oneself as a cultural being, is learning about oneself in the relations of race. When faced with injustice and inequality it seems to be easier to recognise oppression than the privilege and power of the dominant racial and cultural group, which tends to remain normalised and unscrutinised. Fine (Fine 1997) observes that, although there has been extensive documentation of inequality and oppression, there has been little writing about the privilege and power of being white. She argues (1997: 64) that to combat racism we may need to shift gears, and not focus only on the unfair disadvantage accruing to people of colour, but also on the unfair benefits that surround and grow as a result of being embodied as 'white'.

Frankenberg (1993), writing about race relations in the United States, discusses the awakening of her own awareness of the impact of colonisation and oppression on black people, and especially the awakening of awareness of her own white race privilege. She also considers that recognition of white race privilege in the relations of race is more difficult than the recognition of the oppression of others, and that white people tend to conceptualise themselves as neutral (1993). She concludes that seeing oneself as a culturally specific being may require moving away from one's usual situation. In the Australian context, Denborough (1996) discusses his confronting experiences while working with Indigenous people in prison. It was their challenge to him in relation to being white and middle class that lead to his awakening regarding race privilege. He also observes that it is easy to avoid acknowledging the inherent benefits that come with being white, where cultural practices can remain unmarked and unnamed and yet be the benchmark for all.

In a similar way I can identify particular experiences which have been very significant in my learning. I have been very personally and profoundly confronted with my own race privilege as I have encountered and listened to people who have experienced the devastating effects of colonisation and of war, imprisonment, torture, rape, refugee experience, exploitation, exclusion and the persisting day-to-day experiences of racism. Often their experiences have been amplified for me by their startling personal honesty, courage, hope, strength, hospitality and generosity of spirit, little known in Western acquisitive society. Examining and understanding the operations of white privilege and power, and finding ways to challenge and resist these in ourselves, in our professions and at the wider level of society, are at the centre of anti-racist practice.

CONCLUSION

Terrible violence and tragedy linked to racial and cultural difference is evident in various parts of the world today. On the home front, we are challenged to redefine and reshape the place of Indigenous people within Australian society, and at the same time to determine our response to immigrants, refugees and people seeking asylum. We have an urgent need to understand better the operations of racism and cultural difference in order to help build a more just and peaceful society and world. This chapter has canvassed some ways in which critical theories can assist our development of anti-racist and culturally affirming social policies, and theories and practices for social work and the human services. Critical theory approaches will assist us in identifying and challenging racism, especially white power and domination. They will encourage us as students and practitioners to create opportunities to explore and examine our own position within the relations of race and culture, so developing our capacity to recognise and resist white domination and privilege within ourselves (where this is relevant), and in our profession and workplaces. The cultural bases of theories and practices will be made explicit, and more space will be opened for the documentation of new theories and practices based on relevant cultural meanings.

6

INDIGENOUS AUSTRALIANS: TOWARDS POSTCOLONIAL SOCIAL WORK

Linda Briskman

Newly emerging interpretations of colonial history have presented challenges to social work theorising and practice. This chapter explores the historical and contemporary relationship of social work with Indigenous people in Australia. It confronts past and present practices that resist engagement with Indigenous knowledge and theorising. Advocating a decolonising approach to practice requires social workers to recognise their race privilege, to validate Indigenous wisdom and to adopt a professional approach that acknowledges Indigenous rights. Social work educators have a particular responsibility to ensure that social workers leave academic institutions with appropriate understandings and practice tools.

SOCIAL WORK AND INDIGENOUS PEOPLES

The relationship between social work and Indigenous peoples[1] in Australia has been fraught but largely unexplored, evolving in part from experiences of Indigenous groups with the child welfare system, past and present. Aboriginal academic Stephanie Gilbert (2001) points out the dual roles of Australian social workers in the history of the oppression of Indigenous people. For Gilbert, social workers have been part of a long and worthy list of non-Indigenous people who have stood up for the rights of Indigenous peoples. Conversely, they were participants in the process of dispossession and oppression, albeit by default. Furthermore, social workers continue to hold central roles in such areas as child protection and health, sites where great injustices have been carried out against Indigenous peoples (Gilbert 2001).

Notwithstanding isolated pockets of resistance, social work has not generally taken a proactive stance for ensuring Indigenous rights and has not been progressive, activist or outspoken. To a large extent, social workers have colluded with dominant policy paradigms, reinforcing a monolothic viewpoint including the embracing of assimilationist practices. Recent exposure of child welfare policies and practices has forced social work to acknowledge its role, and this arena is explored in this chapter.

The situation is slowly changing. Like the community in general, social work as a profession is starting to take stock of its legacy and endeavouring to redress it. Evidence of recent engagement has occurred through the recognition of Indigenous Australians in the revised Australian Association of Social Workers' (AASW) Code of Ethics (1999), the AASW as a signatory to an Australian Council of Social Service (ACOSS) apology to the stolen generations and through the participation of social workers in the walk for reconciliation across the Sydney Harbour Bridge in 2000. As with other Australians, social workers have recently been forced to come to terms with the least desirable aspects of Australian history. A formal reconciliation process, publicity about land rights and native title, and the release of the Human Rights and Equal Opportunity Commission (HREOC) report on the 'stolen generations' in 1997 have contributed to the awareness. In addition, the attention of the world community, including through the United Nations, has put Australia in the spotlight in relation to its treatment of Indigenous people.

Alongside these developments, critical social workers are gradually turning attention to theoretical constructs which affirm Indigenous world views and reject the privileging of Western paradigms. Consistent with critical social work perspectives are frameworks that reject traditional theorising on citizenship, which recognise whiteness as a form of privilege and which embrace an overtly anti-colonialist stance.

BACKGROUND

The history of invasion, dispossession, murder and destruction of Indigenous people and their society has been well documented (for example, Rowley 1970; Reynolds 1993). Later policies of protection and assimilation had a devastating impact. The emergence of 'protection' policies early in the twentieth century coincided with a belief that Aboriginal people were doomed to extinction. By 1911, most states had introduced specific legislation with the emphasis on protection and restriction of Aboriginal children (Rowley 1970). Segregation and institutionalisation of Aboriginal people were the main instruments of protection (Gale 1973), with control exercised over many aspects of life including child care (Tatz 1979). When it was clear that such extinction was not occurring, assimilationist approaches developed, aimed at a monolithic approach to nation-building. It was only after it became evident that Aboriginal people wished to maintain a distinctive social existence that policies of 'self-determination' emerged (Coombs 1978). However, self-determination for Aboriginal people, which was formally endorsed by the federal Whitlam Labor government in 1972, has had a precarious existence (Briskman 1996). Assimilationist policies, which were subject to their most intensive implementation after World War II, are seen to be the most pervasive, including in the field of child welfare policy and practice.

The legacy of colonisation remains. On every socio-economic indicator in Australia, Aboriginal people fall well below the national average. Many Aboriginal people continue to live in conditions associated with a 'fourth-world' existence, characterised by an experience of being colonised and being a minority in relation to a dominant, encompassing state, with attempts by dominant governments to assimilate them (Reid and Lupton 1991). They experience the worst health, the highest unemployment rate and the lowest degree of participation in secondary and tertiary education of any group. They are over-represented in the prison system and die on average twenty years younger than other Australians. Indigenous communities remain at risk from a range of social problems including high levels of domestic violence (Sam 1992), drug and alcohol problems (Choo 1990; Drugs and Crime Prevention Committee 2001) and child protection issues (Broadbent and Bentley 1997). These factors are symptomatic of a relationship with the state characterised by a lack of understanding of Indigenous culture and aspirations, and dominated by an ethnocentric approach to policy-making and practice. Australia has been listed as being in breach of adherence to international human rights standards in its dealings with Indigenous peoples (Hocking and Hocking 1998). The focus of government and bureaucratic endeavours is largely ameliorative in nature, avoiding such complex issues as land rights, sovereignty, self-determination and the control by Indigenous peoples of their own destinies.

Disempowerment and dispossession still characterise Indigenous peoples' relationships with the state, reinforcing the claim that by being free to determine their own destinies, their circumstances will improve (Dennis 1995). The Indigenous view emphasises that the processes of self-determination are as important as outcomes, and that outcomes must be measured in Indigenous terms (Jones and May 1992). Aspirations toward self-determination, located within a nation state which values homogeneity, have not captured the imagination of either governments or the community at large. In Australia today there is an evident backlash against Aboriginal rights, particularly those rights to land and rights to reparations for past injustices which are seen as intruding on the economic sphere. Mainstream support generally extends only to what may be loosely defined as an equality of opportunity, without recognition of the lack of a level 'playing field'. Reynolds suggests that the question 'Are we not all supposed to be equal?' conceives of equality in terms of the individual, rather than the group, and is hence assimilationist (Reynolds 1997: 33). D'Souza (1994: 27) criticises the social services field 'where we are treated as welfare problems . . . we need to decolonise the field of social welfare'. Tatz (1996: 15) refers to a turning back of the clock to what looks like 'old time Christian paternalism'.

STOLEN GENERATIONS

Until recently, one of the least understood components of the history of post-colonial Australia concerned the forcible removal of Indigenous children from their families and communities, more commonly referred to as the 'stolen generations'. Under a range of legal guises, these practices are seen by many commentators as underpinned by social Darwinist notions of racial superiority. These theories, which explain cultural and social differences largely in terms of 'blood' and physical conformation (Hollingsworth 1997), influenced assimilation policies. Such policies and practices represent a form of social control and engineering imposed by colonial and subsequent governments throughout Australia. In the past, a network of legislation existed which enabled each Australian jurisdiction to exert great authority over Aboriginal children (Grimshaw et al. 1994). Children were removed without consent from their families and placed in white institutions and with white foster and adoptive families, with state and church colluding in the practices (Harris 1994; Summers 1995; Minajalku Aboriginal Corporation 1997). These policies and practices have been described as 'an Australian holocaust, an Australian version of ethnic cleansing' (Katona 1996, cited in McLean 1996), 'genocidal' (HREOC 1997) and as 'the most terrible injustice perpetrated in Australia during the twentieth century' (Manne 1999). Aboriginality was constructed as 'a condition to be transcended' (Rose 1997: 107). As they grew up, the children were expected to think white, act white and be white (Edwards and Read 1992). In Australia today there may be 100 000 people of Aboriginal descent who do not know their families or communities (Edwards and Read 1992). Bird (1998) summarises the themes of removal across all regions of the country:

> The children could be taken away at any age, and many of them were taken from their mothers at birth or in very early infancy. Most of the children so taken were put into institutions where the other children were mostly Indigenous, of mixed race, and where the staff were non-Indigenous. If a child was adopted or fostered out to a family, that family was usually white. The objective of all this activity was to absorb the Indigenous children into white society, to force them to forget and deny their Aboriginal heritage and blood, and to bring about, within a few generations, a form of breeding-out of all Indigenous characteristics (Bird 1998: 11).

These practices are not merely the domain of the past, reinforcing the notion that the process of decolonisation has done little to reshape power imbalances. The HREOC Inquiry (1997) reported that Indigenous children and young people continue to be removed from their families through laws, policies and practices of the states and territories. They are significantly over-represented 'in care' and in their contact with welfare authorities. A high percentage of Indigenous children in long-term foster care live with non-Indigenous carers (HREOC 1997; Australian Institute of Health and Welfare 1997/1998). This occurs despite the fact that all states have implemented, through policy or legislation, an Aboriginal Child Placement Principle which specifies that Aboriginal children should be placed with their families or communities; a principle that is not always uniformly applied. A report by the New South Wales Law Reform Commission (1997) documents its shortfalls. Submissions to an earlier inquiry into children and the legal process were critical of the responses of care and protection systems to the needs of children in Indigenous communities. The three main criticisms were that some workers in family services departments held racist attitudes, that there remained a lack of consultation with communities and that insufficient account was taken of Indigenous child-rearing practices (HREOC and Australian Law Reform Commission 1996).

In their endeavours to change the policies and practices of the state, Indigenous people have established a strong network of Indigenous-controlled organisations. These exist in the fields of health, employment, education, legal services and child welfare. Indigenous child welfare organisations exist in each Australian jurisdiction to provide direct services and to campaign against repressive laws, policies and practices. Despite the growth of such organisations, power still rests with the state. Indigenous organisations are increasingly subjected to stringent funding and accountability requirements, making it impossible to assert their rights to autonomy and community control. D'Souza (1993) argues that there are two child welfare systems operating in Australia, one which is well-resourced and controlled and operated in the main by white people who make the rules; and the other under-resourced, over-loaded and run by Indigenous people who are under-paid and over-worked, whose experience does not count for anything and who are described as unqualified.

The unwillingness to incorporate Indigenous cultural values has characterised the Indigenous relationship with the social welfare system. The lack of understanding, based on the ethnocentric approaches of the dominant culture, has been particularly evident in relation to 'difference' in child-rearing practices, including the importance of the extended family system (Freedman 1989). There continues to be a history of high intervention and interference with Indigenous children and families. In the past it made little difference what the family situation was, because being Aboriginal was in itself a reason to regard children as neglected, with Aboriginal families regarded as 'inappropriate' and 'improper' (Van Krieken 1992). Arguably, similar 'standards' and practices are still applied today, as indicated by the over-representation of Indigenous children in care and in out-of-family placements. The practices' manifestations include interpreting residence in an extended family situation as 'living in overcrowded conditions', and shared parenting as 'neglect' (Minajalku Aboriginal Corporation 1997). The 'neglect' category remains as the main reason for over-representation in child protection statistics, reflecting the high levels of unemployment, poverty and homelessness of Indigenous people (Secretariat of National Aboriginal and Islander Child Care 2001). Of increasing concern is the over-representation of Indigenous people in the juvenile justice system. A 'progression' from the child welfare system to the juvenile justice system to the adult correctional system has been evidenced, and laws seen as discriminatory operate in some jurisdictions. The incarceration of Indigenous people in the juvenile justice system represents the 'new stolen generations' (Cuneen 1997).

SOCIAL WORK RESPONSE

Increasing numbers of Indigenous people are seeking social work training with the aim of increasing their knowledge and skills to work in their own communities. The numbers are still relatively small, which is not surprising given that social work particularly has been described by some commentators as the profession of oppressors (Atkinson et al. 1997), intent on maintaining an apolitical therapeutic approach (Ife 1997) and resistant to activism (de Maria 1997). There is evidence that social workers accepted popular social Darwinist thinking and other doctrines that have harmed the lives of many (Gilbert 2001). According to David Thorpe (1994), the accepted standards of European child-rearing practices grossly distort the judgments workers make about Indigenous children and families reported to child welfare agencies.

These views remain alive within and outside the social work profession, despite endeavours within social work to critically examine the impact of larger economic and political issues, including social dislocation and racism (House and Stalwick 1990: 80). Proponents of critical social work accept and validate wisdom and experience from 'below' as well as from 'above' (Ife 1997). Yet despite good intentions, social work schools have generally lacked an appreciation of the impact of racism on clients, social workers and communities (Carniol 1990).

In some countries, including Canada and New Zealand, there have been more direct endeavours to shift social work from its conventional therapeutic approach and to return power to Indigenous peoples. These include actions to empower people to direct their own social services needs and delivery (House and Stalwick 1990). In recognition of the status of the Treaty of Waitangi, the New Zealand Association of Social Workers adopted a bi-cultural Code of Ethics (Noble and Briskman 1996). Although there is evidence of some reinvention of Australian social work within the critical tradition, little has changed structurally with social work and welfare training; nor has there been extensive engagement with broader critiques about the ways in which Indigenous knowledge is undervalued and even undermined. One example is the marginalisation of spirituality which, according to Ife, is 'to deny or marginalise Australia's indigenous population' (Ife 1997: 10). Drawing on the writings of Edward Said, New Zealand Indigenous academic Linda Smith (1999) speaks also of how the Western discourse of 'other' is supported by institutions, vocabulary, scholarship, imagery, doctrines and colonial bureaucracies.

Professionalism and the entrenched elitism of social work and welfare practice has contributed to resistance to effectively grappling with questions of Indigenous knowledge in the Australian context. Although many educators are aware of the cultural vacuum of their course offerings, attempts to address this are often tokenistic and limited by structural constraints. Unlike New Zealand with its bi-cultural emphasis, Australian social work has not led the way in ensuring that methods of teaching, theorising and practising in complex areas bind together social work expertise and Indigenous knowledge. The scales of knowledge need to be balanced in a way that affirms Indigenous knowledge and expertise, while drawing on 'professional' expertise, largely derived from dominant culture paradigms. In order to avoid undermining Indigenous voices through the legitimisation of Western 'experts', there is a need to incorporate those voices without colonising them in a manner which reinforces patterns of domination (Scheyvens and Leslie 2000). This means that critical social workers must address their lack of knowledge of the processes and experience of colonialism, and work consciously to counter the effects of colonialism, not practising from a colonialist position (Ife 2001).

Social work as a profession is very much in the business of defining needs and working towards having them met. Yet, as Ife (1997) declares, when need is defined from a top-down perspective within a professional discourse, needs are defined by 'experts'. These experts include social workers, as needs definition is seen as requiring professional expertise. From the bottom-up perspective, however, defining needs is a matter for the people or communities directly involved, with expert, professional needs definition seen as disempowering and representing control (Ife 1997). According to Jordan (1977), many social workers have a stake in a style of work which is power-laden, formal and individualised. There is a fear of transition to an approach that involves greater sharing in groups, and more negotiated, informal work.

A prevailing view is that the governance of modern society is too complex to be left in the hands of 'amateurs', the people themselves, and must be turned over to the 'experts' (Sturgess 2001).

Compounding the problem is the fact that professional social work in Australia has largely depended on British and United States' perspectives which have not acknowledged the Australian context, including prior Aboriginal ownership of the land (McMahon, A. 1993). The colonising effect of social work formulations from other cultural and national contexts denies the validity of local experience (Ife 2001). To redress this, social work needs to incorporate 'the voices of the disadvantaged' into curriculum construction and educational experience (Ife 1997: 199). Alongside this, social workers must understand the perspectives on the role of the state, its institutions and organisations, that flow from Indigenous experience (Jones and May 1992). Without this, there will remain a large number of non-Indigenous practitioners with minimal awareness of Indigenous issues.

Changes in the professional discourse do not break down the inherent restrictions of the bureaucracy, and even those existing within mainstream community-sector organisations. Despite the rhetoric of governments in affirming the development of culturally appropriate services, it is still the case that Indigenous Australians are expected to fit within the current structures of child welfare agencies, with expectations to conform with the accepted orthodoxies that govern child protection interventions (Litwin 1997). Referring to the situation in New South Wales, Litwin argues that while the Department of Community Services promotes the ideal of community autonomy and participation, it does so within a context in which such autonomy and participation may be severely circumscribed. Consultation becomes overwhelmingly concerned with the identification of the views of Indigenous Australians in a way that is comprehensible to the outside consulting agencies which control both the agenda and the conceptual framework (Litwin 1997).

THEORETICAL LEADS

Indigenous people have in many ways been oppressed by theory, and emerging theoretical developments from an Indigenous perspective are grounded 'in a real sense of, and sensitivity towards, what it means to be an indigenous person' (Smith 1999: 38). Non-Indigenous people are incapable of theorising from the lived experience of Indigenous cultural worlds (Moreton-Robinson 2000). Decolonisation does not mean a total rejection of all theory or research or Western knowledge, but is about 'centring our concerns and world views, and then coming to know and understand theory and research from our own perspectives and for our own purposes' (Smith 1999: 39). Postcolonial theories and anti-colonialist practices present a major challenge. Shedding colonialism implies a process of overturning the dominant way of seeing the world and representing reality in ways which do not replicate colonial values (McLeod 2000). For Ife (2001), colonialist practice implies any form of practice that assumes the practitioner is coming from a position of superiority, where the world-view of the practitioner is imposed on others and where the practitioner serves to promote the interests and needs of the practitioner rather than those with whom the practitioner is working. Colonialism in social work can be subtle and insidious, and many practitioners are not aware of the colonialist implications of their practice. This is despite the fact that Indigenous people have pointed out the way in which conventional social work practices have effectively colonised and disempowered Indigenous communities (Ife 2001).

Citizenship concepts have been criticised for the perception in modern political thought that the notion of citizen status for all transcends particularity and difference (Young 1994). Although there is an increasing discourse of human rights in the Australian context, the Eurocentric frameworks which shape thinking in the West have an impact on how the dominant society expresses divergent notions of rights. Social perspectives that express alternative values or paradigms have been excluded and marginalised. Australians are generally comfortable with the idea that Indigenous people should have individual rights, but disturbed by the idea that groups have rights because they are groups with a particular history (Reynolds 1997). Although Indigenous communities are entitled to the same basic rights as other citizens, the point of contest lies where justice for Indigenous people conflicts with principles premised conceptually on a paradigm of liberal individualism. This concerns those rights to which they may be entitled by virtue of their cultural specificity and status as Indigenous peoples (Patton 1995). As Young (1994) argues, the inclusion and participation of everyone in social and political institutions sometimes requires the articulation of special rights that attend to group differences in order to deal with oppression and disadvantage. Differences in fact serve as the vehicles for the distribution of statuses, rights, entitlements, obligations, rewards and penalties (O'Brien and Penna 1998b). However, the justifying of exception, with opponents rendering sovereignty into the realm of privilege and handout, becomes unworkable (Mickler 1998), and the question of distinct rights remains highly contested (Dodson 1996).

Although Indigenous people are legally and constitutionally full citizens of Australia, a prevailing discourse among Indigenous leaders is that Indigenous people do not have full citizenship in their own land, and are subject to exclusion, discrimination and human rights abuses. Aboriginal and Torres Strait Islander peoples do not enjoy the rights assumed to adhere to citizenship in general; Chesterman and Galligan refer to Indigenous Australians as citizens without rights (1997), and Dodson has coined the term 'citizen minus' (1996: 193).

Social movements of oppressed and excluded groups have queried why extension of equal citizenship rights has not led to social justice and equality (Young 1994). Contemporary social movements of the oppressed assert a positivity and pride in group specificity against assimilation ideals, and the notion of differentiated citizenship (Young 1994) is gaining momentum. The new social movements have challenged the universal nature of citizenship concepts, as by their very nature social movements are 'particularistic' (Barbalet 1996: 64). This is in stark contrast to the views prevailing in the building of Australian nationhood that Aboriginal people were inferior and their culture incompatible with the modern world (Attwood and Marcus 1997), and that Indigenous people could become worthy citizens only through the erasing of difference and the acquisition of the 'cultural and social competencies' of the colonisers (Peterson and Sanders 1998: 5).

The issue of inclusionary and exclusionary citizenship has been subject to recent analyses which provide tools for exploring the extent of Aboriginal citizenship. In Australia there is some recognition of the increasing rift between the granting of citizenship by the state, and its acceptance by those citizens who consider themselves from the dominant culture (Hage 1998). Dodson (1996) posits that unless one enjoys social rights, it is not possible to enjoy civil and political rights. Citizenship as a force for exclusion (Lister 1997) applies to the stolen generations, where the assimilationist rhetoric was about absorption and rights of Australian citizenship, but where the policies and practices set in place to achieve this set Indigenous people apart from other citizens. The status of Indigenous people as rights bearers was actively undermined (Dodds 1998), and by ridding society of Indigenous peoples there could be justification for the development of a monocultural society. The endeavour to include Indigenous people in the polity resulted in their exclusion, as they never met the conditions of being 'white', or what Frow (1998: 358) refers to as a definition of race in 'self-cancelling terms by a double negative'. The separation of Indigenous children from their families and communities is an example of how a category of people was excluded from full citizenship accorded to other Australians through the imposition of selective and discriminatory legislation, policies and practices. Yet at the same time, the prevailing ideology was to create a society of 'equals', with Indigenous children growing into an adulthood in which they would be white, 'civilised' and Christianised.

In applying these debates to the contemporary context, there is an increasing questioning of how white privilege is rarely explored by the dominant society. Hage (1998: 58) sees 'whiteness' as a 'composite cultural historical construct' which universalises a cultural form of white identity as a means of cultural power. Whiteness was born at the same time as the binary oppositions of coloniser/colonised, developed/underdeveloped and first world/third world were emerging (Hage 1998).

Drawing on the work of Frankenburg (1993), Moreton-Robinson (2000) argues that whiteness is not interrogated or named as a difference, even though it is the standard by which certain differences are measured, centred and normalised. Her work introduces major challenges to social workers, particularly women who still form the majority of the profession, as she sees white women as overwhelmingly and disproportionately dominant, having the key and elaborated roles which constitute the norm in Australian society. White women centre their own experiences, ideologies and practices as part of their invisible race privilege. The phenomenon of white privilege is denied and protected, an invisible package of unlearned assets (McIntosh 1998: 147, 148) and an example of internalised domination. For Moreton-Robinson the identification, interrogation and elucidation of whiteness as 'difference' are missing from most feminist literature, and colonial processes have shaped white feminists' obliviousness to their race privilege and their indifference to the history of their relations with Indigenous women (2000). She calls on white feminists to theorise the relinquishment of power, arguing that until this happens the subject position of middle-class white woman will remain centred as a site of dominance (2000). This site of dominance is no more obvious than in the hegemonic approaches to 'good' mothering and nuclear family values, which act against the interests of Indigenous people and draw the attention of state authorities to those who deviate from the norm.

PRACTICE LEADS

The question of how social work practice affects Indigenous peoples is complex and even contested. With the emergence of Indigenous organisations delivering their own services, some non-Indigenous social workers do not see themselves as having a role. Despite these organisational developments, many Indigenous people still have a relationship with non-Indigenous organisations and a number of clients have little choice but to seek the services of mainstream agencies. Thus there is a need to ensure that non-Indigenous social workers enter into dialogue with Indigenous organisations to ensure that their practices are conducted with cultural sensitivity. In addition, as some Indigenous organisations employ non-Indigenous social workers, there is a need to prepare them adequately for such practice. Although the issue is contentious (Freedman 1989; Clarke et al. 2000), a number of Indigenous people also work in mainstream agencies, and need to have their perspectives understood by those around them.

Those working with Indigenous individuals, families or communities need to acknowledge the reality of Indigenous systems of meaning (Bessarab 2000: 83). This includes taking into account the acquisition of knowledge of a particular culture's values, attitudes and beliefs and adopting appropriate communication styles, content and language (Bessarab 2000: 83-4). In developing practice approaches there is a tendency for culturally different ways to be treated as 'add-ons' to largely unchanged dominant practices (Lynn et al. 1998: 6). Providing prescriptive answers is not helpful, as there are of course variations between Indigenous communities and 'there is not just one Aboriginal way of doing things' (Clarke et al. 2000). Nevertheless, there have been endeavours to articulate principles of practice that can then be refined, developed and adapted to particular situations. For Wingard and Lester (2001), culturally appropriate and accessible services include notions of self-determination and autonomy, consultation, accountability, education and training for Indigenous people, with an emphasis on non-Indigenous people needing to learn about and respect Indigenous ways, knowledges and meanings. Critical social work practices have opened up new ways of viewing clients and embracing alternative world-views. Some of the responsibility rests with social work educators, as the achievement of culturally sensitive practice is bound to the quality of the teaching to which students are exposed (Meemeduma 1994).

Aboriginal and Torres Strait Islander helping styles contrast with the traditional social work approaches that are reinforced by the AASW

Code of Ethics (Lynn et al. 1998: 64). Basic differences include a valuing of the collective rather than the individual, the importance of extended family and different ways of dealing with a range of social issues, including alcohol abuse and domestic violence. In order to set up communication between non-Indigenous staff and Indigenous clients, there is a need to recognise that Indigenous people 'have a strong vibrant culture and their own ways of doing things' (Clarke et al. 2000). It necessitates critical social workers exploring with Indigenous people and organisations what these differences are, and to apply them in their practices. Much of this can be done through familiarisation with the range of Indigenous organisations with which the social worker can consult and cooperate. Bessarab (2000: 84) suggests the use of a 'cultural consultant' working alongside the non-Indigenous worker.

Social work as a profession has a particular responsibility to allow the voices of the marginalised to be heard (Ife 1997). In policy terms there is a need to reverse the 'whites know best' assumption underlying much policy formulation. It is the responsibility of the critical social worker to work towards policy change which fosters the pursuit by Indigenous people for control over their own destinies (Freedman 1989). Clarke et al. (2000: 356) speak of barriers to equality and access for Indigenous families in a hospital setting, arguing that feelings of unhappiness or discomfort about using the service can mean the denial of needed specialist treatment. They refer to problems of communication and lack of understanding of Indigenous decision-making processes: 'We still feel at times that we are judged and stereotyped by different values and a different set of rules' (2000: 357–8). Anecdotal evidence suggests that these concerns are replicated in other fields of practice, although many remain undocumented. To remedy such concerns, a critical social worker has to go beyond changing direct practice to confronting both organisational policies and wider government policies (Cemlyn and Briskman 2002).

CONCLUSION

The social work response to Indigenous concerns must be tackled through ongoing challenges to policy and practice discourses combined with critiques of the wider policy and organisational frameworks which disempower Indigenous groups. Social work, in the main, continues to give credence to universal principles (Briskman 2001) and lacks theoretical development which takes into account the conceptual markers of postmodernist thinking, such as particularism and difference (Williams 1996). Embracing these conceptual markers would help negate criticism from Indigenous people, who argue that the promotion and dominance of chosen systems actively discourage, suppress, marginalise and neglect competing systems (Dodson 1996). The challenge for the profession is to work out how to embrace a critical framework in engaging with Indigenous communities, and to give voice to those advocating alternative approaches. The profession needs to guard itself against trends to cooption by the prevailing discourse, which focuses on individual rights and responsibilities (Briskman 2001), to ensure that 'each voice counts equally' (Flax 1990: 233) and to ensure that a politics of difference (Yeatman 1994) is embraced. In order to do so, critical social work must address the institutionalised and culturally legitimated forms of oppression (Dominelli 1996), so that the organisation of welfare is able to provide spaces for the expression of difference (Leonard 1997). For Gilbert (2001), a competent social worker is one who has examined his or her own beliefs and value systems, understands how racism works and how this can be challenged. Most importantly, critical social workers must engage in a process of overturning dominant ways of seeing the world and representing reality in ways that do not replicate colonialist values (McLeod 2000).

7

WOMEN: DEVELOPING FEMINIST PRACTICE IN WOMEN'S SERVICES

Wendy Weeks

Feminist practice has developed from centuries of women's movement action to achieve equality, social justice and/or autonomy for women. It is a construct which has been coopted by professions such as social work and psychology to inform their work with women and men. This chapter first canvasses and discusses several professional social work accounts, and then turns to the Australian feminist women's services as a source of contemporary feminist practice. I draw on a national survey of 160 Australian feminist women's services to describe principles and strategies of feminist practice used by them.

FEMINIST PRACTICE IN SOCIAL WORK

In Australia, as elsewhere, women were leaders in the establishment of the social work profession, and they continue to comprise a majority of its numbers. Martin and Healy (1993) examined the Australian profession of social work, using national census data, and found women constituted 75 per cent of social workers. Examining census and labour force data, McCormack (2001) confirms that social workers remained 75 per cent female in 2000, and that 89 per cent of new graduates were female. Nevertheless, the tradition of men in senior academic, policy development and welfare administration continues in this profession, as elsewhere in the paid labour force.

The women's movement of the 1970s put many aspects of women's lives on the Australian public policy agenda, achieving some landmark legislation and social policy development which benefits women. Funding for child care, equal pay for work of equal value (still not achieved in practice), sex discrimination legislation, affirmative action in employment legislation, and policy and practice strategies to combat violence against women have been some of the achievements.

Feminist practice came to be understood within the women's movement, as well as in the professions, as resting on a feminist analysis of social issues which emphasises women's experience and names experiences hitherto shrouded in silence, such as father–daughter rape and violence in intimate adult relationships. The first premise of a feminist analysis is seen as making links between the personal and the political. Similar to structural approaches to social work, this explains people's personal experiences as reflecting wider social and cultural conditions and, in the case of women, historically and socially structured gender power relations. What was previously seen as personal choice became understood to be a subtle or explicit maintenance of a social ordering by the state which kept women preoccupied with family life. It became clear that women were first and foremost defined by their family status: as wives, mothers and daughters. In mainstream professional practice, based on assumptions about the normality of a traditional heterosexual family where men are income providers and workers, and women are responsible for care and household labour, women are frequently still identified as 'mothers' rather than as citizen service-users who may be parents within their other adult activities.

A second theoretical premise is that action to change the structural conditions of women's lives should have priority over supporting and assisting women to adjust to their social situations, especially those which threaten their safety. Social and community action to challenge women's lack of access to equal pay, to family-friendly workplaces, to housing, and to relationships free from violence and coercion, have occurred. Women's over-representation in poverty has been a continuing concern: the result of discontinuous labour force participation, part-time and casual work, low-paid jobs, exclusion from occupational benefits including superannuation, and an excessive load of unpaid caring work within extended families and neighbourhoods.

Third, where attention is required to the needs or pain of individual women, perhaps expressing severe emotional reactions to assault or persistent disempowerment, feminist practice defines this as working towards women's emotional well-being. Feminist analyses are reluctant to treat women as victims, recognising women's agency or capacity to act, and are resistant to labelling women as 'sick' when their behaviour is able to be understood as a response to oppressive social conditions and practices.

The fourth premise is that feminist practice requires transformed organisations to deliver appropriate services and responses to women's needs and issues. Hierarchical workplace relations were challenged by an emphasis on collectivity and workplace democracy. Dominelli and McLeod (1989) identified organisational practice as one of the five elements of feminist practice in their British account. This premise was taken most seriously by feminist women's services. Large both-gendered human service organisations, usually directed by men, ignored such challenges.

More controversial was Dominelli and McLeod's (1989) claim that working in statutory work was an element of feminist practice. Working with women as mothers in child protection, where they are unable to perform as socially desirable and supportive parents, or working with women who have broken the law, raise the most contradictions for feminist practitioners. If the location of feminist practice is a women's service or a women's legal centre, the worker can actively remain supportive to the women concerned. However, social workers employed within the state to maintain social control have found this an almost impossible tension.

The conservative 1990s saw a rise of earlier mother-blaming attitudes, and a feminist backlash. Postmodern theoretical challenges questioned 'woman' as a unitary category. This resonated with criticism that the movement had been racist and favoured middle-class women. Others see such challenges as avoiding historical accounts that the women's movement has always reflected diversity among women. Government policies rewarded a focus on individual 'problems', whereby social problems and issues were converted into personal issues, prompting and giving funding priority to therapeutic, individualised responses to women's situations. Women cooperated with such interpretations because of their pain and distress.

From the 1970s there has been an active tradition of feminist social work and women's studies within social work education in Australia. In 1982 a Women in Welfare Education (WIWE) network was established, which operates within the Australian Social Work and Welfare Educators Association (AASWWE). WIWE sponsors a journal and holds annual conferences. University schools of social work typically have at least one feminist scholar on staff, and elective subjects on women and/or gender relations are offered. Still, most mainstream subjects are not imbued with feminist lessons or understandings. This means that a focus on gender and women is present, but often separate, and without the centrality of being a basic organising principle. Alongside feminist women's studies, critical studies of men have begun to develop.

Australian developments in the final decades of the twentieth century reflected action within professional social work associations in many countries. For example, Norman and Mancuso (1980), writing in the United States, on *Women's Issues and Social Work Practice*, identified issues for social workers as women as well as for clients of social work services. A major theme in their book was that 'women cannot be defined exclusively by their family roles' (1980: 5). The authors identified working-class women, ageing women, lesbian mothers, black women and women abusing alcohol as particular populations needing attention. Adopting a systems approach, they identified the health care system, the mental health system, income maintenance and social service administration as worthy of feminist attention. In 1986 the journal *Affilia: Journal of Women and Social Work* was initiated in the United States; it continues to report on research on women and feminist approaches to research and practice. Feminist practice in clinical settings has been extensively reported in the professional literature (for example, Bricker-Jenkins et al. 1991).

As a result of a feminist practice project within the US National Association of Social Work (NASW), the association now requires the teaching of gender relations for course accreditation (Bricker-Jenkins and Hooyman 1986; Van Den Burgh and Cooper 1986; Van Den Burgh 1995). Davis's (1994) compilation of readings entitled *Building on Women's Strengths: A Social Work Agenda for the Twenty-First Century* covers women and public welfare, the experience of low-income women, women in paid employment, child welfare, the experience of older women and women in mental health. Since that time the American state has become more punitive to women on welfare, as Abramovitz (1996) has documented. A range of authors has attended to the gendered nature of social policy and the challenges arising from this (for example, Sainsbury 1994, 1996, 1999).

Canada and the United Kingdom have also had a tradition of feminist social work since the 1970s. The work of Baines, Evans and Neysmith's (1991) work on women's caring was particularly influential in putting the range of caring related issues for women on the policy and social program agenda. Mayo (1977), a British community worker, recounted in *Women in the Community* the different issues for community work arising from women's lives: as community workers, as volunteer activists and as community members. She identified, for example, community women's militancy in the face of housing and unemployment, but also showed how typically women were the support workers in community associations rather than positional leaders. Hanmer and Statham (1988) argue for a code for women-centred practice. Their conception is organised around commonalities between women workers and clients; dependency and poverty; women's caring; and personal identity and self-esteem. This work is valuable in its focus on individual women, but has little to say about community organising and social action, in spite of both authors having a history of such action. This underscores the separation between social work strategies and the professionalisation of feminist practice into individual work, showing the influence of the conservative 1990s. Dominelli and McLeod's (1989) work has been referred to above, and Dominelli also authored *Women and Community Action* in 1990. At the same time Dominelli and others, including Australian women, have been active in the International Federation of Social Workers, seeking to introduce a feminist perspective into international social work. In Australia, Marchant and Wearing (1986) published a collection of practice accounts entitled *Gender Reclaimed: Women in Social Work*. Specialisation of feminist practice has been a feature of the late 1980s and 1990s. For example, in her writing on sexual assault (one area of feminist practice) Carmody (1990), herself a social worker, draws attention to the numbers of social workers in the sexual assault services in New South Wales; a phenomenon also true in Victoria.

Specialisation has been a feature of feminist theory and practice in the 1990s. There are now extensive bodies of theory on work in situations including violence against women; working with young women, older women, lesbian women; caring, reproductive issues, labour force discrimination and exploitation; and a wide range of women facing multiple disadvantage, such as women with disabilities and Indigenous women. Many women's services publish reports on their work, and women's association journals and newsletters contain a wealth of practice knowledge. The CASA House (1995) manual *Breaking the Silence: A Guide to Supporting Adult Victims/Survivors of Sexual Assault*, and the *National Standards of Practice for Services Against Sexual Assault Manual* (National Association of Services Against Sexual Violence,

Hardiman and Dean 1998), provide excellent accounts of feminist practice principles and standards.

The International Federation of Social Workers (IFSW) published a policy position on women in 2000. This responds to the call from the United Nations World Conferences on Women that women's rights are human rights. It adopts the Beijing Platform for Women: the 'Areas of Critical Concern' include poverty, the economy, education and training, health, violence, female infanticide or abandonment, childhood sexual exploitation, and limited access to adequate nutrition and health care.

FEMINIST PRACTICE IN AUSTRALIAN FEMINIST WOMEN'S SERVICES

In the absence of systematic research on the activities and practices of social workers who identify as 'feminist', it is from the feminist women's services that much can be learned about feminist practice. Small feminist women's organisations developed in Australia in the 1970s, as elsewhere, and have been remarkably tenacious in their survival, in spite of efforts by conservative governments to promote larger, more generalist amalgamated services.

Feminist women's services are defined as 'run by and for women, and are either community-based or autonomous units of an auspice organisation, usually a non-government organisation' (Weeks 1994: 36). They typically claim to operate on a feminist philosophy of social change and have a triple purpose. In addition to working with individuals and/or women's groups, they take social action to change the structural conditions of women's lives and engage in community education to change myths and negative attitudes about women. These organisations are special in that they put women's experience and situations at the centre of their work, rather than being focused on families or children. They responded to women and children escaping violence, to women who had been sexually assaulted or raped, to women's working conditions or special health needs. They became places where women could explore and identify their needs and how these might best be met in state policies and programs. Once they obtained funding to operate as services, they continued to have women staff. Committed to the assumption that the social relations of gender power, and associated attitudes and practices, were a central problem for women, they created safe spaces for women and supported women's culture and ways of doing things. They celebrated women's history and achievements, so often invisible in the public realm. They brought women together in groups to see that they, as individuals, were not 'the problem', but that the conditions of their lives were difficult and sometimes hazardous. Individual counselling developed, with feminist principles which put women's needs and issues at the centre of their practice. Women's personal lives were understood to be political, and practices avoided victim-blaming or pathologising the women. The feminist women's services became sites for women's voices.

A national study of Australian feminist women's services was undertaken in 1999.[1] The sample was built from earlier research undertaken in 1993[2] which was supplemented by searches of directories and lists from each state and territory. The research design was canvassed with large women's associations and comprised a mail survey with follow-up interviews with spokespersons for the services in one state (Victoria) and one territory (Northern Territory). The responses to questions on principles of practice and strategies for change are reported here.

WHO WERE THE PARTICIPATING WOMEN'S SERVICES?

Women's services in Australia include refuges and shelters, of which it is estimated by WESNET (a national network of women's emergency services) that there are 320 across the country, with some having more than one house. Refuges are houses where women can stay while they are rebuilding their lives after escaping serious violence from their husbands or male partners. Since 1986 they have been funded by the national Supported Accommodation Assistance Program (SAAP). There are also women's housing services which offer assistance with a range of housing options. Women's health centres focus on women's special health needs, such as challenging female genital mutilation, issues related to birthing and menopause. They provide direct health services in some states, and in others work to change the mainstream health system and engage in a range of health promotion and community education projects. CASAs (centres against sexual assault) respond to women who have been raped, sexually assaulted or harassed. They have worked with churches to challenge sexual abuse and set up grievance procedures, and have challenged the entertainment industry to provide entertainment venues which are safe for women. CASAs in Victoria have been under pressure to expand their service delivery to men, small numbers of whom have always been seen, and then usually referred. CASAs are included in this research because of their main focus on women, and their self-declared adherence to feminist philosophies and principles of practice. The sample includes some multipurpose women's centres, particularly in rural or regional areas. An example is North Queensland Combined Women's Services in Townsville, which provides a meeting place for women and many projects they undertake and develop, such as the sexual assault service. Most states have at least one women's legal service, assisted by a government funding program introduced by the Labor Federal Government before it lost office in 1996. All states and territories have a women's information telephone service, with domestic violence, sexual assault and women's health services also operating crisis telephone lines. The survey also included a range of specific-focus services, such as Children by Choice (abortion counselling), working women's centres, single mothers' associations such as Council for Single Mothers and their Children (CSMC), Association of Relinquishing Mothers (ARMS), Sisters Inside (an organisation for women in and after prison), Indigenous women's organisations and an international women's development organisation. All have been developed by and for women, specialise in their particular needs, and are run by women staff.

The participants in the research described in this chapter include a representative range of the services available, with no major omissions of service type: refuges (25, or 15.6 per cent); centres against sexual assault (30 or 18.8 per cent); women's health centres (41, or 25.6 per cent); women's housing services (8 or 5 per cent); women's legal services (10, or 6.3 per cent), multipurpose women's centres (15, or 9.4 per cent), and smaller numbers of specific services such as those listed above.

WOMEN'S SERVICES' PHILOSOPHIES

The services were asked to update the relevant elements of their philosophies identified earlier (using grounded theory) in the 1993 research, and 155 of the 160 organisations reported on their philosophies. The services' most frequently reported pro-women values were:

- Supporting women's control over their decisions (94 per cent). For example, Ruby Gaea Centre Against Rape, Darwin, notes: 'We seek to use counselling which sees women as the experts in their own experience and provides them with control over their own recovery. The counselling is informed by a commitment to a feminist interpretation of rape.'

- Responding to the special needs of women (90 per cent). For example, CASAs recognise the particular needs of previously neglected groups, such as those from non-English-speaking backgrounds, Indigenous women and women with disabilities.
- Empowering approaches to practice (89 per cent). In the face of continuing medical dominance and the associated stigmatising and medicalising of abuse and professional expert models of working, services seek to empower women to take control in their situations. For example, Charmian Clift Crisis Accommodation Service, New South Wales, for women typically labelled as having serious psychiatric disabilities, has 'a focus on empowerment of all women— especially those disadvantaged by experiences that have affected their ability to cope, grow and make decisions on their lives and the lives of their children'. This means knowledge of rights, skills and lifestyles, and ensuring respectful response to all women, avoiding victim-blaming (85.8 per cent). Validation of women's experiences has been argued to be critical in a society where they do not have the power to define experiences and social roles. For example, the Domestic Violence and Incest Resource Centre, Victoria, offers 'non-directive, non-judgemental support'. Hobart Women's Health Centre, Tasmania, states, 'Women have a right to dignity and respect'.

These principles suggest a valuing of diversity and a continued commitment to women's dignity and empowerment.

Since the 1993 research there have been some interesting changes. In 1993, 'a feminist or women-centred analysis of issues' was the predominant element, but this ranked only eighth in 1999. There was near-universal support for a 'social model of health' in 1993, yet it was ranked last in 1999; and a 'social analysis of violence' was ranked tenth in 1999, whereas it was frequently mentioned as part of the 'feminist analysis' which topped the list in 1993. In the 1999 data, the highest rating elements do not mention the word 'feminist'. These shifts all suggest sensitivity to a climate of feminist backlash, and possibly less comfort with the term 'feminist' in some of the services. It may also reflect a shift to meet the needs of 'all' women, not only those who identify with the word 'feminist': this is a particular issue among some minority ethnic communities.

The next highest ranked elements of service philosophy referred to efficient organisational practices reflective of the more challenging managerial environment of the late 1990s, where organisational responses became critical to survival. These responses also emphasise the extent to which organisations which survived (the great majority) were efficient, and valued being well organised in service delivery. For example, aiming at excellence, quality, accuracy and relevance (86 per cent); accessibility (85 per cent); cooperative and constructive inter-organisational relationships, in the interests of women service users (82 per cent), were identified as service principles.

During the 1990s the organisational networks, sometimes in associ-ation with government funding departments, put a lot of time into developing 'standards of practice' for work with victim/survivors of sexual assault or violence against women, to ensure access, equity and quality service provision. Services therefore were asked whether the basis of their principles was derived from their own service, from state-wide or national standards of practice, or a combination. Twenty-four per cent reported that their principles were derived from their own service; 11 per cent drew them from statewide or national standards (such as the National Standards of Practices for Services against Sexual Assault); 63 per cent said they relied on a combination of their own and other standards. 60.4 per cent of the services also reported that they have an organisational code of ethics or practice.

WHAT DO THE SERVICES DO?

The main activities of feminist women's services provide guidelines for strategies or 'methods' of feminist practice. Most (147 or 96 per cent) offered women information, support and referral by telephone. Women's health services, domestic violence centres, information services and centres against sexual assault all provide support and infor-mation on the telephone. All but two of these (145 or 95 per cent) also provided face-to-face information, support and referral. The philoso-phical basis for this is that women can cope with their situations with information, resources and support, and that it is their environment which should be made to change, by social action.

Community and professional education was the third most frequent activity, with 131 or 86 per cent involved in using this strategy. This suggests that education, and endeavours to challenge myths and change attitudes, continues to be alive and well as a strategy, alongside working with individual women. Community education has been important to challenge popular myths which blame women, such as the myth that women are to blame for rape and domestic violence.

Particular educational strategies are employed:

- Public speaking is a major strategy in 126 (91 per cent) of the 152 services responding. Talks to schools and community groups present the facts rather than the myths about women's lives and experiences.
- Educational pamphlets, posters or stickers are another major strategy in 117 (84 per cent) of the services. For example, one Queensland service has put colourful information stickers about violence against women, the law and women's rights in women's toilets in all public shopping and entertainment venues in their region. The stickers also indicate where women can seek help.
- Production of kits, manuals and booklets is the third most used strategy, in 100 (72 per cent) of the services. Easily accessible information on women's health issues and rights, legal rights and setting up self-help groups for women who have experienced violence are some examples.
- Use of media was reported by 97 (70 per cent) of the services. This includes regular and occasional radio programs, including ethnic radio in community languages addressing women's concerns and where they can seek help.
- Regular newsletters were produced by 84 (60 per cent) of the services to inform their membership and others about events and resources for women.
- The production of educational videos was an activity reported by 36 (26 per cent) of the services. For example, a number of educational resources about women's right to say 'no' to incest and date rape have been made for young women. CASA House, Victoria, has prepared booklets, a video and postcards to empower young women with the right to party safely. Sisters Inside, for women in and after prison, has made videos telling women's stories to increase public understanding of the tragic events of abuse and exploitation in their lives.

Counselling face-to-face is the fourth major activity of the range of women's services (126, or 82 per cent). In addition to the activity in providing 'information, support and advocacy', this suggests a lot of work with individual women toward their emotional and social well-being is undertaken. While the extent of this work may reflect increasing professionalisation, further research would be necessary to explore this.

The fifth type of activity is policy advocacy, that is, attempts to change social policies, in which 125 (82 per cent) of the services are engaged, indicative of their historic commitment to social change. One of the methods reported refers to engagement with state policy reform and development processes, with 124 services sitting on committees of review and policy development. Examples include developing state/ territory policies and strategy plans to respond to the needs of Indigenous women; reforming rape and sexual assault legislation; developing state/territory plans for women's safety, health and mental health strategies, with 125 services involved in making policy submissions to government, typically on similar issues for reform, and 124 (82 per cent) reporting participating in campaigns. Services give examples such as Stop Domestic Violence Day and Reclaim the Night marches. Other campaigns have been more specific, such as the Release Heather Osland Campaign directed at releasing a woman thought to be wrongly jailed; or the national campaign against mandatory strip-searching women in prison, coordinated by Sisters Inside, which sees mandatory strip-searching as a re-victimisation of women, many of whom have previously been raped or physically assaulted.

Telephone counselling is provided by 125 (82 per cent) of the services. Nearly as frequent is the provision of educational resources, by 121 (79 per cent) of the services, consistent with feminist assertions that women need information for empowerment. Often women's social isolation within family homes makes them atypically dependent on the telephone for social contact.

Women's groups and skills programs are offered by 114 (75 per cent) of the services. This reflects a continued commitment to groups as an important feminist strategy to provide support for change, rather than individual counselling. Often these are specific-purpose groups, with a health focus, or support after escaping violence, lesbian support, or support for Indigenous women or women from minority ethnicities. The use of women's groups has increased since 1993, when only 46 per cent of services reported that they ran groups (Weeks 1994). In early accounts of feminist practice, groups are proposed as more appropriate than working with individual women, on the assumption that women can more easily see the shared structural barriers to their full citizenship. Further, they can work together to make changes in women's interest.

Outreach was named as an activity by 105 (69 per cent) of the services. This includes outreach programs to geographic areas without services of their own, outreach to particular populations, such as home-less young women, or outreach which may lead to establishment of new services. Sometimes this involves joint auspice of a particular project or initiative, such as an after-hours service in a rural region. For example, Ballarat CASA has undertaken an outreach initiative towards Aboriginal women in their region and they have worked together on a range of cultural and service development activities.

Just over half of the responding services (88 or 58 per cent) are involved in offering multilingual services and support for immigrant women. A similar number (87 or 57 per cent) identified themselves as offering cultural support for Indigenous women. These figures show a significant increase from the 1993 survey, when only 13 of the 78 serv-ices studied (17 per cent) reported offering cultural support (Weeks 1994). This is consistent with other research which reports on access and equity strategies for Indigenous women, women from ethnic minor-ity communities and their children, undertaken by the services against sexual violence (National Association for Services Against Sexual Violence 2001). The services are engaged in a number of educational, community development and outreach strategies, as well as employ-ment of Indigenous and bi-lingual workers from minority communities.

Research is undertaken by just over half the services (82 or 54 per cent). It is likely that larger services and state-wide services are most active in research, though some smaller services work with higher degree students or women in local universities (for example, Orr 1997). This strategy has been important to uncover previously hidden aspects of women's lives: in the labour force, the extent of part-time and casual work, the silence about maternity leave and other carer leave; in fami-lies, the extent of incest and violence against women; and in the serv-ices, evaluations to determine the most successful practices and strategies.

The question which gave the opportunity to list other activities undertaken elicited some useful information. One-third of services (42 or 32 per cent of the 130 answering) were engaged in some way with the provision of housing for women. This included women's housing services, the largest number of which are found in New South Wales, which may be engaged in property management and development as well as information and referral for women to appropriate housing. Refuges, shelters and refuge referral services were well represented in the sample. A number of services were engaged in housing cam-paigns and development. This indicates a significant issue for women, especially those escaping violence, in view of high private rental and long waiting lists in public housing.

- Women's services planning and development is a category which covers a range of organisational and women's movement development activities. Thirty (23 per cent) of the services were involved in such activities. Those counted in this category include those developing state-wide plans, supervising and resourcing workers in other services, establishing a community newspaper and a feminist anti-violence journal, providing industrial relations advice to other services, running volunteer training, developing national standards of practice and starting new services.
- Specific health or medical or alternative health services were offered by 24 (19 per cent) of the services. These included provision of a doctor, nurses, physiotherapists or alternative therapies, such as massage, acupuncture and naturopathy. Other women's health services, such as those in Victoria, focus on community development and policy advocacy, and work to improve the experiences of women in mainstream health services.
- Legal service and court support were named by 22 (17 per cent) of the services. These included specific legal services offered by the women's legal services and supplementary services offered by refuges or domestic violence resource centres.
- Children's and youth programs were provided by 19 (15 per cent) of the services. This is a new development since 1993, and includes programs for girls and young women and programs in or associated with schools, and homeless young people.
- The smallest group of new activities, comprising just 4 (3 per cent) of the services is the provision of men's programs. Those mentioned were specifically for male survivors of sexual assault; Canberra Rape Crisis Centre has overseen the establishment of a separate service for male survivors of sexual violence. It is a new development since the research in 1993.

ADVOCACY

Because social change activities have been one of the historically valued features of feminist organisations, the services were asked whether or not they were involved in advocacy. In the years of conservative federal government, advocacy has been discouraged, and funding formulae have favoured direct service. Nevertheless, the women's services have maintained considerable advocacy activity, and the question was answered by 151 services.

Fifty (33 per cent) of the services indicated that they spent 10-30 per cent of their time on advocacy; a further 39 (26 per cent) said that they spent between 31-50 per cent of their time engaged in this activity, while 19 (13 per cent) reported that they spent over 70 per cent of their time on advocacy. These respondents included Immigrant Women's Domestic Violence Service, Victoria; Council for Single Mothers and their Children; three refuges; and the Domestic Violence Action Group in Tasmania. Another nine (6 per cent) reported that they spent 100 per cent of their time on advocacy—these included state-wide services, the International Women's Development Agency and some services against sexual assault. These responses indicate that advocacy is alive and well in the women's services, even in a policy and service delivery environment which actively discourages it.

Of the 132 services commenting on whether they spent the same, more or less time on advocacy than in 1993, 50 (37 per cent) spent the same time; 34 (25 per cent) considered their advocacy activity had decreased; 46 (34 per cent) thought their advocacy activity had increased. Some in the third category commented that the more hostile political environment required that they be more active. Those whose social change activities had decreased pointed to increased direct service demand, associated with penalties for advocacy (see Weeks 2001 for a more detailed discussion of this).

CONCLUSION

This chapter has reported on research on the activities of feminist women's services to bring to life feminist practice by Australian organisations. Feminist practice is a dynamic concept, clearly articulating principles for practice. The common features of feminist social work frameworks include a feminist or gender analysis of social issues, including the assumption that the personal is political; and a commitment to changing the structural conditions of women's lives in addition to working towards women's individual emotional well-being. Transforming organisational practices has been considered a necessary feminist principle, and the feminist women's services have been able to develop organisations by and for women, with an emphasis on low hierarchy and democratic decision-making. Over time there has been considerable specialisation in feminist practice.

The reported research on Australian women's services gives a glimpse into present feminist practices and priorities and there are many qualified social workers employed across the national services network. The services have maintained the significance of working with women in groups identified in early accounts of feminist practice. They favour information, support and advocacy above counselling, thus continuing to affirm women's capacity to solve their own problems and address issues when provided with information and support. More than half the services have maintained or increased their systemic advocacy, which indicates that their social change agenda continues. Community education has been retained as an important strategy, as has influencing social policy and running campaigns. These activities offer practice strategies to those committed to develop women-centred or feminist practice.

The research shows that women's services have survived, in spite of pressure from funding bodies to amalgamate into larger generalist services. While they have increased their children's and young people's programs, very few are developing men's programs, or capitulating to funder pressure to become mainstream family services.

Feminist practice faces a number of future challenges. First, Indigenous women and immigrant, refugee and asylum seeker women continue to experience poverty, powerlessness and marginalisation. To what extent can feminist practice be developed with or by such groups to address their needs? Second, the emphasis reported on working with individual women in the research described above raises questions about the extent to which professionalisation and a focus on therapeutic work might challenge or reduce the historic, though still maintained, commitment to giving priority to structural social change? Third, to what extent do the frontline feminist services for individual women ally with the national women's movement organisations to create change for women? Women's health centres are typically members of the national women's health lobbying associations. The CASAs have formed their own National Association for Services Against Sexual Violence. The refuges unite nationally in WESNET (women's emergency services network). They are tireless in their campaigns for women's well-being, but there is all too little documentation of their work. Fourth, to what extent can the women's services, and those espousing feminist practice, work with men and men's organisations to challenge and redress gender power relations? This is especially urgent in the arena of violence against women and children, as ultimately men's behaviour change is essential to the safety of women and children. And finally, what can future research tell us about feminist social work practice, and the particular contribution it might make to women's lives?

8

MEN AND MASCULINITIES: PROFEMINIST APPROACHES TO CHANGING MEN

Bob Pease

In this chapter I explore the implication of postmodern critical theory for social work practice with men. Such a perspective recognises structural inequalities in men's lives but also emphasises the importance of dominant discourses in shaping men's diverse subjectivities. This means that we must locate men in the context of patriarchy and the divisions of class, race, sexuality and other forms of social inequality, while at the same time exploring the ways in which patriarchal belief systems become embedded in men's psyches. This dual perspective draws upon the theoretical frameworks of Connell (1995), Hearn (1998) and Kimmel (2000) in the critical studies of men and my own experience in profeminist masculinity politics (Pease 1997, 2000).

I have written elsewhere about the limitations of traditional approaches to working with men in social work, and the importance of adopting a postmodern critical theory and a profeminist commitment among men to challenge sexism in the human services (Pease 2001). In this chapter I extend that analysis by examining men's practices in personal and public life, in the context of social difference and inequality in men's lives. I also outline the practice implications of a critical approach to men in the areas of male social workers' social location, and in working with individuals, groups and communities.

PROFEMINISM AS A BASIS FOR PRACTICE WITH MEN

A critical approach to work with men necessitates an explicit profeminist commitment; this is consistent with structural (Moreau 1990; Mullaly 1997), anti-oppressive (Thompson 2000) and postmodern critical (Leonard 1997; Pease and Fook 1999; Healy 2000) approaches to social work practice. For men, profeminism involves a sense of responsibility for our own and other men's sexism, and a commitment to work with women to end men's violence (Douglas 1993). It acknowledges that men benefit from the oppression of women, drawing men's attention to the privileges they receive as men and the harmful effects these privileges have on women (Thorne-Finch 1992). Profeminist men also recognise that sexism has an impact on men as well as on women. To oppress others it is necessary to suppress oneself. Systemic male dominance deforms men, as evidenced in stress-related illnesses and emotional inexpressiveness. Furthermore, not all men benefit equally from the operation of the structures of domination. Issues of race, sexuality, class, disability and age significantly affect the extent to which men benefit from patriarchy.

Over fifteen years ago, Tolman et al. (1986) articulated twelve principles for a profeminist commitment among men in social work: to develop a historical, contextual understanding of women's experience; to be responsible for themselves and other men; to redefine masculinity; to accept women's scrutiny without making them responsible; to support the efforts of women without interfering; to struggle against racism and classism; to overcome homophobia and heterosexism; to work against violence in all its forms; to not set up a false dichotomy between oneself and other men; to act at individual, interpersonal and organisational levels; and to attend to process and product. They noted at that time that very few men had been proactive in promoting feminist values such as these in social work and that men had contributed very little to ending sexism (Tolman et al. 1986). Dominelli (1999) made a similar observation thirteen years later. Along with Thompson (1995) and Pringle (1995), I believe that men in social work have an important part to play in challenging sexism. This chapter builds upon two recent initiatives in developing a new agenda for profeminist practice with men (Christie 2001; Pease and Camilleri 2001).[1]

UNDERSTANDING MEN'S PRACTICES

McMaster (2000) argues that issues associated with masculinity underlie the problems that men present at social work agencies. The general consequences of traditional masculinity that have been identified include: emotional inexpressiveness, poor health, distant fathering, family breakdown, stress associated with competitiveness and over-work (Brooks 1998), the over-representation of men in substance abuse, high risk behaviours, homelessness, suicide and criminality (Lichtenberg 1999).

A number of writers have suggested that men will change when they consider these costs of masculinity for themselves. I have argued previously, however, that the focus on the problems facing men has placed too much emphasis on the costs for men associated with patri-archal relations and given insufficient attention to the costs to women and children of men's practices (Pease 1999, 2000).[2] In this regard, Cowburn and Pengelly (1999: 198) make the distinction between 'men with problems' and 'men as problems'. The latter include rape and sexual assault; violence against women in the home; sexual harassment and sexual misconduct as a group norm. Brooks (1998: 2) refers to these practices as 'the dark side of masculinity'.

Hearn (1996) has developed a critique of the concept of masculin-ity itself, however, arguing that it may divert attention away from gendered power relations between men and women. He prefers the concept of 'men's practices' to describe what men do, think and feel. This is consistent with Pringle's (1998a) three central principles for critical social work practice with men: maintaining a focus on the rela-tions between men and women rather than on men alone; examining the complexities of masculinity while grounding these in the materi-ality of men's practices; and maintaining the issue of power at the centre of one's analysis of men's practices.

I have been guided by Hearn and Pringle on this matter, in arguing that men's practices should be the focus of critical social work with men. This focus enables us to move beyond the dichotomising portrayal of men as either 'victims' or 'perpetrators'. I suggest here that there are six main arenas in which men's practices are enacted: sexuality; inti-macy and emotional expressiveness; health and well-being; family and care of others; paid work; and violence against women.[3]

Sexuality

Objectification and fixation are key processes in many men's sexual relationships with women, in which often a part of the woman is seen as representing the whole (Kaufman 1993). Some writers argue that there is a connection between the construction of men's sexuality along the objectification, fixation and conquest lines, and the prevalence of sexual assault and rape (Schacht and Atkinson 1992). Male heterosexual socialisation leads to the assumption that men should take the initiative in sex and be dominant. Sattem et al. (1984) argue that it is male sexual socialisation that helps to predispose some men to rape. Lisak's (1991: 243) research demonstrates 'an association between rape myths, stereotypical sex role beliefs and attitudes, the culture's misogynist messages and both the propensity for and actual perpetration of sexual aggression'. Thus culturally supported attitudes and norms are seen to foster sexually aggressive behaviour.

If this is so, male sexual coercion can be prevented by challenging the cultural values that promote aggression and male domination over women as a natural right. This involves confronting the mythology that sees sexual coercion as an inevitable product of male needs, otherwise there is a danger of unintentionally endorsing the 'naturalness' of men's urge to dominate women, rather than challenging the way in which our society condones male coercive sexuality.

Changing the basis of men's sexual desire will require challenging men's sense of entitlement through consciousness-raising and therapy (Segal 1990). In order for men's sexuality to be non-oppressive, it would have to incorporate becoming aroused without exerting power over the other (Hester 1984). The centrality of male power within heterosexual relations is not static or unchangeable. Sex does not have to be about domination and submission. Eisler (1996) has outlined a model of partnership sex that constructs new images of men's sexuality encompassing passivity, sensuality, joy and generosity. While many men appear reluctant to relinquish control in heterosexual relations, partnership sex is possible.

Intimacy and emotional expressiveness

Many women have expressed dissatisfaction with their intimate relationships with men. In Hite's (1987) survey in the United States of 4500 women, 98 per cent of them said that the biggest problem in their current relationships was a lack of emotional closeness. The most commonly expressed complaint (77 per cent) was that 'he doesn't listen'. One of the constant requests from heterosexual women is for men to express themselves more than they do. Most men have been constantly challenged for not giving enough of themselves in their relationships. Men's inability to express emotions has serious consequences for their relationships with women, their friendships with men and their capacity to provide for the nurturant needs of their children; it also has consequences for men themselves because they are robbed of potentially rich emotional experiences.

But is men's emotional inexpressiveness a tragedy, as many writers suggest (Balswick 1982), or is it a way in which men maintain their social power? Sattel (1989) argues that inexpressiveness is a strategy for men to maintain their positions of privilege. To exercise organisational power, one must be able to guard against one's own emotional invest-ment in the consequences of the decision, that is, one must be blinded to the potential pain one's decisions may cause others. Inexpressiveness validates the rightness of one's position. The social positions of highest power demand veneers of inexpressiveness. In this view men are in-expressive as a defensive strategy enacted by them to maintain their power (Sattel 1989).

Men's primary model for relationships tends to be hierarchical. Men have a tendency to either dominate women or withdraw from them in their intimate relationships (Rabin 1996). If men have difficulty giving up power and control in their relationships, it will hamper their capac-ity for intimacy (Dienhart and Avis 1990). hooks (2000: 41) argues that only when men repudiate 'the will to dominate' will they be able to experience love and intimacy. Thus men's relationships with women will be impoverished as long as they continue to control and subordi-nate women (Sattel 1989).

Health and well-being

The issue of men's health started to surface publicly in Australia in the early 1990s. Numerous studies have drawn attention to sex differences in health status between women and men (Fletcher 1997; Mathers 2000). According to gender group averages, life expectancy for men in Australia is six years less than for women. A significant number of commentators draw attention to this and related statistics to indicate that on average, Australian men die from nearly all non-gender specific causes at higher rates than women (Were 1998).

Men's health status is used by some segments of the men's movement to claim that men are a disadvantaged group and are discriminated against in health services compared to women. However, men's health conferences and men's health policy documents often ignore the social divisions between men and the relationship between men's health status and men's relationship to gender-based power. A profeminist approach to men's health emphasises diversity and difference in men's lives and the costs of men's adherence to forms of social domination. Thus we must encourage men to develop a critical consciousness of the material and ideological factors that impact on their health and acknowledge the circumstances of men marginalised by class, race and sexuality.

Family and care of others

Research demonstrates that women's involvement in the paid labour force does not significantly affect the amount of unpaid work they do at home. An Australian study published in 1997 showed that women in full-time paid employment completed over 65 per cent of the household's unpaid labour (Dempsey 1997). This is not counting the invisible work of thinking about and planning meals and other psychological responsibilities for domestic life that women carry more than men. Resentments and disputes over various forms of marital inequality such as these are among the factors that men and women cite as contributing to the breakdown of their marriages (Dempsey 1997). One-third of all marriages in Australia end in divorce. Many women want their husbands to do more housework and child care, they want more opportunities for leisure and they want a greater say in decision-making (Dempsey 1997). It would seem that marital breakdown may be related to men's sense of marital entitlement and their sexism.

There is a prevalent view in the human services literature in Australia that greater involvement of men in child care is important to heal the 'father wound' that is caused by fathers' remoteness and absence (Biddulph 1994). However, while this literature advocates greater involvement of men with their children, it also encourages clear distinctions between men's and women's roles. For example, fathers are expected to be the main transmitters of culturally approved masculinity to their sons. McMahon (1999) has pointed out in his analysis of 'new father' writing that only a minority of such texts argue for equity in child-care work.

Women's sense of personal and relationship well-being increases and their depression decreases if husbands share the housework (Dempsey 1997). In a Melbourne study, 80 per cent of the wives said that if husbands shared responsibility for domestic tasks this would contribute substantially to marital happiness (Dempsey 1997). Men can also gain from an improved relationship and from a sense of partnership by being equally involved in domestic work (Goodnow and Bowes 1994). When fathers take on significant responsibility for children, they develop sensitivities associated with women. Such men report that the experience of child care makes them more complete people and enables them to develop more caring and emotional dimensions of themselves (Coltrane 1996). It is thus important that critical social work with men emphasises equity in household work.

Paid work

Men have been socialised to pursue work as their central life interest and consequently regard child-rearing and domestic responsibilities as secondary. Work-related behaviours influence men's personalities and carry over into the home setting, the competitive world of work encouraging them to estrange themselves from their feelings as a way of surviving. Furthermore, given the masculinised nature of some men's work, the aura of masculinity is sustained by keeping women out or 'keeping them in their place' if they get in.

Some men are 'now less willing to spend endless hours at work, to subordinate their family life to the interests of the corporation; to lead an unbalanced life in which personal well-being comes last' (Edgar 1998: 3). Thus there is pressure on workplaces to become more family-friendly. In response to these issues, in recent years we have seen the development of anti-sexist educational programs targeted at men in the workplace (Russell 1999). The purpose of these workshops is to encourage male managers to work more cooperatively with their staff and to place a higher value on family issues.

If more egalitarian relationships between women and men are to emerge, however, significant alterations to the nature and structure of paid employment are required. Such alterations should include the flex-ible restructuring of work to take account of child-care needs, parental leave which leaves either partner the option of selecting child-care as a priority, increased availability of job sharing and part-time work, and changes in the nature of career values.

Men's violence

It is widely acknowledged that almost all the perpetrators of violence are men. However, while most violence is male, not all men are violent. In contrast to the socio-biological arguments that explain men's violence by reference to testosterone and hormonal patterns (Turner 1994), I believe there is nothing inherent in men that leads them to be violent.

In numerous cross-cultural studies, research shows that the greater the level of gender inequality in a society, the higher the level of violence against women (Klein et al. 1997). Studies of societies in which there was little violence 'found that the definition of masculinity has a significant impact on the propensity toward violence' (Kimmel 2000: 245). Those societies where gender inequality was highest were those where masculinity and femininity were seen to be polar opposites. This analysis has significant implications not only for preventative approaches to men's violence but also for the establishment of gender democracy across all levels of society.

Intervention with perpetrators of violence is too often aimed at men's abuse of authority in the family rather than at the nature and constitution of this authority itself. The organisation of the family is untouched by this approach (Walker 1990). Interventions may help the man control his violence while leaving the basic power structure of the marriage unaltered (Bograd 1984). Empirical research indicates that 'men tend to abuse women when they have much greater power and/or status than women' (Gondolf 1987: 316). Thus, in the longer term, we must eliminate the imbalance of power between men and women if we want to eradicate violence. Until the power inequity of a marriage is altered, there is greater likelihood of male coercion and domination remaining.

SOCIAL DIFFERENCE AND INEQUALITY IN MEN'S LIVES

Men are not a homogeneous group and variations among men are central to the understanding of their lives. This diversity entails differences in relation to class, ethnicity, age, sexuality, bodily facility, religion, world views, parental/marital status, occupation and propensity for violence (Collinson 1992). It is important to always consider which men we are talking about. I now look at some of the implications of this question in relation to class, race and sexuality.

Class

Power is not shared equally among men, and men's class locations influence the nature of their dominance over women. Most working-class men do not experience work as a satisfying or rewarding experience, and the promise of masculine independence and power is not fulfilled (Leach 1993). Many aspects of working-class men's work erode their sense of masculinity. The pressure of production targets, being controlled by foremen and supervisors and having to put up with constant noise and dirt are common experiences for workers. Because of the way it is socially organised, the experience of manual work poses a constant threat to masculinity (Tolson 1977). As working-class men lack social power in the class hierarchy, it is claimed that they are more likely to treat women as underlings in order to compensate. They are quicker to resist changes in the balance in sex roles at home and at work (Astrachan 1989). Having women to dominate can be seen as part-compensation for having to put up with the indignities and oppressions of the workplace. Domestic tyranny can be a spin-off from oppressive experiences in the workplace and a damaged masculinity (Connell 1982).

Pyke (1996) argues that working-class men's masculine identity and self-esteem are undermined by their subordinate position in the social order. As their jobs do not provide satisfaction or social power, they need to maintain their dominance by other ways. This may result in asserting their power and reproducing their masculinity through more extreme methods of controlling women. Working-class masculinity becomes strung between the contradictory poles of the powerlessness of men's wage labour and the power and privilege they have over women of the same class. As most male social work clients are likely to be working class, this contradictory location in relation to power needs to be considered in developing strategies for challenging sexism.

Race and culture

The writings of black men in North America emphasise the role of racism in the development of masculinity. Due to their exclusion from satisfying paid work, most black men do not expect to attain the benefits of traditional masculinity. As prevailing definitions of masculinity imply power, control and authority, these attributes are seen as being denied to most black men since slavery (Mercia and Julien 1988). Black men and white men differ in terms of their power relations with women because of black men's tenuous position in the relations of production. According to Staples (1989), black men's subordination as a racial minority has more than cancelled out their advantages as males in the larger society.

Issues of culture and race have played little part in Australian men's literature. There has been no attempt to analyse the changing modes of masculinity resulting from migration to Australia and we know little about the effects of migration on men's work, leisure and domestic relations (Chambers 1989). Poynting et al.'s (1998) research with Lebanese young men in Sydney, however, points to some of the key issues. They found a highly developed solidarity against 'Aussie' males that took forms of what Connell (1995) calls 'protest masculinity'. This protest masculinity involves exaggerated claims of potency and hypermasculinity as a result of marginalisation. This strong nexus of masculinity and ethnicity has implications for critical social work practice with men of non-English-speaking backgrounds.

In relation to Indigenous men, there has been no analysis of the changing modes of masculinity among Indigenous men in the move from traditional societies to an urban, capitalist society. Studies of Indigenous men do not address masculinity and sexual identity, although obviously they have lost their traditional power and authority since white settlement. Many have embraced alcoholism and become the recipients of welfare (Flynn 1986). Historical processes have devalued the Indigenous male role in both the family and the community. When Indigenous men were confined to reserves, many lost respect and self-esteem (Davis 1992). It is thus argued by some that Indigenous men have suffered more than Indigenous women from the consequences of colonisation (Bolger 1991).

Within this context it is claimed that Indigenous women in contemporary society are not characteristically subordinate. There is evidence that Indigenous women are more highly educated than men (Davis 1992). Atkinson (2000) argues that 'Aboriginal men not only had unequal relationships with dominant mainstream culture but also with Aboriginal women, particularly those who forged dominant roles in family and community affairs' (Atkinson and Pease 2001: 187). There are, however, conflicting views about the impact of colonisation on Indigenous women and men, the extent of Indigenous men's violence against Indigenous women and the extent to which this violence is a product of colonisation. White social workers need to be aware of these debates. They also need to be sensitive to the separate areas of men's and women's business when working with Indigenous men.

Sexuality

From the gay viewpoint, heterosexual masculinity is a privileged masculinity that is created and maintained by homophobia at the expense of homosexual men and women (Nierenberg 1987). As homosexuality is not the norm, gay men have had to question the association of masculinity with heterosexuality. In response to this equation of homosexuality

133

with femininity, some gay men have attempted to create alternative representations of gay identity, what Humphries (1985) calls 'gay machismo'. Gay machismo involves the adoption by gay men of hyper-masculine gender characteristics. In their attempt to counter the associ-ation of masculinity and real men with heterosexuality, some gay men have therefore reinforced hegemonic forms of masculinity. As Messner (1997) notes, however, one of the costs of this hard and tough gay masculinity is the further marginalisation and subordination of effemi-nate gay men.

It is said that homosexual men suffer oppressions similar to those inflicted on women by heterosexual men (Kinsman 1987). As gay men do not dominate women sexually, they do not benefit in the same way from the oppression of women. On the other hand, while gay men are in a subordinate position in the institution of heterosexuality, at the same time they stand with straight men in the privilege of being in a dominant position in relation to women (Kinsman 1987). Gay men are known to dominate lesbians in activist groups and women generally in work places, which can be seen either as a compensation for their own oppression or as a reflection of their masculinity. Ward (2000) challenges the view that gay men have a special understanding of sexism simply because they are gay men. She argues that a shared experience of gender-related oppression does not mean that gay men are not sexist. Rather, she suggests that sexism takes on a speci-fic form in gay communities, what she calls 'queer sexism' (Ward 2000: 171).

Tolman et al. (1986) have emphasised the importance of under-standing the ways in which issues of class, race and sexual preference influence men's commitment to gender equality. In their view, men do not have the same resources or responsibilities to promote an end to male privilege. The fact that men are divided among themselves along the lines of class, race, ethnicity and sexuality makes the task of analysing men's power more difficult (Brittan 198). Brod (1994: 89) suggests that one way through this dilemma is to theorise men simul-taneously 'along two axes, the male–female axis of men's power over women within the marginalised groups, and the male–male axis of non-hegemonic men's relative lack of power *vis-à-vis* hegemonic men'. This is consistent with Collinson and Hearn's (1994:11) exhor-tation that 'both the unities and differences between men and masculinities as well as their interrelations' should be examined.[4]

CRITICAL SOCIAL WORK PRACTICE WITH MEN

Pringle (1995: 45) identifies four levels in which male social workers should engage in anti-oppressive practice: one's own behaviour, individual work, group work and structural change at the community and societal levels.

Working on one's own social location and behaviour

Many writers have drawn attention to the gendered patterns of employment in social work (Martin and Healy 1993; Christie 1998, 2001; Camilleri and Jones 2001). The starting point for men's profeminist practice with men must involve a critical reflection upon the privileges associated with one's own position in the gender order and the gendered division of labour within social work. Christie (2001) has stressed the importance of male social workers critically reflecting upon their gendered privilege and the gendered nature of their work. Pringle (2001: 45) similarly argues that male social workers 'have a particular responsibility to engage in challenging those oppressive structures of power from which they may benefit directly'. This requires male social workers to monitor and challenge their own behaviour. It also means that male social workers need to recognise the contradictions and dilemmas arising from their position.

Cree (2001) has suggested that men in social work should consider engaging in consciousness-raising work. Anti-patriarchal consciousness-raising with men can clarify the social dimensions and historical shifts of masculinities. It can provide a link between personal experiences and the wider social context of men's lives. Men can come to understand their own sexist behaviour, to develop emotional support with other men and encourage their anti-sexism.[5]

Individual work with men

As previously discussed, when gender issues facing men are noted in social work, the tendency is to focus on how men may be oppressed by traditional masculinity and sex roles. Longres and Baily (1979) first drew attention to this issue in their review of social work journals in 1979 and little has changed since then. As Thompson (1995: 460) has pointed out, however, 'understanding the costs of sexism will not in itself, provide a platform for male anti-sexist practice'.

Men often want things to change but they do not want to relinquish their power. A profeminist approach encourages men to re-think their power. This means, as Connell (1987) has suggested, disrupting men's settled ways of thinking. It involves what Cree (2001: 161) calls 'critical engagement'; how to 'build open connection with men while at the same time not being seen to condone their behaviour or attitudes'.

Many of the beliefs men hold are the cause of the troubles in their lives. Thus the starting point for work with men is to assess their beliefs. What beliefs does the man hold about masculinity? What are the sources of these beliefs? What are the potential harmful effects of these beliefs? How are these beliefs associated with the difficulties the man is experiencing? (Allen and Gordon 1990).

Men's socialisation leads to the individual beliefs that can promote abusive behaviours (Russell 1995). Men need to be helped to acknowledge their tendencies to act oppressively and they should be assisted to devise strategies for avoiding those situations and changing their behaviour. They should also be encouraged to develop wider repertoires of behaviour and models of masculinity not associated with violence, control and objectification (Pringle 1995).

Russell (1995), in her work with men who hold abusive beliefs, has articulated a set of respectful beliefs and behaviours. A respectful belief system about relationships is seen to involve: a belief in one's connectedness and interrelatedness with one's partner, a belief that the partner is an equal person whose differences are valued and a belief in the necessity for mutual exchange. To reconstruct masculinity means that it is possible for men to feel good about being men without the negative repercussions of traditional patterns of aggressive masculine behaviour (May 1998).

Group work with men

There are many positive claims made for men's groups. Andronico (1999) argues that men's groups are ideal forums in which to raise issues relevant to men in the coming years. He suggests that the sense of community fostered by groups leads men to feel less isolated and alone. Brooks (1998: 104) similarly argues that because 'men learn to be men in front of other men', then it is in front of other men that men 'can unlearn some of the more unproductive lessons about manhood and relearn and reinforce some of the more positive lessons'.

The psychological and therapeutic literature on men's groups, however, tends to ignore the dangers and the problems associated with such groups. Profeminist writers have drawn attention to a range of issues that need to be addressed in group work with men. Funk (1993: 130) cautions social workers 'to be careful not to get caught in the habit of focusing on the support and on feeling good about being men'. Similarly, Rowan (1997: 222) notes that whatever the intentions, men's groups have a tendency to 'slide into some kind of warm self-congratulation'. He says that while such groups can provide moving experiences for the men, they seem to contribute little to challenging the patriarchal arrangements between men and women. McBride (1995: 89) has argued that any therapeutic benefit for men meeting in groups needs to be 'set against and indeed counter the history of male dominance, collusion and violence' experienced in such groups.[6]

The last fifteen years in Australia have witnessed a dramatic increase in the development of education and counselling programs for violent men. The provision of services to violent men has proved controversial, however. While they have been seen by some as constituting a viable alternative to legal sanctions, they have been condemned by others as psychologising and decriminalising men's violence. Many of the early programs focused on childhood precedents of violent behaviour, anger management and communication in relationships, and failed to adequately address issues of gender inequality, women's safety and accountability. More recently, explicitly profeminist educational programs that challenge patriarchal belief systems have predominated.

Profeminist group work emphasises the importance of working in groups with men who oppress and disempower others, where their prejudices and oppressive behaviours can be challenged (Pringle 1997). As Hearn (2001) comments, profeminist models educate men about the oppressiveness of their beliefs and behaviours and involve them in analysing their use of power and control tactics to enable them to move towards more equal relationships with women.

Creating change at community and societal levels

Feminist and profeminist writers in social work emphasise that personal change does not go far enough, and advocate the importance of connecting personal change with cultural and structural change (Thompson 1995; Cree 2001). Thus work with men should be one aspect of a broader strategy for changing unequal power relations between women and men.

Eisler distinguishes between 'dominator societies' and 'partnership societies' (1987). A dominator society ranks the male above the female, has a high degree of institutionalised social violence, including wife-beating and rape, and has a hierarchical and authoritarian social organisation. A partnership society values the sexes equally, has a low degree of social violence and an egalitarian social structure (Eisler and Loye 1990).

In working towards the goal of creating change we need to raise consciousness, especially among men, about the human costs of men's violence and how the eroticising of such violence reinforces men's domination (Eisler 1996). We also need to develop collective political actions to challenge institutional violence. While feminism has been the underlying foundation of social movements against men's violence, if such movements are to succeed they need to involve significant numbers of men as well as women (Hayward 2000). Men need to become more actively involved, as partners with women, in social movements against violence against women.

In the Australian context, Men Against Sexual Assault (MASA) has been in the forefront of social action against men's violence. MASA was formed at a public meeting in Melbourne in December 1989 to challenge the attitudes that legitimate sexual violence by encouraging men to take action against sexual assault through community education, social action, public media work and sexism awareness workshops. The primary purpose of MASA is rape awareness education for all men. This is based on the premise that there is a relationship between the dominant model of masculine sexuality in Australian society and the prevalence of sexual assault. MASA has been involved in organising public forums on the societal factors that perpetuate and maintain sexual assault, facilitating patriarchy awareness workshops, organising marches and a white-ribbon campaign against men's violence, and commenting in the public media on sexism in popular culture.

CONCLUSION

Working with men to eliminate sexism and violence against women is an emerging field of practice for critical social work. Such a practice needs to be informed by a profeminist agenda that recognises both the institutionalised power that men hold over women and the way in which many men are also marginalised by class, race and sexuality. It is suggested that analysing men's practices in key sites of sexual politics provides the best starting point for social workers to challenge the reproduction of patriarchal relations and to work towards gender equality with women.

9

FAMILIES: RECONSTRUCTING SOCIAL WORK PRACTICES

Susie Costello

The family is the basic unit of identity, connection and care in Australian society. Most people live in some kind of family and Coalition Prime Minister John Howard, has described the family as 'the best social welfare program yet devised' (Department of Community Services 2001). Yet the family means different things to different people. Families can be nurturing, validating, confusing or damaging, and many people spend much of their time trying to make sense of their own family experiences and relationships. Vulnerable family members often experience oppression within their own families. Family forms that diverge from the norm—single-parent, homosexual, Indigenous and other ethnic or cultural minority forms—live constantly with discrimination, homophobia, racism and other forms of oppression.

This chapter critiques traditional ways of conceptualising the family, and discusses the limitations of conventional social work responses to families. The family is examined as a social construct, in which family relationships and situations are influenced by and influence the structural and policy contexts in which they are located (Mason 2001). The chapter explores empowering social work practices with case examples relating specifically to families with children.

SOCIAL WORK AND FAMILIES

Social work's long history of family work has been recently acknowledged and documented (Wood 1996, 2001). Beginning with the charity organisation societies in the 1870s in the United Kingdom, and the settlement houses in the 1880s in the United States, early social case-work pioneers established forms of structural social work with families. Addressing and advocating for the material needs of poor families and their communities, they lobbied actively for the rights of marginalised people and persuaded politicians to improve public health standards, child-care, housing and other practical aspects crucial to family well-being (Wood 1996). Australian social work was strongly influenced by these models.

Despite these encouraging beginnings, social workers have not always been effective in addressing the full range of issues affecting families, from the personal to the structural levels. Employed by state and federal governments, as well as by non-government agencies, many social workers have acted as agents of social control, making decisions about which families gain access to resources, and who lives where and with whom. Other social workers have responded therapeutically to families, providing family counselling, therapy and parenting programs on the assumption that improving 'family functioning' would improve family situations. A re-focusing of government policy in the 1970s, under the Australian Assistance Plan, led some social workers to work along-side families in community participation and development projects (Weeks 2000). A central tenet of critical social work practice is to respond to families at all levels: personal, social and political.

WHAT DO WE MEAN BY 'FAMILY'?

> Nothing in our society brings us greater joy than being part of a happy, supportive family: nothing in our society brings greater devastation than being part of a family that is destructive of the individual personalities of its members (McDonald 1994: 4).

In 1983, Eichler contested the 'monolithic family' myth of one form of family relationship and activities (cited in Bessant and Watts 1999). The Latin word *familia* means 'household', and includes everyone who lives under the same roof (Bessant and Watts 1999). In 1994 the National Council for the International Year of the Family formally re-defined the concept of 'the family' to include:

> . . . two parents with dependent and older children, sole parent families, step-families, siblings caring for each other, spouse/partners caring for

each other, networks of relatives extending well beyond the household, families caring for elderly members and those with a disability, families whose structures and relationships may differ according to race, ethnicity, religious faith and cultural background (Cass et al. 1994: 7).

Despite the actual diversity of Australian families, the traditional family concept prevails in the Australian culture. Drawing on Barrett and McIntosh's (1982) definition, Mason (2001: 70) identifies this as familism, the view that the white nuclear family, with a breadwinner husband and a homemaking wife taking care of their children, is the most important unit of society and the basic household unit. Familism is evident in advertising and in popular television shows such as *Neighbours*, where there is little challenge to the homogeneity and universalising of the traditional family. Such television programs seldom represent or address issues faced by single parents living in poverty, Aboriginal people or Torres Strait Islanders, refugee or migrant families, gay and lesbian couples, or people with disabilities.

Compare the nuclear family with Indigenous families, which include all relatives who are obliged, through kinship, to accommodate each other whenever requested (Byrnes 2000). Children are cared for by a wide range of relatives, often grandmothers. Children and young people are regarded as responsible for, and having the right to make decisions for, themselves from an early age. This might include seeking assistance and sustenance from relatives if it is not available at home (Byrnes 2000). Lacking a critical understanding of such differences, particularly the role of the extended family, social workers played a significant part in removing Indigenous children from their families, colluding with the discourse of the time that living with non-related white people in children's homes or foster families was better for these children than living with their own families.

An examination of figures from the 1996 census challenges the myth that the traditional family still prevails:

- Only 53.7 per cent of the population lived in two-parent families
- Two-parent families with their own offspring made up only 36.4 per cent of the population
- 9.7 per cent of all families were single parent families, 84 per cent of which were headed by mothers
- 33.6 per cent of all families were childless
- 48 per cent of married couples divorce
- 7 per cent of children live in step or blended families

- 1.6 million women were married with children
- 2.2 million women were married and had no children
- 50 per cent of all women were in the paid workforce
- 29 per cent of married women were in the paid workforce
  (cited in Bessant and Watts 1999).

The statistics reveal that while the traditional nuclear family is an important style of family, it represents only about half the population's experience. Families have changed dramatically from the 1950s to the 1990s (Probert 2001). Fertility control, contraception and divorce laws have given women the choice to participate in paid work, with a new sense of identity as citizens in their own right. Women, however, now work in casual and/or part-time jobs, are generally lower paid than their male counterparts (Bryson 2000), and continue to do the 'second shift' of housework, child and community caring (Hochschild 1989; Bittman and Pixley 1997; Gilding 1997).

Exploring the impact of these changes on young children reflects competing discourses about family responsibilities. The collapse of full-time secure employment and the rise of casual and contract jobs has reduced breadwinning options for fathers also. Yet, says Probert, opinions about parents' roles have not kept up with these changes, due to the 'ideology of domesticity' which requires mothers to be selfless, with their sense of self 'organised around being able to make, then to maintain, affiliations and relationships' (2001:9). McCain and Mustard's (1999) research, emphasising the first three years as crucial to a child's development, raises questions for many mothers, not just for the 'selfless devotee'. A recent survey indicates that most Australian mothers think they should stay home to raise their children instead of joining the paid workforce (Saltau 2001). Is this about the 'ideology of domesticity', and how does it reflect the changes to work culture and its impact on families? Taffel's (2001) research with young teenagers and their families in the United States has concerning implications for families in Australia, where working hours and pressures are increasing (Jackson 2001). Overworked, overstressed parents, with few connections with their neighbours, are unable and unavailable to relate to, much less supervise, their children, who are establishing a 'second family' with peer groups, online communities and large corporations selling lifestyles (Taffel 2001). Young people lacking 'the anchor of steady, reliable adults in their lives' are engaging in far more risky behaviour than they did a decade ago, with disturbing rates of substance addiction, male suicide and high rates of youth homelessness (Mitchell 2000).

At the other extreme, 19 per cent of couple and sole-parent families with dependent children have no one in the paid workforce (ABS 1998). Many women are unable to take up full-time work because, with little available or affordable alternate care for family members, the burden of care falls on them. With the current global economic instability, work opportunities and security are diminishing. This is challenging to the 'provider anxiety' experienced by fathers as part of the internalised 'ideology of domesticity'. Emerging out of the 'absent breadwinner' notion of fatherhood are new models of fathering (Camilleri and Jones 2001; Hood 2001), and debates about fathers' roles in constructing their sons' masculinity have been explored elsewhere (Pease 2000a). The role of single mothers in bringing up sons is also being explored, questioning the notion that boys must have a father in their life, regardless of his commitment (Silverstein and Rashbaum 1994; Howard 2001). Yet this remains one of the constraining beliefs that many women describe as their reason for staying with abusive men (Costello 1997).

With work and gender relations continually evolving, couples have the opportunity to develop egalitarian relationships that are fair, share power in decision-making and share household and parenting roles (Rabin 1996). Yet counteracting the prevailing gender-role prescriptions requires the luxury of time to talk and reflect, and the absence of hunger, debt, violence and grief, as well as the availability of a support network. Prescriptions for 'ways of being' are embedded and transferred through family interactions and culture, and divergence from the norm is often challenged both subtly and overtly. Critical social workers can play a role here in working with families as they reconstruct themselves. Speedy (2001) describes the freedom from prescriptions about 'how to be' that she and her partner experience as a lesbian couple. They are enjoying 'making it up as they go along', marred only by the perceptions and discriminatory responses of others.

Khisty's (2001) examples of her dilemmas in trying to balance her internalised Indian culture with her adopted Australian identity demonstrate the complexity, pervasiveness and random nature of influences shaping the migrant experience. Both cultures (the culture of origin and the adopted culture) give conflicting messages: 'Be Australian like us (but you shouldn't really have come here in the first place)'; 'Don't lose your culture—but don't be one of those Indians who refuse to adapt' (Khisty 2001: 19).

Immigrant families in Australia face many similar issues: differences in language and religion; the migration experience; unrecognised qualifications; intergenerational conflict and stress in establishing themselves in a foreign environment. Yet within this set of common issues, their experiences are enormously diverse. Categorising 'migrants' as a homogeneous group reduces the opportunity to respond to families' individual needs. Workers in ethno-specific agencies frequently have to remind mainstream workers of this, as well as how to access interpreting services, in response to referrals for services such as housing, financial assistance or family support for families who do not speak English (Sadowski 2001). Ethno-specific workers' 'expertise' in working with migration issues derives from their listening to individual stories of immigrant families rather than from the education process. Advocating for these families can make a significant difference, as illustrated in the following case. A school contacted the local Migration Resource Centre to discuss the risks for a five-year-old boy who walked home on his own. The boy's Iraqi lone father, based on his experience in his own country, had not considered walking home alone a risk. He described his isolating situation in not being able to bring his wife and other children from Iraq because of Australian government policy. The worker explained the Australian practice of collecting children after school to the father, and the role of the state Protective Services to protect children's rights and safety. This intervention averted a notification to Protective Services and a complex period of misunderstanding and further trauma (Sadowski 2001).

No form of family guarantees a loving connection between people. Searching for a family of choice is an option for adults but is seldom available to children, who have very little power in making choices. In terms of age, size, knowledge, authority and society's expectations, children are clearly in a position of least power in families. When that power is abused in families, it operates on the basis of the strongest victimising the weakest, with the greatest volume of abuse directed at children under the age of six (McGoldrick et al. 1999). Abused by the people they love, children are likely to feel confused, anxious, ashamed and self-blaming (Joy 2001), and simply finding another family is no solution. Stories of sexual abuse within foster families and children's homes destroy the myth that foster families always provide a safe and caring alternative to a destructive family situation (Morgan 1999).

Children need laws and policies to protect their rights as citizens. The Chief Justice of the Family Court in Australia urges the establishment of a dedicated commission for children and young people to protect their rights (Nicholson 2001: 15).This challenges the private domain of the family and the ideology that children 'belong' to their parents. The notion of social parenthood (Edgar 2000: 31), or 'socially distributed parenting' (McGurk 1996), considers children the responsibility of all citizens. Family policy swings between extending the responsibility of caring for children to the community, via family and community-strengthening initiatives (Department of Community Services 2001), and placing greater emphasis on individual families taking full responsibility for and supporting their own family members.

The National Drug Strategy, for example, focused on the family's responsibility for 'talking to your children' as a means of preventing drug addiction. The campaign assumed all families have the safety, comfort and skills to match the predominantly white families portrayed on television and in the promotional booklet (Abetz 2001). Although unemployment, poverty, abuse and homelessness have been identified as predeterminants of heroin use (Abetz 2001), the campaign implicitly blamed the family for the associated loss of hope and choice (Mendes 2001).

An analysis of social and structural factors reveals a dramatic increase in the number of Victorian families who are homeless, around 47 per cent of which are single-mother families. A third of all people housed by refuges are children, many escaping domestic violence (Rogers 2001: 1). The failure of police and legal systems to ensure the safety of women and children indicates a prevalence of patriarchal ideas within those systems (Murphy 2001). Government policies and initiatives to strengthen families and communities often overlook the institutional barriers facing families in Australia. In this policy climate, what role do social workers have in working alongside families in challenging inequalities and oppression?

CRITICAL SOCIAL WORK WITH FAMILIES: EMPOWERING PRACTICES

In chapter 4, June Allan adapts Parsons et al.'s (1998) model of empowerment. This section analyses the model's application to critical social work practice with families. The first aspect considers the dynamics of power between the worker and the family. The position of an educated, employed social worker is imbued with socially ascribed meaning and power. How that is enacted in relationships with clients is influenced by dominant beliefs from one's own family culture, thus it is important to engage in ongoing critical self-reflection of one's own racism, classism, agism, homophobia and familism. Part of this reflection includes reviewing one's professional past to see how the ideas and theories that are held have changed over time (White and Epston 1989). With such understanding, social workers can question ideas that they currently hold: 'Do these ideas lead to creating or closing space in conversations with families?' (Fine and Turner 1991). Positioning oneself by taking a 'not knowing' stance (Furlong 2001), using self-disclosure, and making the processes and bureaucratic formalities transparent, can begin to minimise power differentials between workers and families.

The second aspect of empowering practice is addressing the distribution of power within families. It is essential to take into account the hidden ways that abuse and intimidation may be organising family behaviour, and to be attuned to the patterns of violence in different contexts of class, cultures, gender and age (McGoldrick et al. 1999). Critical social workers recognise that migrant and non-English-speaking families experience double jeopardy from institutional racism and patriarchal oppression; in families where the woman has less power by virtue of not being in the labour force or having less education, she is at higher risk of abuse (McGoldrick et al. 1999).

How can social workers maintain a dialogical relationship in working with families where there is violence and abuse? Ignoring it is not effective, as Stanley and Goddard (1993) found in research where some child protection workers minimised the level of violence in abusive families, with the result that children were removed from their home for lack of care, rather than the violence being named and the perpetrator removed. Using a 'dialectical analysis', on the other hand, provides a way of addressing these contradictions (Fine and Turner 1991). A dialectical analysis names contradictions as an impetus for change. Taking a 'both-and' approach means contradictory ideas can be spoken about and explored (Fine and Turner 1991: 317). In confronting an abusive father, a protective worker might name the contradictions in his stated love for his family and his abuse in the following way: 'You seem to care about your family and yet your behaviour has hurt them and broken their trust in you. Are you interested in working with us and your partner to stop being violent, so your children can live without fearing you?'

Consistent with structural and postmodern approaches, the strengths-based principles outlined by Elliott et al. (2000) provide ways of discovering strength to challenge oppressive principles. To work sensitively with families, it is necessary to:

- Be sensitive to the impact of material and structural realities on families' lives. Be aware of and prepared to challenge legal and welfare structures and the family policy framework. Be informed about resources, laws, rights and the processes to access and influence them, such as debt and bankruptcy laws, the income security system, intervention orders procedures and appeals processes.
- Explore, validate and celebrate the diversity of family types as well as acknowledging individuals' experiences within families, using narrative and strength-based approaches within a critical framework.
- Look for and enhance positive connections between family members and significant others. Acknowledge and include the influence and roles of absent members (children, siblings, fathers and grandparents) by including their views in family discussion. Acknowledge the impact of transgenerational legacies and expectations (McGoldrick et al. 1999).
- Seek the voices of children and include them in decision-making processes. As the youngest and least powerful citizens, children are often overlooked in social work practice.
- Be aware of the power dynamics within family relationships, between the family and the worker, and between the family and the community. Name and challenge oppressive situations such as racism, homophobia, abuse and violence.
- Make administrative and legal processes transparent and ensure there are opportunities for families to participate in decision-making processes affecting their lives.
- Share knowledge and skills and advocate alongside families facing issues of oppression.
- Establish and maintain effective networks, and work collaboratively for change with other child and family-focused agencies such as maternal and child health centres, schools and youth centres.

USING STRENGTH-BASED APPROACHES IN CRITICAL SOCIAL WORK PRACTICE WITH FAMILIES

Working with families towards social justice involves naming and challenging practices and policies that oppress individuals in relationships within families, as well as within the broader social and political contexts (Mason 2001). Strength-based orientations (Elliott et al. 2000) such as narrative (Monk et al. 1997; Morgan 1999) and solution-focused approaches (de Jong and Berg 2002) can be used as forms of critical questioning, using respectful curiosity about people's beliefs in order to explore taken-for-granted familistic assumptions that limit choice and deny individual or family realities.

It can be informative and empowering for family members to hear each other's views. Naming differences and strengths and creating space for alternative stories from a structural analysis such as class or gender (or other disabling dominant discourses), has an impact on families' stories. Competing views can be identified. One way is to separate the person from 'the problem' by 'externalising' the problem as a separate 'thing'. Family resources can be mobilised against 'the problem' and its influence over the person and their family and others. This entails listening carefully for any hint of an experience where 'the problem' does not dominate. The worker then celebrates this 'unique outcome' as the beginning of an alternate story that can be expanded or co-authored by the client and worker. Recruiting an audience to listen or bear witness to the preferred new story can ensure its ongoing performance (Drewery and Winslade 1997; Elliott et al. 2000).

Another way of exploring strengths is by asking solution-focused questions. Believing that people can find their own solutions, workers ask questions to find 'exceptions' to dominant problem-focused stories. Conversations focus on personal skills or qualities that have been overlooked because of the dominance of oppressive stories in someone's life. The focus is on what is going well and how things will be when the problem is not there, rather than looking for causes of the problem (Elliott et al. 2000). A series of questions has been developed to foster hope and the possibility of other outcomes. The 'miracle question' defines a picture of what will replace 'doing the problem' when it no longer dominates the person's life:

> Suppose you go to bed tonight and while you are sleeping, a miracle occurs. The miracle is that the problems you've been telling me about are solved. What do you suppose you would notice tomorrow morning that would be different and would tell you things are better? (de Jong and Berg 2002: 14).

As a new picture begins to emerge, the worker's task is to notice and collect examples of what is working, or has worked, in the past. Scaling questions can be used to rank someone's energy for challenging an issue or to trace the severity of a situation over time.

Violence, poverty, disability or loss cannot be wished away by miracles, however. These questions are useful tools when used in conjunction with a critical approach, where they can be used for setting priorities with families facing multiple issues, by acknowledging family achievements and involving families in decision-making.

For example, Tranh, a young Vietnamese new mother with a heroin addiction, was referred to a family support agency by Child Protective Services. An assessment of her situation alerted the worker to some of the concerns she might be experiencing: inconsistent responses to her baby, alienation from her community, loneliness as a new mother, shame, fear and racism in an unfamiliar place, as well as the effects of her addiction. Following the guidelines for developing trust and rapport suggested by Nguyen and Bowles (1998), the worker presented in a friendly and caring way, explaining her role as helper and asking: 'If at the end of my visit, you felt our time had been useful, what might have happened?' Tranh responded that no one could help her, then talked about her fear of contact from her ex-boyfriend. She described her life with him where his drug-dealing, theft and abuse meant she lived in constant fear. She had tried to leave him in the past but had no supports outside the drug circle. Tranh feared her addiction would result in her baby being taken by 'the welfare'. Responding to a 'miracle question' about her life without heroin, she spoke of her dreams of caring for her son and studying journalism. This provided a strong basis for developing alternate stories about her, for herself and hospital staff and later, her family, with whom she had cut ties because of her shame about her addiction.

Listening to Tranh's story involved several critical aspects: normalising her loneliness as an 18-year-old Vietnamese woman alone in a foreign country; identifying and honouring her vulnerability which had led to her depending on an older man for protection which turned to abuse; naming the unfairness of her experience and the illegality of his actions (Nguyen and Bowles 1998). On a practical level, the new story involved Tranh reporting the violence to the police, finding safe housing, having financial security and linking with other young mothers, some of whom were also fighting addictions. Work with Protective Services entailed clarifying expectations about what was needed to close the case. Externalising heroin and Tranh's heroin-related lifestyle became a useful mechanism for providing an open process of monitoring her fight against her addiction.

Solution-focused narrative approaches are useful in establishing hope and clarifying goals for families and workers to aim at together. Without a critical understanding of situations, however, they can minimise families' experience by ignoring the impact of structural factors and disabling discourses. Carter and McGoldrick's (1992: 22–3) 'questions to help raise issues' heighten critical awareness to encourage new and constructive ideas. For example, they suggest that workers ask routinely who manages the money, how financial decisions are made, what impact a disparity of income has on a family's overall decision-making processes, and how couples decide who would do the paid work and who would be at home caring for the children. Such questions challenge the dominant traditional family discourse that men are the breadwinners and women do the 'home' work. They address issues of power, oppression and meaning, which are embedded within financial arrangements, or relate in other ways to material conditions.

Consciousness-raising can alert families to the impact of power abuses of racism, sexism, classism and homophobia, and leads to new forms of social accountability (Carter and McGoldrick 1999), and creates an understanding of the multiple combinations of power and oppression. All forms of abusive behaviour should be challenged, even when there are multiple forms of oppression, as in the case of lesbian violence, women's violence to children (FitzRoy 1999), violence in the Indigenous community, adolescent abuse of a parent or elder abuse. Consciousness-raising is more effective in a collective approach, as in group work or community meetings. An example of this is the reflection of a young woman at an evaluation session of a group for women who had experienced domestic violence. She wrote: 'I thought violence was a normal part of adult relationships until I came to the group and heard that you don't have to put up with it.'

Mullender and Ward (1991) describe principles of empowering, self-directed group work that are applicable in working with families or issues affecting families. This approach involves people in the process from the beginning; from the identification of the need for a group, through the planning, goal setting, conduct, recording and evaluation of the group. One example of an empowering group for families which draws on some of these principles is the Families and Schools Together (FAST) group program, implemented in Melbourne by Kildonan Family Services. Based on a 'strengthening families and community' philosophy, schools invite eight to twelve families with children 'at risk' to participate in a program aimed at increasing families' self-esteem. The team consists of a teacher or welfare coordinator from the school, local family support workers, a drug and alcohol worker, the FAST facilitator and a parent graduate. Families prepare and share a meal together, then join in strength-based interactive games, such as designing a family crest, family photos and singing. The evening is fun, empowering and educative. With financial and practical support, each family takes a turn in cooking and serving the meal. The FAST program is one group program that has involved fathers successfully. At the conclusion of the ten-week course, some families have formed lobby groups to address local issues (Barrett 2001).

DEVELOPING AND SHARING ORGANISATIONAL COMPETENCE

Social workers can help families develop organisational competence by acting as a resource for information and access to services, and by providing clients with an understanding of agency processes such as writing letters to organisations and professionals. Residents' meetings can provide an empowering forum for families to meet as a self-help group to address collective concerns, such as stopping violence and crime in the community. It is important to establish good working relationships with other workers to mobilise support at the local level. The Ecumenical Migration Centre in Fitzroy, Melbourne, for example, provides training and volunteer work experience for newly arrived refugee and migrant families. Volunteers are seen as equal participants in the agency, developing skills in administration, reception and community projects. Strong links with the local community can lead to employment for people on temporary protection visas, a category which offers minimal support (Sadowski 2001).

SOCIAL ACTION FOR POLITICAL CHANGE

Working towards the elimination of oppression using social action methods is an important dimension of working with families from a critical perspective. Families and groups living in situations of extreme poverty make constant and important efforts to improve their living conditions, but these efforts largely go unnoticed by the dominant society (Genugten and Perez-Bustillo 2001). Promoting the voices and views of marginalised people can be achieved in several ways. Keeping records, collecting information and analysing data about client families and the issues they are facing is an important aspect of practice, as the information can be used to lobby about trends or gaps in the service system. National peak bodies, such as the Australian Council of Social

Service and the Australian Association of Social Workers, can play a crucial role taking responsibility for coordinating and promoting information. For example, in Victoria, the Domestic Violence and Incest Resource Centre gathered information from refuges and welfare agencies via questionnaires about the ineffectiveness of police responses to reports of violence against women. The data was used as part of a submission to the Victorian Chief Commissioner of Police, who subsequently announced a plan to review police procedures in dealing with domestic violence (Murphy 2001). Other organisations, such as the Brotherhood of St Laurence and The Family Centre in New Zealand, involve families in researching issues affecting their lives.

PARTICIPATORY DEMOCRACY AND COLLECTIVE ACTION

Social workers can maximise families' participation in broader political aspects of citizenship through consciousness-raising and collectivisation in response to issues that emerge from working with families and communities. Involving families in policy activism is one way of connecting people with each other to address local and global issues. For example, since the 1970s, the Brotherhood of St Laurence has involved families directly in efforts at social reform (Taylor 1990; Gilley 1990, 1995). One example was a project to explore low-income, sole-parent families' views on the quality of available services. Weekly small group discussions were held with mothers of young children over a four-month period. Service providers from three levels of government and the community sector were consulted throughout the project. The parents' experiences, views and recommendations were used as the yardstick for defining families' needs at the conclusion of the project (Gilley 1995).

Research and policy activism are central to the approach of The Family Centre in New Zealand, as is the commitment to a sharing of power and resources within the Centre. Consequently, salaries are the same for all employees, with bonuses paid for policy work. Work with families reflects the analysis of the distribution of power and accountability, and culturally appropriate ways of working are integrated into the processes and culture of the agency (Law 1994). The model of 'Just Therapy' addresses a commitment to social justice, taking account of the impact of gender, culture, and the social and economic context on people's lives. It also explores the manner in which people give meaning to experience and create their reality (Waldegrave 1990). Waldegrave, for example, invited a group of families on low incomes to develop a process to research the impact of poverty on families' lives. The consultant group developed a questionnaire that was used to conduct nationwide research into the impact of poverty. Using the New Zealand network of welfare and family therapy agencies, Waldegrave made the questionnaire available for workers to use in focus groups with clients across the nation. The Family Centre collated the responses into a report which was submitted to the national government. Strong in evidence-based data, the report provided an alternative to the government's analysis of poverty and income security, and became one of the key platforms for the next national election (Waldegrave and Stephens 2000).

A similar project at Good Shepherd Youth and Family Services in Melbourne illustrates a feminist research approach: doing research 'for' women as opposed to 'on' them (Sutherland 1986). Anticipating the impact of proposed changes to sole parent payments in the upcoming Budget, Good Shepherd sought the views of single mothers before and after the changes were implemented. It was a tripartite approach. Sole parents, workers and policy-makers were interviewed, revealing dramatic drops in the income of single mothers as well as relationship implications, as women supporting children were forced to renegotiate maintenance payments with (often violent) ex-partners. The agency has since established strong links with the Federal Child Support Agency, which administers family payments, and is proposing developing a pilot study to gather the views of sole parents across the nation (Webster 2001). Such large-scale participatory research projects can empower, connect and mobilise people as well as change the social structures that limit their choices and lives.

CONCLUSION

The family is in transformation with the traditional heterosexual, white, male-headed nuclear family no longer dominant in Australian society. Its legacy lingers on, however, in the ideology of domesticity, with prescribed gender, parenting and policy implications. Children's rights and parents' responsibilities are being reconsidered, with the notion of 'socially distributed parenting' at the basis of current 'strengthening families and communities' policies. This is at odds with a concurrent policy expectation of increased parental responsibility for children and young people. Families are acknowledged as the key site of identity and connection in our society. Individual families' access to power and choice is limited according to family type, gender, race, class, age, ability and sexual orientation, as well as by multiple forms of oppression, within and outside families. Social workers therefore have a significant role in identifying the beliefs, assumptions and prejudices affecting families, as well as raising families' consciousness about structural impediments to equity and participation. Part of this involves social workers' critical self-reflection to locate their own position and to identify situations that may constrain equal relationships with clients. Narrative, strength-based approaches provide empowering ways to develop alternative stories respecting the diversity of families' experiences. Involving families in participatory research and action can take this further by validating families' 'lived experiences' in challenging policies and practices that oppress families and family members.

10

MENTAL HEALTH: RETHINKING PRACTICES WITH WOMEN

Jennifer Martin

This chapter is a discussion of women and mental health from a feminist perspective. Attention is drawn to the social construction of mental illness and mental health, and the medicalisation of women's distress. Patriarchal power structures and sex stereotypes are discussed, highlighting the gender biases operating in the formulation and application of psychiatric diagnoses. Issues of violence and sexual assault are included, as a high proportion of women who use mental health services have experienced abuse. Anti-oppressive and anti-discriminatory practice highlights the links between race and other forms of exclusion or oppression. Consideration is given to gender-sensitive practices that acknowledge the social and political context of women's lives. A discussion of women, mental health and the criminal justice system raises the question: Who is deemed 'mad' or 'bad', by whom and on what basis?

A FEMINIST PERSPECTIVE ON WOMEN AND MENTAL HEALTH

Critical perspectives of mental health arose in the 1960s and 1970s in the sociology of deviance literature, questioning the validity of biological definitions of mental illness and mental health asserted by mainstream psychiatry at the time (Goffman 1961; Laing 1961, 1965, 1967; Szasz 1961, 1963; Scheff 1966; Foucault 1967, 1977; Scull 1979). The concept of mental illness was refuted, and the power of psychiatrists to define 'normal' and 'abnormal' behaviour was challenged. Critical theorists focused on the social construction of mental health and mental illness and the impact of class, gender, sexuality, race, ethnicity and age.

Since the mid-1970s, feminist writers have opened up the debate of gender and mental health. The focus has been on the over-representation of women as service users in the mental health system, exploring how women enter the mental health system, and their subsequent treatment. There are a variety of views of women and mental health within feminist theory. From a social constructionist perspective, mental illness is seen as a label assigned to women who transgress acceptable notions of femininity. Patriarchal power structures are used to explain the over-representation of women diagnosed as mentally ill. Chesler (1972: 56) argues that what is considered mental illness is—'either the acting out of the devalued female role or the total or partial rejection of one's sex-role stereotype'. This predicament places women in a precarious position whereby they can be considered 'mad' if they accept or reject sex-role stereotypes.

Numerous studies have found a gender bias within the formulation and application of psychiatric diagnoses (Chesler 1972; Sheppard 1991; Coppock and Hopton 2000). This serves to further exclude women from patriarchal social structures, with women's anger or unhappiness viewed as psychological disturbance. The social construction of such labels is reflected in changing patterns of psychiatric diagnoses over time. In the nineteenth century women who did not conform to female social expectations were labelled hysterical, whereas later labelling included anxiety and depression (Showalter 1987).

The connection of women's mental health with biology is a major concern of feminist theorists. Biological explanations of mental health continue to dominate psychiatry, with an emphasis on reproductive biology and women's genetic and hormonal predisposition to mental disorder. Within this framework there is an emphasis on pre-menstrual tension, post-natal depression and menopause. Feminist writers refute these assertions, claiming that they are merely a reflection of sexist assumptions and ideologies with no scientific basis (Chesler 1972; Caplan 1995; Sheppard 1997; Ussher 1997; Coppock and Hopton 2000). Alternatively, feminist theorists focus on women's lives within an oppressive patriarchal society, and the impact of gendered sources of stress on women. These stresses include economic dependence, family caring responsibilities, physical and sexual abuse and social isolation

(Stoppard 1997). Women are not only socially disadvantaged in these role expectations; they are also psychologically disadvantaged as a result of the socialisation process that prepares them for these roles.

THE MEDICALISATION OF WOMEN'S DISTRESS

Women continue to be placed in subservient roles that necessarily impact upon their levels of health and well-being. The distress expressed by many women in relation to their social, economic and political subordination is often viewed as a clinical problem. This biological response to women's distress has legitimated medical interventions in responses ranging from highly invasive surgical procedures to high rates of prescription of highly addictive tranquillisers that maintain women in this deferential position. A number of studies have found that when men and women present with similar symptoms of anxiety and depression, women are far more likely to be prescribed tranquillisers and to receive electro-convulsive therapy (ECT) when compared with men (Ettore and Riska 1993; Gerrand 1993; Busfield 1996; Ussher 1997). If women succumb to the medicalisation of their distress, they can become further disempowered and experience even greater difficulties and distress in fulfilling expected social roles.

The traditional structure and delivery of mental health services has been rigid. Women experiencing mental distress, particularly those from Indigenous and ethnic minority backgrounds, have often been met with statutory services that are neither appropriate nor responsive to their needs.

When a woman is deemed mentally ill this has a major determining influence on the manner in which she is subsequently treated. One of the major assessment and diagnostic tools of psychiatrists is the *Diagnostic and Statistical Manual* (DSM), now in its fourth edition (DSMIV), produced by the American Psychiatric Association. General practitioners also use the DSM, as well as those commonly referred to as allied health staff: this includes social workers, psychologists, nurses and occupational therapists. It is also used by lawyers and insurance companies when deciding on eligibility for reimbursement of patient costs. It is sold world-wide and has been translated into numerous languages, including Chinese, Italian, Japanese, Portuguese, Russian and Turkish, to name a few (Caplan 1995: xix). Caplan's work exposes the biased and unscientific manner in which the American Psychiatric Association determines what is deemed 'normal' as opposed to 'abnormal' behaviours. In her critique of the DSM

Caplan focuses on what she describes as,'the disingenuous and dishonest process of constructing the world's most influential handbook of mental disorders' (1995: xvi). Her experience as a psychologist concurs with my own as a social worker, with many people ending up in psychotherapy or counselling and believing that there is something wrong with them, when in fact their distress is often due to disempowerment or discrimination. This may be in relation to their gender, age, mental health, physical condition or appearance, class or sexual preference (Caplan 1995: xx).

Sex stereotypes are reflected in the psychiatric diagnostic categories assigned to women, with those who do not conform to traditional female stereotypes viewed as experiencing an even greater level of disturbance (Gerrand 1993;Teplin et al. 1997).Women are more frequently diagnosed with depression, with men more likely to be diagnosed as having an alcohol or drug disorder or a personality disorder. When women in the community are diagnosed with personality disorder it is most likely to be a diagnosis of histrionic or dependent personality disorder (Gerrand 1993).

Some general practitioners and psychiatrists, particularly males, have been found to become more anxious and frustrated when treating women than they do with men. Women are seen as presenting with vague and difficult-to-understand complaints (Gerrand, 1993; Saxon and Emslie 1998). Many women have expressed feelings of frustration from being patronised and not taken seriously by their general practitioners. Chesler comments:

> Clinicians, most of whom are men, all too often treat their patients, most of whom are women, as 'wives' and 'daughters', rather than as people: they treat them as if female misery, by biological definition, exists outside the realm of what is considered human or adult (1992: xxi).

A major issue is the high prevalence of sexual abuse of women who are diagnosed as mentally ill.

VIOLENCE AND SEXUAL ABUSE

A high proportion of women who use mental health services have experienced physical and/or sexual abuse. Some studies estimate as many as 50 per cent of women using mental health services are survivors of sexual assault (Cox 1994). Many of the symptoms attributed to having been sexually abused are evident in the psychiatric diagnoses of personality disorder, schizophrenia and post-traumatic stress disorder. Women have been portrayed as both passive victims and active seducers.

Women with mental health issues are at risk of sexual harassment from hospital staff and others. The issue of sexual relationships between male workers and female psychiatric patients is often dismissed, 'because it is seen as too controversial, or trivialised as unduly subjective or ignored as irrelevant' (Gerrand 1993: 3). Invasive surveillance and the supervision of personal hygiene by male staff are distressing for women, particularly for those who have been sexually abused.

Self-harm and attempted suicide is high among women who use mental health services. The figures are even greater if the eating disorders of bulimia and anorexia are included (Quadrelli 1997). From a feminist perspective self-harm is a response to feelings of anger, hostility and impotence, and is an attempt to regain internal control and power (Alder 1997). The response from some hospital staff to self-harm has been harsh and unsympathetic, with women viewed as attention-seeking and being punished rather than assisted (Wadsworth 2001).

ANTI-OPPRESSIVE AND ANTI-DISCRIMINATORY PRACTICE

Mental health services do not adequately meet the needs of people from non-Anglo cultural backgrounds. The DSMIV has little relevance or applicability to non-Western cultures, with diagnostic categories generally assigned after acculturation processes (Bainbridge 1999). Service provision has been characterised by longer hospital stays and greater use of involuntary treatments in locked wards and secure units. The participation of people from non-Anglo backgrounds in community mental health programs is also problematic. This is due to the lack of bilingual staff, cultural limitations placed on interaction between females and males and, 'the unwitting ethnocentric nature of service delivery and culturally inappropriate programs' (Gerrand 1993: 69). This results in higher rates of crisis intervention and hospital admissions. Once hospitalised, medical responses, such as high doses of neuroleptic medications, or ECT, are often used in preference to 'talking therapies'.

Only a small percentage of Indigenous people use mental health services relative to the general population. However, services developed by the specialist Indigenous mental health network have seen greater usage. The success of these services is attributed to their cultural appropriateness, the employment of Indigenous workers and the establishment of effective linkages with other services.

Anti-discriminatory and anti-oppressive practice reveals a connection between poverty, racism and isolation, and the experiences of Indigenous women and women from non-English-speaking backgrounds. Racism is both pervasive and persistent in contemporary Australian society, dating back to the invasion of Indigenous society by the British in the 1700s and subsequent colonialism. Racism is embedded within definitions of mental health and mental illness, and in the services and treatments provided. Racism permeates the organisations and institutions within the mental health system, and the training of mental health professionals. Ethnocentric bias in diagnostic practices leads to the inappropriate psychiatric labelling of non-Western people and greater usage of involuntary procedures (Fernando 1991).

Western notions of health and illness predominate, with a medical biological framework imposed upon emotional and social concerns. From a non-Western view an illness model of mental health can be both alien and alienating (Fernando 1991). Western notions incorporate individualist ideologies, in contrast to notions of health and well-being that stress a holistic and collective approach integrating the individual, the family and the community. Anti-discriminatory perspectives note the impact of the structural oppression of poverty, racial discrimination and harassment, discrimination in housing, education, employment and health on the mental health of Indigenous women and women from ethnic minority groups. Yet resistance to oppression has been defined as deviant behaviour to be punished or treated as mental illness.

The experience of racist stereotypes and practices within mental health and community settings necessarily influences the self-concept of Indigenous Australians. The experience of being treated as inferior within their own country can result in Indigenous women either fighting against or internalising these negative stereotypes. Outcomes of both processes can lead to labels of 'mad' or 'bad'. Feminist theory advocates for collective consciousness-raising and the reframing of the position of Indigenous women, located within Indigenous history and culture (Coppock and Hopton 2000).

Racism manifests itself in many different forms and guises within mental health and community services, including individual or institutional responses. These forms of racism have led to the development of equal opportunity policies within services and professional organisations.

However, what these measures fail to address is the centrality of racism as the key issue, rather than simply a case of lack of 'opportunities'. An anti-racist approach acknowledges the links between race and other forms of exclusion or oppression. It is thereby geared toward tackling the multi-faceted and complex nature of oppression (Orme 1998). The development of anti-racist practices needs to be broad and strategic, addressing both personal and institutional racism. It must be reflected at all levels of education, policy development and service management and delivery, beyond the level of 'ideal intentions', to actions that can be implemented in practice. Coppock and Hopton (2000) assert that a truly anti-oppressive and anti-discriminatory model of mental health care must embody four essential elements. Firstly, a dialogue needs to be established within and between the biological, psychological and social perspectives. Secondly, while recognising the limitations of each of these perspectives, there should be an explicit challenge to the notion that any one of these perspectives has supremacy above the other two. Thirdly, strong historical roots are required to legitimate practices to avoid the following of popular fads and trends. And finally, the model must incorporate an explicit anti-racist and anti-discriminatory framework.

FEMINIST PRACTICE

Comprehensive gender-sensitive policies that acknowledge the social and political context of women's lives are required. A major challenge for social workers is how to provide services in a respectful and empowering way, particularly if a woman's initial involvement with mental health services, and subsequent treatment, is involuntary. In the 1960s, radical critics of social work in statutory settings claimed that the enforced nature of social work activity was aimed at maintaining conventional social standards of normative behaviours, rather than being responsive to women defining their own needs (Goffman 1961; Laing 1961, 1965, 1967; Szasz 1961, 1963; Scheff 1966). However, critiques of this period did not provide solutions to the dilemmas faced by social workers in statutory settings. Later, Dominelli and McLeod (1989) developed a feminist model of social work practice in statutory settings.

The model developed by Dominelli and McLeod (1989) requires a feminist presence that can contribute both to how problems are defined and to the nature of the responses. The focus of direct practice is on the emotional empowerment of women on a one-to-one and small-group basis. Activity is directed toward influencing the working relations in an endeavour to tackle male-dominated management structures, lessen the authoritarian style of workers, promote collaborative work and address other social divisions, including gender. Community development activity is directed at campaigns organised on a feminist basis. Dominelli and McLeod (1989: 129) assert that the application of this model is 'not impossible, only extremely difficult'.

Empowerment

The planning and delivery of mental health services for women must be developed in ways that are non-threatening, responsive and sensitive to their age, cultural background, physical, emotional and social circumstances. A humane approach, and the maintenance of a reasonable quality of life and hope, is essential. Women in mental health services have complained about staff attitudes and of not being treated as 'human' when what they have wanted is support, understanding and nurturing. In the words of a woman in a forensic psychiatric hospital unit, 'Treat us like human beings, not as if we're stupid. It's just we have not been given opportunities like other people' (Martin 1999: 54).

Attention needs to be given to the valuing of staff activities. Talking to women is a key component of social work direct practice and crucial to the development of effective working relationships. Unfortunately other workers in mental health services sometimes view this activity as 'slacking off' (McGuiness and Wadsworth 1992). This is within the context of increased cutbacks in health and welfare services resulting in demands for greater output in terms of numbers of people seen, with little attention to the erosion of service quality.

A creative, individual response to each woman's needs is paramount. A focus must be on exploring the uniqueness of individual women as well as their shared experiences as women. Encouragement and efforts at increasing self-esteem, grief work and dealing with family issues is required. Issues of empowerment, and maximising choices and decision-making processes for each individual, are particularly important when working with women due to high rates of abuse. Adequate and appropriate housing and income support are a priority. Accommodation needs to be secure, safe, affordable housing suited to each woman's individual needs and circumstances. It is futile investing time and energy into counselling and psychotherapy if the woman is homeless and without an adequate income.

Consumer involvement and participation of women who have first-hand knowledge, and experience of mental health services is crucial to the re-development of these services. It is important that social workers develop strategies that facilitate and strengthen partnerships with consumers. Good practices embrace consumer involvement in joint decision-making on a number of different levels. The involvement of women who have received psychiatric services is particularly important for ongoing broader policy and planning initiatives. The challenge for social workers is to facilitate consumer involvement and develop and translate espoused organisational values and policy directions into actual practice (Epstein and Wadsworth 1994).

Community

Prior to de-institutionalisation, and the closure of the major psychiatric hospitals in Australia in the mid- to late 1990s, the critique of psychiatry focused on detrimental practices in psychiatric hospitals. The debate has now shifted to the community and is primarily concerned with issues of dangerousness. Although much policy development in mental health has been based on notions of community care, the reality for many in late-capitalist, post-industrial societies such as Australia is that the notion of community, based on mutual caring and shared values, is hard to find. Community development and the re-building of community, including establishment of 'connectedness' and mutual support, is a central concern of critical social work practice.

Although it has been established that there is no connection between psychiatric diagnosis and dangerousness, perceptions of dangerousness persist (Coppock and Hopton 2000). This unfounded fear of violence within the wider community has resulted in the development and implementation of repressive policies and legislation, with systems of increased surveillance and control. Examples of this are the increased powers given to psychiatrists under mental health legislation and an increase in assertive outreach services in recent years. Restrictive community treatment orders, for example in the *Victorian Mental Health Act* of 1986 (amended 1997), give psychiatrists decision-making power over where a woman lives. This gives rise to the question: What is the purpose of increased regulation and in whose interests is it? (Busfield 1996). While politicians and professionals focus on provisions that allow for the forcible treatment of women in the community, what many of these women want is access to appropriate and affordable housing, a sustainable income, education and employment, friendship and social supports, information and choice, and trust and respect (Martin 1999; Coppock and Hopton 2000).

Egalitarian and democratic alliances are required between social workers and women who use mental health services. Interventions are more likely to succeed if they are the result of honest negotiation, rather than the imposition of professional power. While practices that include negotiation, and the funding of appropriate advocacy services, may reduce the level of distress a woman is experiencing, they do not address the fact that discrimination and prejudice may be significant causal factors contributing to the woman's distress. Any service will ultimately reflect the dominant values, beliefs and prejudices of Australian society. Social workers can challenge these dominant ideologies by joining movements that unite women service-users and professionals in political struggles against oppression and discrimination.

Advocacy and service linkages

Advocacy for policy and service development in health and welfare services is required, focusing on gender-sensitive practices. Advocacy for rights and entitlements, and anti-discrimination for active community participation are necessary, as there is a high level of social disadvantage and stigma associated with having a psychiatric diagnosis. Goffman (1961) highlights the central feature that the question of acceptance has in the life of the stigmatised individual and the social construction of deviant identities. More recently the effects of stigma have been seen as contributing to an overwhelming sense of fear and isolation for the individual affected (National Mental Health Strategy 1995: 1; Burdekin 1993: 445).

Strong linkages, within and between services, are required for effective service delivery (Martin 1999). It is important for links between the woman and significant people in her life to be fostered and maintained to the greatest extent possible. Social workers need to be sensitive to the needs of family members and other significant people in the woman's life and seek their involvement where appropriate. It may be that referrals are made to services in the community that are able to provide the support and assistance that family members require during a woman's hospitalisation.

Appropriate responses and specialist services must be put in place with an emphasis on preventative health programs. It is important for social workers to be familiar with services in the community that have past or ongoing involvement with the woman, as well as other services that may be of assistance. Access to medical practitioners, particularly female doctors, is necessary to cater for women's physical health care needs. Social workers must treat reports of abuse with the seriousness they deserve. Because of the high levels of sexual abuse among women who use mental health services, strong linkages also need to be developed with specialist services in this area (Martin 1999).

Traditionally, the non-government sector, including services commonly grouped under the umbrella of 'psychiatric disability support services', has supplemented mainstream mental health services. However, the increased privatisation of and managerial approach to the delivery of health and welfare services, combined with the de-institutionalisation of psychiatric services, has seen the role of these services change to one of key service provision. Changes to funding mean that many of these services are now in a precarious position. This undermines the traditions of innovation and enthusiasm that characterised the non-government sector, with traditional roles of advocacy and campaigning increasingly eroded. Arising from the growth in recent years in the number of mental health and community service providers, the need for effective communication between services has become increasingly important (Martin 1999).

The following discussion of women, mental health and the criminal justice system raises the question of: Who is deemed 'mad' or 'bad', by whom and on what basis?

WOMEN, MENTAL HEALTH AND THE CRIMINAL JUSTICE SYSTEM

There has been a tendency to view female crime predominantly as a function of psychological disturbance. Even when contextual factors may be used to explain women's offending behaviours, they tend to be discounted or subsumed into psychological explanations. Evidence in support of psychological dysfunction is often weak or questionable. An over-emphasis on psychodynamic explanatory factors produces a distorted view of both the woman concerned and the offending behaviour (Henning 1995). As women prisoners in need of medical or psychiatric care are labelled as 'mad' (Ingram-Fogel 1991; Teplin et al. 1997), medication is routinely dispensed in lieu of counselling or other support (Easteal 1992; Raeside 1995).

Prisons in Australia and the United States have been criticised for 'a failure to translate service models designed for men into treatment programs appropriate for women' (Acoca 1998: 57). The provision of fewer programs for women has been attributed to their low numbers compared with male prisoners. However, this is more to do with the fact that the forensic systems in both countries were developed by males for males (Belknap 1996). This position of male privilege, and its protection, continues to be a central feature of the criminal justice system in Australia.

Numerous studies have reported extremely high rates of mental illness within female prison populations, with some as high as 100 per cent (Raeside 1995; Jordan et al. 1996; Teplin et al. 1996). The enactment of the view of female prisoners as mentally ill, in both policies and practices, has seen major prisons for women at Holloway in England and Cornton Vale in Scotland transformed into secure forensic hospitals. This model of care is problematic, as many of these women did not see themselves as mentally unwell and resented being treated as such (Maden et al. 1994).

Epidemiological and anecdotal evidence raises concerns about the extremely poor prognosis of women diagnosed with a mental illness, in custody and post-release. In particular there are grounds for concern about high death rates in the first twelve months post-release (Carnaby 1998). While these women constitute a relatively small proportion of the overall prison population, their numbers are increasing following the introduction of harsher legal penalties for drug-related crimes. The situation of these women is particularly disturbing because of the limited knowledge and information about their experiences, in custody and post-release, with very little support provided. It is known that with few exceptions these women are among the poorest and most vulnerable members of our society (Teplin et al. 1996; Martin 2001).

It is also known that a significant proportion of women prisoners are mothers with dependent children. The majority of these women have sole care and responsibility for their children, providing emotionally and financially for them. When a woman is imprisoned she may lose her home, and subsequently lose custody of her children. Housing is a priority due to a significant proportion of women being homeless on admission to prison (Carnaby 1998).

Issues of loss and grief from being separated from her children, fear and uncertainty about care arrangements, and the possible loss of custody, are important considerations for a woman prisoner with dependent children. Many women are unsure of their rights concerning the custody of their children, as well as being uninformed about the processes involved in protective services interventions (Easteal 1992). These women have been described as receiving a double sentence. They are punished not only for the offence but also for 'betraying their children and womanhood' (Quadrelli 1997: xx). The high proportion of women who are mothers with sole care of their children means that imprisonment has major implications for these children and society (Singer et al. 1995; Rutherford 1997; Carnaby 1998; Martin 1999, 2001).

Women prisoners do not conform to stereotypical diagnostic categories, with an overwhelming representation in the diagnostic categories of substance abuse and anti-social personality disorder, which is generally associated with males (Teplin et al. 1996). The usefulness of the psychiatric labels applied to women in the forensic system is questionable, with the diagnosis of personality disorder resulting in detrimental stereotypes and stigma. The debate as to whether these women require 'care' or 'control', and whether they should be dealt with in the criminal justice or mental health systems, continues to rage.

Like women who use mental health services, a significant proportion of women prisoners are survivors of sexual and/or other physical abuse as children or as adults (Raeside 1995; Belknap 1996). They too are vulnerable to further abuse. A Queensland study found that women prisoners, in desperation to make a phone call, can find themselves trading sexual favours with unscrupulous male officers. When they complain, those women labelled as 'bad' are viewed as liars, and those construed as 'mad' are seen as victims (Quadrelli 1997).

A woman's experience of prison is closely related to submissive behaviours towards prison officers and dismissive behaviours in response (Wilson and Leasure 1991; Easteal 1992). Prisons and forensic hospitals promote the socially sanctioned 'feminine' behaviours of passivity and obedience in women. In both settings every action is under surveillance. Women are treated like children, reinforced by prison officers calling them 'girls', with no responsibility or control over their lives. They are patronised and spoken to in condescending and disrespectful ways (Easteal 1992).

Women in these settings are categorised and individualised. The architectural design of modern prisons and forensic hospitals results in the women having no privacy, with every aspect of their lives open to scrutiny. Women prisoners are subjected to a range of oppressive techniques such as seclusion, totalitarian tactics and emotional abuse. Further factors impacting on the mental health of women prisoners are general overcrowding and poor conditions, lack of contact with family, drug usage and drug withdrawal, violence and abuse. All of this occurs within the context of generally inadequate health, welfare and counselling services available to women prisoners (Quadrelli 1997). This can result in women engaging in self-harming behaviours or, less commonly, open anger and aggression. This can in turn develop into depression, despair and withdrawal, with medication used to numb the emotional pain. This resistance is important in unravelling the regulatory processes imposed upon women prisoners. Women retain their ability to act despite what appears like overwhelming powerlessness (Healy et al. 2001). As in mental health services, estimates of attempted suicide and self-harm are higher among women prisoners than in the general community. Similarly, the response to suicide attempts and self-harm can be unsympathetic, with those in the prison system sometimes seen as endeavouring to get a hospital transfer (Easteal 1992).

Women who have been in prison and also have a psychiatric diagnosis experience high levels of social disadvantage and stigma. Alternatives to litigation need to be considered at the time of arrest. For those convicted, alternatives to prison need to be creatively explored at the time of sentencing. Policy development that is inclusive, and respectful, of all aspects of women's lives is crucial for the future, particularly given the disturbing increase in the number of women prisoners in recent years. It is important that women who have direct experience of forensic services contribute to policy development. Unfortunately however, consumer participation has been described as 'forgotten within forensic services . . . These women need to be given the opportunity to contribute their hard-won experience, an invaluable input in formulating policies or recommendations for change' (Sisters Inside, 1994: 6).

CONCLUSION

From a feminist perspective, the focus of direct social work practice is on individual and group empowerment, with community development activities and campaigns organised on a feminist basis to address structural inequalities that necessarily impact on women's mental health and well-being. The starting point in planning for service provision is the recognition of ways in which gender permeates psychiatric diagnoses. A shift in practice in mental health settings is required that moves away from individual pathologising of women's lives to the acceptance and recognition of the social and political factors that necessarily impact on women's mental health. Services need to be developed in a coordinated manner that is responsive to the diversity of women's lives, in consultation with women who have direct experience of mental health services. Services in the community need to give priority to preventative strategies as well as being able to respond in a timely and appropriate manner to women experiencing severe mental distress who are not effectively engaged with services elsewhere. Social workers have a responsibility to increase public awareness about the mental health needs of women, as the stigma of a psychiatric diagnosis can result in discrimination and marginalisation affecting all areas of a woman's life.

11

LOSS AND GRIEF: WEAVING TOGETHER THE PERSONAL AND THE POLITICAL

June Allan

Loss and grief are part of the life experience for each of us. Anecdotal evidence from practitioners suggests that the circumstances of people who see a social worker are frequently complicated by losses that have had a profound and enduring impact on their own and others' lives. Critical social work has previously paid little attention to practice issues concerning loss and grief, which have been dominated by psychological theories such as psychoanalytic, stress, attachment and psycho-social transition theories (Parkes 1998, in Walter 1999). However, increasing recognition of ways in which people are linked to and influenced by their social world, and new theories for understanding grief shaped by sociological and social constructionist perspectives (for example, Klass et al. 1996; Walter 1999; Neimeyer 2001; Small 2001), are resulting in richer understandings of loss and grief at the personal and social levels. There is a developing reorientation to ways of working at the grassroots level with people and their communities that acknowledges the deep penetration of social arrangements, culture and history into people's emotions and intimate internal experiences (Small 2001).

In this chapter I invite readers to reflect on the assumptions made in relation to loss and grief in our society, and to question taken-for-granted ideas and practices in this aspect of work in the human services. Modern Western literature typically depicts only isolated individuals and families dealing with their own private grief, yet these experiences are social. This can be seen in events such as the tragic loss of life in the United States on 11 September 2001; the catastrophic daily loss of life in parts of Africa as a result of the AIDS pandemic; the disastrous loss of lives that has occurred in places like the Balkans, the Middle East and Rwanda; the mass movement of people across the globe, displaced and homeless, their ideals shattered; and much less 'dramatic', the huge numbers of people who visit cemeteries each year in Australia[1]; the women and men struggling with the breakdown of an intimate relationship (Gee 2001; Martin, S. 2001); the distraught widow with whom I am working to assist her to make meaning of her life following the sudden death of her life partner. Loss and grief are experiences of everyday life, arising from a multitude of events, both ordinary and extraordinary.

Frameworks upon which social workers have tended to draw in understanding and responding to loss and grief have traditionally focused on individualistic, pathologising approaches. Approaches that integrate individual experience with the broader context are needed, incorporating social and political understanding and educative, empowering and collective ways of working that facilitate healing and respectfully work with the meanings those who are grieving give to their experiences. I explore contemporary understandings of grief in the context of social, political and cultural influences and the influences of dominant discourses regarding grieving processes. Themes and contradictions are teased out, and implications for practice discussed. Grief, and working with people to live constructively with their grief, can only be understood through the knowledge that the personal, political and cultural are intimately bound together.

THE LANGUAGE OF LOSS AND GRIEF

'Loss', a term that is typically viewed negatively and often used interchangeably with 'death', takes many different forms. The notion of loss can be thought of simply as no longer having something or someone that we used to have (Miller and Omarzu 1998: 4). The types of loss people experience can be understood in two general ways: physical, 'where something tangible has been made unavailable' (Miller and Omarzu 1998: 6), such as the death of a loved one, or loss of a body part such as a breast or limb. The second, symbolic, occurs 'where there are abstract changes in one's psychological experiences of social interactions' (Miller and Omarzu 1998: 6). This includes circumstances such as the loss of a sense of self-worth experienced through retrenchment, loss of a sense of peace, through wartime trauma or victimisation in family violence, or loss of dreams and ideals. 'Bereavement' is specifically associated with loss from death, signifying 'the situation of an individual who has recently experienced the loss of someone significant through that person's death' (Stroebe et al. 1998: 83).

'Grief', the response to loss, is customarily deemed to be natural, universal, psychological and physiological (Marris 1996; Walter 1999). Usually linked to sadness, grief covers a broad range of emotional, physical and behavioural responses, including anger, regret and a sense of betrayal and injustice. 'Mourning' is commonly associated with the process of grief (for example, Walter 1999; Harvey 2000; Hagman 2001). It refers to the behaviour expected by social groups after bereavement occurs. Cultural norms about how people should behave and feel, such as customs and rituals that are customarily part of mourning processes (for example; Marris 1996: 50; Walter 1999: 127–53), serve as a mechanism for the regulation of emotion and grief within societies. This regulation will be further discussed in the section on the 'rules' of grieving.

LOSS AND GRIEF AS SOCIAL, POLITICAL AND CULTURAL EXPERIENCES: THEMES AND CONTRADICTIONS

A number of significant factors in Australia's past and present have influenced attitudes to loss and death and shaped professional responses to people who are grieving. Kellehear's book *Death and Dying in Australia* (2000a) has made a major contribution to our understanding of some of these factors. Despite the difficulties of defining an 'Australian way', Kellehear (2000b) maintains that there are some common influences, often taken for granted, which underpin our social experiences of loss, death and grief. Other socio-political and cultural themes are also evident. The factors discussed here are Australia's race relations, multiculturalism and Americanisation, medicalisation, secularisation, gentrification and the development of 'grief and bereavement care', a term used to cover the counselling services and mutual help groups tailored to loss and grief.

Australia's race relations history and institutional racism are important factors in understanding the pattern of public grieving and remembrance of loss and death. In honour of the tragic loss of life and injuries sustained in World War I, communities across Australia established memorials. The Australian War Memorial was built as a sacred and spiritual symbol of the sacrifice of Australians in war. Only recently has the impact on Indigenous Australians of policies of the colonial government and later, the federal and state governments, been recognised. Acknowledged are the cumulative and adverse effects of the experience of massive and continuing losses of land, culture, identity, family and children (Kellehear 2000b; Raphael 2000), as documented in the *Bringing Them Home* report into the forcible removal of Indigenous children from their families (Human Rights and Equal Opportunity Commission 1997). Kellehear claims that 'the grief of indigenous peoples, . . . reopened or exacerbated with every Aboriginal death in custody or legal and political setback over land right claims, has not only provided no therapeutic response but given no ritual or otherwise social and political response' (2000b: 2).

Although responses have been delayed, the growing movement for reconciliation and response is now resulting in the development of programs of support for reunion of families, and counselling and healing programs for the trauma and grief that Indigenous people have experienced (Raphael 2000). An Indigenous people's centred approach to decolonisation that includes the healing needs of individuals, families and communities is developing (Atkinson and Ober 1995; Fredericks 1995; Brown 2001; Wingard 2001a, 2001b). The We Al-Li program[2], for example, has emerged out of the need for healing the 'individual, family and community pain and trauma resulting from colonial domination and power abuse' (Atkinson and Ober 1995: 201). This program uses the shared group experience to enable a healing journey for those people who have been oppressed by colonisation. It is based on the belief that to address the abuses and losses that have occurred it is insufficient to address only the systems and structures of oppression, itself crucial if Indigenous people are to be allowed to achieve social justice and equal human rights (McKendrick and Thorpe 1998). Drawing on Howson et al. (1994), Raphael (2000) asserts the value of the development of a culturally appropriate model of narrative therapy with its focus on story telling and oral tradition and its orientation to families and social groups.

In their discussion of grief and loss arising out of racist experiences in a multiracial context, Rosenblatt and Tubbs (1998) describe the losses and feelings of grief that result from racism. They draw attention to the significance of language and ask, 'Who are we to say people have experienced loss?' The words people use in talking about their experiences of racism are complex and various, representing different perspectives from those expressed in the usual discourses and language of loss and grief. Rosenblatt and Tubbs (1998) ask whether people grieving a racist situation would say they are grieving losses or betrayals, attacks, frustrations or deprivations? Practitioners need to be careful not to automatically categorise experiences as losses, or feelings as grief, as this may result in particular responses and actions. Agencies that typically help people manage their emotions may be ill-suited to people whose needs are practical or economic or who require justice. Rosenblatt and Tubbs suggest that in the case of structural forces like racism, the most important question might be 'How can racism be eradicated?' rather than 'How can people best cope with the losses they experience as a result of racism?' Particular care must be taken to ensure that the perspectives of people who may be grieving are understood and respected (Rosenblatt and Tubbs 1998). A critical social work approach, combining activist practices that challenge the structures of racism with postmodern narrative practices and discourse analysis, can help prevent inappropriate and dichotomising ways of working.

Australia's increasing cultural diversity has also been a most important influence on attitudes and responses to major loss. Postwar European immigration and further waves of immigrants from many different cultural and racial backgrounds[3] have contributed to a growing recognition and acceptance of difference and diversity in human behaviour and social responses. People from some of these cultures have brought with them values and norms requiring openness and outward expression of grief as respect for the dead. Over the years this, along with other factors favouring the expression of feelings, has changed the nature of Australian society and the ways it has dealt with loss (Raphael 2000).

Noting the wide range of cultural and religious patterns and behaviours now seen in contemporary Australia, Campbell et al. (2000: 69) draw on Kagawa-Singer's (1998) metaphor of weaving cloth to describe 'how many cultures may use looms and threads (universal aspects of behaviour)' to create a 'great diversity of recognisable patterns or styles (culture-specific behaviours)'. Campbell et al. (2000) warn that workers may fall into the trap of superimposing parts of their own tapestry onto those with whom they work unless they have sound transcultural understanding. They point out that cultures are not static and that the process of migration and resettlement can alter attachment to traditional beliefs so that after migration, rituals may be fewer but of greater significance to those who continue their practice. Similarly, Jonker (1997) discusses the importance of memory for migrants, and Fukuyama and Sevig (1999) note the importance of understanding the diversity of spiritual concerns in transcultural settings.

Apart from the impact of multiculturalism, however, the process of Americanisation is also impacting on norms about, and structures for dealing with, grief and death in Australia. The British-influenced middle-class values that dominated the colonial Australian way of grieving—stoicism, privacy, reserve and avoidance of discussion of taboo topics such as sexuality and death—persisted after the overwhelming loss of Australian lives in World War I, becoming eroded somewhat first by the impact of a strong Irish influence and later by the post-World War II immigration (Griffin 2000; Raphael 2000). More recently, however, these values are being altered through an increasingly strong influence from the United States (Kellehear 2000b) in relation to matters of loss, death and grieving. Two ways in which this has occurred are seen in the prominence of a dominant model of grief, and the corporatisation of the funeral industry.

First is the profound influence of the 'stage theory' of dying and loss, popularised by the Swiss-American psychiatrist Kübler-Ross (1970). She promoted the belief that people need to express their grief to resolve their loss and avoid complications, an idea that has been firmly followed by many American and Australian professionals. Second, through amalgamations and the reorganisation of global capital to ensure profits, American business practices have influenced the funeral industry in Australia. Small family-owned funeral businesses have been taken over by larger companies and international corporations, one example being the United States-owned Service Corporation International, which now owns 25 per cent of the Australian funeral industry (Howarth 2000). While the economies of scale that result are not in themselves necessarily problematic, Howarth (2000) warns of the risk that funerals could become more impersonal and standardised, and less culturally responsive.

The processes of medicalisation, secularisation and gentrification have all contributed, among other things, to the emergence of pro-fessionals whose focus is grief and death. The rise of modern medicine saw the health and disease issues of people ('patients'), and hence dying and death, become the province of medical experts. This paved the way for professionals with expertise in helping people deal with these matters, typically focusing on individuals. During the 1980s a more participatory style of health-care culture developed, with healers, patients and their communities working together on health outcomes. Through these developments, death came to be seen as a health matter, to be aided through palliative care or medically assisted suicide in the pursuit of the 'good death' (Kellehear 2000b: 6-7).

The gentrification of Australian society (Kellehear 2000b) through the growth of the middle class contributed to the development of professionals as a group. Smaller social networks, medicalisation, and a rising life expectancy have all contributed to the fact that families experience death less frequently in contemporary Australia. With the development of the isolated nuclear family, individuals know less about what to expect regarding loss and death and, increasingly, academic and professional information has outweighed personal experience in the provision of advice and direction.

At the same time, the secularisation of Australian society through the separation of church and state (Griffin 2000; Kellehear 2000b) has resulted in understanding, processing and managing death commonly becoming matters for medicine and law rather than for religion. Deaths are typically explained in medical rather than religious terms, and disasters are commonly regarded as occupational health and safety issues rather than as 'acts of God'. Volunteer rescuers, police and firemen become the 'angels' and 'saints'. Death and the funeral moved out of the family home during the twentieth century (Griffin 2000). Materialist ideas in which death is 'a product of physical processes' (Kellehear 2000b: 5) have become popular, although religious ideas about death remain popular, albeit in different forms such as New Age concepts, or spiritual notions emerging from a combination of Eastern religions and Western mystical traditions. Secularisation, along with the growth of professionals and the process of medicalisation, increasing affluence and women's growing independence, has fostered an individualistic counselling approach.

Thus 'grief and bereavement care' has taken the place of social mourning as an accepted way for people to grieve in contemporary Western life, with modern-day therapy substituting for many of the functions once played by religion (Walter 1999).[4] But the culture of professional experts and counselling is a contentious issue. Some authorities regard counselling as a useful resource to assist people to grieve, as attested to by the vast array of literature on grief counselling (for example, Worden 1991; Lendrum and Syme 1992; Rando 1993; Gunzburg and Stewart 1994; Attig 1996). Others question it. Little (1999), for example, describes what he considers to be the inappropriateness of

176

professional support in the immediate aftermath of the Thredbo land-slide in 1997 in which a number of people were killed, commenting that 'at the start the handling of the disaster looked like a disaster itself'. Grief and mourning became a fashionable topic in the media, and public and professional expectations inappropriately rushed and managed the grieving process. All of which, argues Little, may have 'inhibited genuine grieving, which takes its own time and proceeds in its own way' (1999: 88). Bereavement care can be quite prescriptive and may or may not suit individuals, depending on how much freedom they seek for themselves. However, it may also offer a refuge from a society that many grieving people feel has policed them too harshly, having had 'bad experiences with families and professionals who they feel do not and cannot understand' (Walter 1999: 202–3).

These differences and contradictions become more complex because of the rules and norms relating to how we are 'allowed' to grieve, who is 'allowed' to grieve, and who we are 'allowed' to grieve for.

THE 'RULES' OF GRIEVING

The emotions of grief are often raw, disturbing, volatile and unexpected. People who are grieving are prone to feelings of anger. These emotions are therefore to be regulated, a phenomenon thought to occur in all societies (Rosenblatt 1997, cited in Walter 1999: 119). How and why regulation should occur, however, are matters of considerable debate, and opinions are divided on whether the emotions of grief should be contained or expressed. Whereas there were once clear guidelines for grieving, in the Western world this is no longer the case. The lack of regulation that traditional mourning rituals once provided is bemoaned. The position affirmed by popular culture is that the emotions of grief should be contained, at least in public, with distractions being provided as a way of getting over the pain of grief (Walter 1999). Holst-Warhaft (2000) takes the argument further to suggest that grief not contained can become political outrage and translate into violence, noting that revolutions and riots have often begun with funerals in different parts of the world. Mourning rituals and memorials attempt to 'bring order to the emotional chaos of grief' (Holst-Warhaft 2000: 18).

Yet at the same time the view persists that grief should be allowed to express itself naturally and that its expression may be appropriate and healing (Walter 1999; Raphael 2000). It must be talked through if the person is to recover, a position reinforced by the received wisdom of practitioners and by certain religious and self-help cultures (Walter 1999). Damousi (2000) maintains that the shift from denial to public recognition of grief stems from a belief that this is necessary and desirable, citing as examples the 1987 Vietnam Veterans' Parade and the public mourning of those killed at Port Arthur in 1996. Both governments and activist groups use disasters, public mourning and rituals as political tools to capture world opinion, draw attention to issues, or hasten progress and legislative change. For example, United States President George W. Bush's global television appearances and pronouncements following the September 11 hijackers' attacks have been used to elevate his image and status around the globe. However, as Holst-Warhaft (2000: 19) asserts, if our grief is to be 'managed', individuals and communities should at least be aware of it. Grief, an empowering and enabling force, can be effectively mobilised for political purposes to give the bereaved a political voice (Damousi 2000). The disaster at Port Arthur, which hastened tighter gun controls in Australia, and the campaign against AIDS, are clear examples of this.

There is debate in the literature as to whether males and females grieve differently (for example, Cline 1996; Golden 1997; Walter 1999). Walter (1999) maintains that there is a considerable body of evidence to suggest that males have a more contained way of grieving and that females prefer to express their grief. However, there is another view emerging, that there are ways of grieving that are not necessarily tied to the gender of the grieving person, associated with the knowledge that some women may use action-oriented healing, and some men may seek relational skills to heal their grief (for example, Doka and Martin 1998; Golden 1999). A so-called 'feminine' style centres on the open expression of feelings, is social and support-seeking and relational-oriented. A 'masculine' style is more instrumental, demonstrating an action-oriented, cognitive and solitary style of grieving (Golden 1997). In my view it is inappropriate to perpetuate the stereotypes of 'masculine' and 'feminine'. Terms such as 'expressive' and 'instrumental' may be more appropriate to describe the styles of grieving which individuals adopt.

Reflecting on some of the practice implications of these debates, Walter (1999) provocatively suggests that what men and women want in bereavement care may not be what they would most benefit from. Drawing on the work of Stroebe and Schut (1999) and Schut et al. (1997), he proposes that bereaved people benefit from assistance with both emotional and practical problems, but that as women tend to focus on the former and men on the latter, they should be encouraged to deal with the problems with which they are less comfortable or familiar. Clearly, the issue of gendered grief will continue to be the focus of continuing research and debate, but it is important that practitioners understand and respect people's individual styles of grieving.

If an event is not defined as a socially significant loss, it can cast people into disenfranchised grief, that is, 'grief experienced when a loss is not or cannot be openly acknowledged, publicly mourned, or socially supported' (Rando 1993: 498). This arises because societies have sets of norms about who and for whom people should grieve. These norms or grieving rules may not correspond to the nature of relationships, the sense of loss or the feelings of the grieving person (Doka 1995). Grief is disenfranchised for four main reasons. First, it may occur where the relationship is not recognised by society, especially if it is not based on familial ties, such as lover (including homosexual or extra-marital relationships), friend, colleague, caregiver or step-parent, reflecting in part the legal status accorded to these relationships. Second, the loss itself may not be recognised because it is not regarded as socially significant (for example, an abortion, relinquishing a child for adoption or foster care, loss of a pet). Third, grievers themselves may not be recognised as they may be considered to be socially incapable of grief, such as the very old or the very young, or people with intellectual impairment. Finally, the death itself may be disenfranchising where its circumstances create shame and embarrassment, such as death from a disease like AIDS or from self-destructive causes like suicide. Practitioners and communities need to be sensitive to the needs of those whose grief is not acknowledged by society (Doka 1995, 1999).

It is clear that the discourses on loss and grief contain many contradictions for grieving people to negotiate—at a time when they are likely to be at their most vulnerable. I now consider more closely actual grieving processes and the practice implications of dominant and changing theoretical discourses.

GRIEVING PROCESSES: THEORIES AND PRACTICES

Three sets of competing discourses, each touched on in the preceding discussion, are evident in the conceptualisation of grieving processes. These concern, firstly, the notion of grief as a series of stages, following a linear trajectory to completion or resolution, as popularised by the 'stage theory' developed by Kübler-Ross (1970) and later by others such as Worden (1991) and Parkes (1996). Second is the culture of containment and control compared to the culture that supports the expression of grief. Finally, there are competing discourses concerning the social integration of the dead in society: whether the living should leave behind their relationship with the dead, or maintain continuing bonds.

The notion of continuing bonds has been supported by a range of research studies and evidence from bereaved people themselves, suggesting that rather than detaching themselves and moving on from deceased persons, individuals instead need to develop meaningful symbolic ways of holding on to the dead (White 1988; Wortman and Silver 1989; Klass et al. 1996; Walter 1996, 1999; Foote and Frank 2000; Neimeyer 2000; Klass and Walter 2001). The notion of grief or bereavement as something that 'ends' no longer fits, and is being replaced by the idea of negotiation and renegotiation of the meaning of the loss over time. There is recognition that major losses impact on people for the rest of their lives and that as they change they experience a changed but continuing relationship or bond with the deceased person (Silverman and Klass 1996). New connections with the deceased are constructed and reconstructed as the meaning of the loss is negotiated and renegotiated.

The modernist view of grief that dominated among Australian health professionals in the twentieth century provides people with some idea of what to expect when they are grieving, but is now being challenged. Postmodern views claim that everyone grieves differently, and there is no single way to deal with grief reactions (Walter 1999; Kellehear 2000b). What are the implications of these different perspectives for work with individuals and communities?

Individual counselling

In the dominant modernist discourse of the grieving process, time is expected to heal and the bereaved are expected to restrain their displays of grieving to appropriate times and places (for example, White 1988; Wortman and Silver 1989, 2001; Walter 1996; Foote and Frank 2000; Neimeyer 2001). If the expression of grief is too short, too long, delayed, too demonstrable or not demonstrable enough, then the mourning is judged to be 'complicated' and is pathologised (Foote and Frank 2000). Individuals are then expected to participate in some sort of mutual help or therapy to bring about resolution of their mourning.

An alternative narrative proposes that the story of the person who is seen to have problems should be reinterpreted as the dominant discourse exercising power over the person's life. The 'problem' story is reinterpreted as a form of resistance to the power of the dominant discourse, and counselling is then seen as nurturing resistance to the dominant discourse (White and Epston 1990 and White 1993, cited in Foote and Frank 2000: 177-9). As most people's stories draw on the dominant discourse, the personal problems they bring to counselling can be seen to emanate from the 'lack of fit' between their lived experience and the dominant socio-cultural story being imposed on them. This is a view shared by Shapiro (1994, 1996 cited in Walter 1999:152). Discussing family bereavement in the context of immigration and inter-ethnic marriage in America, Shapiro recognises that the way in which a person feels most comfortable grieving may not fit with the dominant cultural expectations of the community in which they live. She suggests that the aim for practitioners is therefore to focus with the person on the goodness of fit between their own style and the cultural expectation.

The aim of narrative work is to assist clients to critique the imposed story, freeing them to develop their own story to give meaning to their experiences, and recognising how the dominant discourse works to deny this story (Foote and Frank 2000). Neimeyer (2001) suggests that meaning-making or meaning reconstruction in response to a loss is the central process of grieving. It involves making sense of the loss, and finding benefits and positives that follow from the loss experience (Davis 2001). An experience of profound loss shatters the assumptions we hold about the world and our place in it. Neimeyer (2000, 2001) suggests that with such an occurrence we seek to make meaning within the narrative of our lives and the core assumptions that we hold. We do not do this in isolation, but by negotiating with family and broader society. In the process we are influenced by norms and expectations about how to grieve.

A woman who has experienced a stillbirth, for example, may be encouraged to reflect on ways in which dominant discourses are impacting on her and how her own responses and feelings can be understood as resistance. She may believe, for example, that she 'should' openly express her grief, 'get over' the stillbirth and 'get on with it', especially since she can 'always have another baby'. The emphasis in such a situation might be to encourage the woman to develop other potential stories, giving her the fullest possible choice to give meaning to her own experience. The objective of the counsellor's role with such a person would be to witness her experience and hear what parts of it the dominant discourse has sought to make invisible, while naming her resistance against the unhelpful dominant discourse as a strength. Such a process would assist the woman to better support herself, freeing her to resist the dominant discourses and make new meanings of her experiences.

Groups, communities and activism

While individual counselling has its place in supporting individuals and countering dominant but unhelpful messages received from the community, family or professionals, a sense of community is important for those who grieve (Klass and Walter 2001). As Little (1999) asserts, a robust social fabric is fundamental to people's well-being. Social workers can contribute much by helping to build stronger communities and social infrastructure that help when grief strikes, and by linking those who grieve with existing communities of support. Mutual or self-help groups[5] for loss and bereavement, such as Solace and The Compassionate Friends, can provide such communities of support for many, and have become popular in Australia. These groups are valued for their reliance on experiential rather than professional knowledge, forming communities of experience not shared by mass society, professionals or families. They have their own subculture in which continuing bonds are affirmed, providing an alternative to dominant discourses in mainstream culture.

There are at least four different types of mutual help groups (Walter 1999). First are those groups for people whose relatives died in a common event, where members feel bonded through their trauma. Second are the groups where the losses came out of totally separate incidents but are of the same kind, such as loss of a partner or sibling. Members may join such a group if they feel alienated from family, friends or professionals. The third type is for people linked to those who died because of unlegitimated violent actions such as murder (for example, the Homicide Victims Support Group, based in New South Wales). Such groups often have activist aims, channelling emotions such as anger into political activity (for example, tightening of sentencing laws). This contrasts with much bereavement counselling, which focuses mainly on the person's difficult emotions rather than activism. The fourth type of group is that initiated and facilitated by professionals, and is numerous throughout the community.

Much can be learnt from other alternatives to Western individualistic approaches. More communal ways of working, such as those described by Howard Kasiya (1996), working in partnership with local communities in central north Malawi to address issues of HIV/AIDS, are of interest. Gupta's (1999) work with UNICEF in Rwanda following the genocide also illustrates varied and innovative ways of working with experiences of profound trauma and loss. The Memory Box Project (Morgan 2000) provides another example. This project with HIV-positive women in Uganda encourages the women to create memory boxes to leave for their children. The memory box of Maki Lufhugu, for example, who died on 27 April 2000, contains among other things her skaf-tin (lunch box), her favourite hat, a memory book of photos and press clippings, and her life story written in her own handwriting. Detailed information about the women and their origins decreases the risk of fear, confusion and loss of identity for their children, thereby lessening the distress of their grief (Morgan 2000).

Grief can be a powerful motivator for bringing about change and striving for a more socially just society, and practices drawn from structural as well as postmodern perspectives are useful in such situations. Not only can the power of disabling discourses be challenged through individual counselling and groups, as already discussed, but social workers can also work with or advocate for people who grieve to work towards change, and can encourage people themselves to take action. Activism has several functions—healing, education, awareness-raising, attitudinal and social change. It can occur through lobbying and campaigning for legal and other reform, public rituals, speaking out on issues, public storytelling, setting up new support or action groups, and publishing (for example, Cracknell 2000; Ryan 2000; McLean 2001; Wingard and Lester 2001).

There are numerous examples of effective activism apart from those already mentioned. Some individuals decide to care for others or do volunteer work, all of which serves in some way to develop a sense of community. This is illustrated in the longitudinal study of caregiving and bereavement among partners of men with AIDS in the San Francisco Coping Project (Richards 2001). Others, through their own experience and disaffection with existing services, establish new support groups. Following the death of her father in a construction incident, Liz Moyabad founded Industrial Death Support and Advocacy (IDSA) in 1995 in Victoria. This organisation assists families, employers and industrial organisations on matters concerning industrial deaths. Other initiatives include Red Nose Day, a well-known fundraising event for Sudden Infant Death Syndrome (SIDS), the AIDS Memorial Quilt Project, a world-wide project that memorialises people who have died from AIDS, and Walk for Wigs (Hull 2001), an annual event initiated by a widower to raise money for the Wig Library in Canberra, established to assist women having chemotherapy treatment. These are all examples of successful political campaigns which have raised public awareness and helped to change attitudes and meanings.

CONCLUSION

The field of loss and grief is a complex and contested area in which to work. This chapter has illustrated the political and socially constructed nature of grief and grieving processes, and has highlighted some of the inherent contradictions. The relevance of structural and postmodern practice approaches is clear. From a postmodern perspective, social workers can assist grieving individuals in their journey of healing by working in sensitive, respectful and culturally appropriate ways. They can also nurture individuals' resistance to disabling dominant discourses and help them to support themselves by assisting them to make meaning of their experiences and negotiate the contradictions that they encounter during their journey. Structurally, assisting those who grieve to link up with mutual help groups can help create communities of support, often lacking in today's fragmented society. Work with individuals and groups can ensure that people who are grieving have access to information and personal experience, to practical and emotional resources, and to justice. Social workers can also challenge unjust attitudes and processes that precipitate grief or discriminate against those who grieve, and contribute to the strengthening of the social fabric that is known to be so important for supporting people when grief strikes.

PART III

Facing the challenges for critical social work

12

RETHINKING THE RELATIONSHIP BETWEEN THE SELF AND SOCIETY

Bob Pease

Numerous social work writers have claimed that the relationship between the individual and society is both the rationale for the social work profession and the primary focus for intervention. This was first conceptualised as 'person-in-situation' (Hollis 1964) and later as 'person-in-environment' (Green 1999a). Green (1999a: 2) argues that all social work practice 'is anchored in a common paradigm to reshape the context of the person-in-environment configuration'. She further argues that the basic mission of the profession requires this dual focus on both the person and the environment. This approach is sometimes articulated as 'the bio-psycho-social perspective' and is presented as an analysis of 'the interplay of biological, psychological, social and cultural elements of development in the life space of individuals' (Green 1999b: 36).

From the outset, social work has distinguished itself from other helping professions by claiming 'that social policy and practice must build on and inform each other as evidence of the person-in-environment focus' (Ramanathan and Link 1999: 33). Thus the person-in-environment approach has been an important conceptual reference point in constructing the role of social work practice. This conceptualisation has a number of difficulties, however, not the least of which is that no single theory to date has been able to provide an adequate analysis of the relationship between the person and the social context.

There have also been a number of challenges to this conceptualisation from within the critical theory tradition. Over 25 years ago, Galper (1975) argued that social casework theory contained a conservative vision of human beings in the context of their social situation. He maintained that social casework was 'essentially conservative because it failed to examine the influence of the social order on the individual in a systematic way' (Galper 1975: 121). Even the conceptualisation of 'psychosocial diagnosis' operated within a conservative theoretical framework. By conceptualising society as environment, family, occupational structure and residential community it became a form of 'socio-psychologism' (Galper 1975). Social casework then was seen as being unable to move beyond the specifics of human psychology in the social context to a consideration of the totality of the human condition. What progress has been made in addressing this issue in social work theory since then? In this chapter I identify the limitations of the 'person-in-environment' configuration for critical social work and explore attempts within the critical tradition to theorise the relationship between self and society, with a particular emphasis on the concepts of oppression and domination, and on agency and resistance, in the context of the material and discursive constraints on critical practice.

SYSTEMS AND ECOLOGICAL APPROACHES TO THE INDIVIDUAL AND SOCIETY[1]

A number of writers have endeavoured to address the link between the individual and society by constructing the person-in-environment framework from within systems and ecological perspectives. Green (1999c: 220) argues that systems theory can overcome the false dichotomy between the person and the environment due to 'its emphasis on the multiplicity of systems with which people interact'. Thus systems theory is presented as a unifying framework or a conceptual bridge between the individual and society.

The major aims of systems and ecological approaches are to enhance the adaptive capacities of individuals in their transactions with their environments and to facilitate a more adequate fit between the individuals' needs and the resources in those environments. Thus systems and ecological approaches promote an adaptive evolutionary view of human beings in constant interaction with all elements of their environment. People change their physical and social environments and are changed by them through processes of continuous reciprocal adaptation (Germain and Gitterman 1980).

It is claimed that all human beings, like all living systems, must maintain a goodness of fit with the environment. When all goes well, this reciprocal adaptation is said to support people's growth and development. However, in the transactions between people and their environments, upsets to the adaptive balance or goodness of fit can occur and create stress (Germain and Gitterman 1980). It is argued that these maladaptive patterns can be restored by social workers with a dual concern for the adaptive potential of people and the nutrient capacities of the environment (Gould 1987).

The person–environment interaction is described by the ecological systems model as being in dynamic equilibrium (Brower 1988). Thus the ecological approach promotes an equilibrium model of human development. It argues that a state of balance, stability and rest is more desirable than a state of upheaval and change. In fact, this notion of equilibrium as a desirable goal for human development has permeated social work theory.

Systems theory has endeavoured to integrate the two levels of micro and macro social work practice into a more generalist approach that encompasses multiple levels of intervention. However, as Fisher and Karger (1997) point out, this has not been successful. They identify a number of limitations in the ecological framework for understanding the individual and society: a bias towards the private troubles of individual clients, the lack of attention given to the role of power, and the tendency to explain most problems as those of communication and linkage of interactions and transactions between people and environments. Further, Kondrat (1999) argues that ecological perspectives place the individual over and against the social structure as two separate integrating elements. They cannot account for the way in which the self is interconnected with society.

The ecological approach is more focused on stability and the status quo than on conflict and change. It assumes that problems are caused by deficits in communications between individuals and the systems. The model assumes no conflict between the goals of different groups and no clash of interests between marginalised groups and the wider society (Gould 1987). It is argued that it is always possible or desirable to strive for a goodness of fit between the person and the environment.

To the extent that sexism, racism and poverty are acknowledged, they are interpreted within an interactional framework as processes created by people as they endeavour to reach a goodness of fit with their environment (Gould 1987). From an ecological perspective, change is permissible within the system, but not within the wider structure, because the system has to harmonise with the wider structure (Langan 1985). By emphasising only those aspects of the social environment considered amenable to social work practice, the ecological system model loses sight of the broader structural social forces (Gould 1987) and thus fails to challenge class, gender and race based social, political and economic arrangements.

CONCEPTIONS OF PERSONAL AGENCY IN STRUCTURAL SOCIAL WORK

As noted in Chapter 2, structural social work was first formulated by Moreau (1979) in Canada. The term 'structural' indicates that 'the focus for change is mainly on the structures of society and not solely on the individual' (Mullaly 1997: 104). Early conceptions of the structural approach were informed by Marxism and we have witnessed a return to the Marxist emphasis with Mullaly's (1997) reformulation of structural social work. While Marxist analysis has made a significant contribution to a critique of the structural basis of capitalism, as Hayes (1996) has pointed out, it has had very little to say about how individuals subjectively experience their lives under capitalism.

Leonard (1984, 1997) has argued that the individual has often been relatively untheorised in structural social work. This has meant that 'many social workers tend to see welfare recipients only as victims of an oppressive and monolithic social order' (Leonard 1984: 5). In this view, the individual is portrayed as having little opportunity to challenge social arrangements. Rossiter (1996: 26) sees this as a result of structural social work theory being 'caught in dualistic conceptions of individuals and society'. In emphasising the structural causes of people's problems structural social work theorists have constructed a view of society as overly determining individual experience. As a consequence, structural social work has little to contribute to prescriptions or a knowledge base for individual practice in its social change approach (Payne 1997). Fook (1993: 32) argues that 'if we are to develop a truly radical casework, we must concentrate on the interplay between individual and society'. I would add this is necessary for the development of a critical social work practice as a whole, not just radical casework practice.

Where can social workers gain knowledge of an integrated practice that more adequately links the individual with the social? How do we move away from the dichotomy that portrays individuals either as being responsible for their own oppression or as passive victims with no agency to struggle against their oppression? What is missing, as Leonard (1984: 5) has noted, 'is detailed attention to the dialectic between the individual and the social order whereby the former is socially consti- tuted but within a context of struggle and resistance'.

Thus we need a theoretical framework that acknowledges the importance of both agency (people's capacity to act in the world) and structure. Structural theories have under-emphasised 'the role of agency, by concentrating on social structures almost to the exclusion of issues of choice, intentions, wishes, fears and aspirations' (Thompson 1998: 36). On the other hand, some forms of radical humanist and post- modern theory have tended to over-emphasise the role of agency, and failed to recognise the limitations on action by the social structure. What is needed, Thompson (1998: 65) argues, is the articulation of 'a dialectical approach, which relates the interaction of individuals with the wider socio-political context of their lives'.

Various writers in critical psychology have endeavoured to break out of this dichotomised view of the individual and society. Nightingale and Neilands (1997: 73) argue that 'critical psychology generally views the individual and society as so fundamentally intertwined that they cannot be separated'. Spears and Parker (1996: 4) similarly state that 'the social does not have to be used in contrast to the individual or a back- ground against which individuals act but can be seen as constituting their very being'. McNay (2000: 19) also notes that recent feminist theory has also attempted to overcome the conflict between psyche and society by 'replacing it with the idea of a relation . . . where neither side is reducible to the other'.

However, what does a dialectical conception of the relationship between the individual and society mean for people's capacity to resist oppression? As Leonard (1997: 32) asks: 'To what extent, if at all, is the individual relatively autonomous, a moral agent able to act upon the surrounding world in his or her own interests? What external forces might affect such potential and actual autonomy?' Is individual agency possible within the context of dominant ideologies and social practices?

TOWARDS A CRITICAL PSYCHOLOGY OF OPPRESSION AND DOMINATION

In 1984, Leonard saw the disjuncture between our understandings of the social order and of the individual as one of the major barriers to a critical social work practice with individuals and families (1984: 3).

Nine years later, he argued that a critical social work practice 'must be based on an adequate critical psychology which has still to be developed' (1993: 167). In the remainder of this chapter, I want to outline some theoretical contributions to the development of a critical psychology for social work.

Fox and Prilleltensky (1997) see oppression as a central concept in critical psychology. Sloan (1997: 97) also argues that 'the aspects of the person that concern critical psychology are those that are systematically produced by social relations characterised by domination and oppression'. Gil (1998: 5) articulates the point well when he says: 'Relations of domination and exploitation and conditions of injustice . . . come to be reflected not only in socio-economic, cultural and political institutions and in all spheres of everyday life but also in the consciousness and behaviour of the victims and perpetrators.' Thus a critical social work practice must address the processes by which oppression and domination become internalised in the psyches of individuals.

Fanon (1978), a black psychiatrist in Algeria at the time of the Algerian revolution, was one of the first to talk about the internalisation of oppression. He described it as 'the process of a non-conscious acceptance of one's own inferiority and powerlessness' (Fanon 1978: 64). He argued that the internalisation of oppression in daily living also entailed an internalisation of the oppressors' values, norms and prohibitions. As a result of this, the oppressed become agents of their own oppression. He thus perceived an inferiority complex in black people where they accepted the reality of their inferiorised position and aspired to be white.

There is a tendency to describe oppression primarily in economic and political terms. It is of course also possible to be oppressed psychologically, to experience what Bartky (1975: 56) calls 'psychic alienation'. Psychic alienation is 'the estrangement or separating of a person from some source of the essential attributes of personhood' (1975: 57). Psychological oppression breaks the spirit of a people and renders them incapable of understanding the nature of the structural arrangements responsible for their subjugation.

Freire (1972) argues that until they discover their oppression, the oppressed nearly always express fatalistic attitudes towards their situation. Because they do not perceive clearly the social order which serves the interests of the oppressors, oppressed come to identify with the oppressor. By internalising the opinion the oppressors hold of them, they come to lack confidence in themselves and believe in the invulnerability and power of the oppressor.

A number of writers have noted that despair and apathy inhibit action for change. Macy (1998: 26) defines apathy as 'the inability or refusal to experience pain'. Pain is the price we pay for our consciousness of suffering in the world. Thus 'the problem lies not in our pain for the world, but in our repression of it' (Macy 1998: 27). Murphy (1999: 3) also observes that 'a central dilemma of contemporary activism is despair and political disorientation' and Gil (1998) notes that because of the power of the dominant ideology, people tend to feel powerless to initiate collective action. Rather, they focus their energies on individualist efforts to get the most for themselves within the established way of life.

The task then is to transform the mechanisms of repressive consciousness in such a way that, as Freire (1972: 83) suggests, people in their everyday lives can discover the oppression in their lives and struggle to become 'self affirming subjects of their own destiny'. To reclaim the right to live humanly, oppressed groups must confront, in praxis, those institutions, processes and ideologies that prevent them from naming the world. Thus while consciousness usually involves a form of adaptation to established ways of life, it can also evolve into critical consciousness, which can 'challenge internalised images of established ways of life' (Gil 1998: 48).

The discussion of agency in sociology most often refers to the agency of oppressed groups. Little attention is given to the agency of dominant groups, particularly those who want to subvert their dominant position. However, the concept of critical consciousness also contains the ability to examine regressive values such as sexism, racism, class-elitism and homophobia which are internalised into consciousness (Shor 1993).

As noted in Chapter 4, internalised domination is 'the incorporation and acceptance by individuals within a dominant group of prejudices against others' (Pheterson 1986: 147). There are many forms of internalised domination. Frankenburg (1993) says that one of the effects on white people of race privilege and the dominance of whiteness is their structured invisibility. The predominant comment of whites is that they are not aware of themselves as white. Whites are taught not to be aware of themselves in racial terms. Similarly, in relation to gender domination, Brittan and Maynard (1988) argue that men are exposed to a socialisation experience that turns many of them into male supremacists. In this view, men are under pressure to internalise beliefs and feelings which natu-ralise their commitment to the subordination of women. Similar processes operate in relation to class-elitism, heterosexual dominance and ageism.

A key question here is whether it is in the interests of the dominant group to change.[2] Lichtenberg (1988) argues that those at the top of an exploitative relationship are also miserable. Wineman (1984) has used the concept of 'negative consciousness' to describe the process by which people become conscious of their internalised domination and react against it. According to him, 'equal relations can be experienced as more rewarding than top-down relations' which constitute the posi-tive foundation for negative consciousness (Wineman 1984: 187). When one dehumanises people, one denies one's own capacity for emotional connectedness.

In addressing these issues of internalised oppression and internalised domination, in recent years, we have seen the development of a variety of critical psychologies. Fox and Prilleltensky (1997) have identified a number of theoretical influences in the attempt to develop a critical psy-chology, including feminism, neo-Marxist psychology, South American psychology, social constructionism, discourse psychology and post-modernism. I have identified four critical theoretical perspectives that I think contribute most to the development of a critical psychology for social work in a Western context: radical humanism, materialist psy-chology, Marxist-Freudianism and postmodern critical psychology.[3]

RADICAL HUMANISM AS A BASIS FOR A CRITICAL PSYCHOLOGY

Payne (1997: 181) argues that 'social work values are essentially human-ist', and Ife (1997: 115) comments similarly that 'social work is inevitably bound to a humanist vision, given its value base'. Humanism is based on a premise 'that human beings share essential properties which define them from all other creatures' (Rojek et al. 1988: 114).

Can humanism provide a basis for a critical psychology? It has been criticised by a number of writers as treating 'human action as the expression of innate, timeless human properties', of being 'ahistorical and asocial' (Rojek et al. 1986: 115) and as 'missing a structural analysis of oppression' (Ife 1997: 116).

However, there are many different versions of humanism. Ife (1997: 130) formulates a notion of critical humanism which 'incorporates a power analysis alongside a humanist vision'. Similarly Mullaly and Keating (1991: 61) articulate a radical humanist position that focuses on 'raising people's awareness about how society's inequalities shape, oppress, limit and dominate their experiences'.

A number of writers have drawn upon the early work of Marx in advocating a radical humanist position. Fromm (1971), for example, argues that Marx's work enables us to distinguish between genuine human needs for relatedness to each other and to nature, and imaginary or false needs which are socially created to consume a mass of alien products. The key concept that Marx used to elucidate this process was alienation. In Marx's view, society is reflected back upon the individual as an alienating force dominating his or her essential being and nature. Thus he uses the concept of alienation to lament the loss of humanity associated with capitalism.

Marx was concerned with the individual's need for development and of the development of individual's capacities. However, to fully develop their humanness, individuals have to be active, self-conscious agents in producing the social conditions that will lead to the end of alienation. From a radical humanist perspective, 'many of the problems people experience personally, psychologically and socially can only be understood in terms of dehumanising characteristics of modern society' (Howe 1987: 121). Thus 'people should become aware of how social experience . . . limits them, shapes their outlook, dulls their senses and channels their desires' (Howe 1987: 124). This means people reclaiming 'their own subjectivities' and recognising 'how others define us to suit their interests' (Howe 1987: 129). Thus social change requires a psychological transformation of oppressed people towards a new subjectivity. This involves identifying and criticising the psychological effects of all forms of domination and oppression.

The underlying theme of the radical humanists is that people become trapped within a dominating society that they sustain in their everyday lives and thus come to live alienated, inauthentic lives. Radical humanists are concerned with understanding how these processes occur so that human consciousness can be freed and transformed into critical consciousness. Critical consciousness is based on the premise 'that we can move from the distorted to the accurate representation of how things really are' (Webb 1985: 97). This notion of awareness beyond ideology has been criticised by postmodern writers, however. The post-modern critique of consciousness-raising is that it is a modernist project based on the premise that people can come to recognise ideological and material domination and can struggle collectively towards egalitarian and socially just relations (Gore 1993). I argue, however, with Janmohamed (1994) that consciousness-raising can be reconceptualised in post-modern terms, that the process can encourage people to redefine the way in which their subjectivity is constructed and assist them to reject the dominant definitions of their experiences. In recognition of the post-modern critique, Sloan (1966) says that the development of critical consciousness does not need to represent a transcendent perspective.

TOWARDS A MATERIALIST PSYCHOLOGY?

Although structural social work is informed by a materialist position, neither Moreau (1979) nor Mullaly (1997) have attempted to construct a materialist theory of the individual. Would a materialist psychology overcome some of the limitations of structural social work previously discussed?

The main tenet of materialism is the view 'that people's experiences and sense of themselves will reflect their economic position or forms of consciousness will reflect the currently dominant human solutions to the material problems of life' (Edley and Wetherall 1995: 97). The materialist argument is that to understand an individual in society one needs to understand the social groups to which this individual belongs, the history of the groups and the individual's economic and social position in relation to these groups. Thus people's personalities emerge from their social practices; this means that investigations of personality formation must study the structure of social activities and relations in which individual lives are embedded.

Perhaps the most elaborate attempt to develop a materialist theory of the individual is seen in the work of Seve (1978), who argues that the main limitation of psychology is that it portrays the individual as an abstraction. The individual is not related to the social relations of particular societies in particular periods of history. To understand individual people, Seve argues, we need to focus on particular individuals in context. He demonstrates how social relations are fundamental to the formation of subjectivity and shows how social forces affect a person's life and personality. Seve's (1978: 347) alternative is to construct a theory of 'the concrete individual' by analysing how individuals spend their time in relation to the institutionalised social practices that they are embedded within.

Murkitt (1991: 193) argues that Seve's approach 'has been limited in its almost exclusive focus on the relations of production and the capacities learned in social labour'. A number of writers have criticised Seve's work for ignoring the domestic division of labour and the way in which unequal gender relations also influence the personality development of men and women (see, for example, Leonard 1984). However, domestic work could be incorporated within Seve's analysis. What is more relevant here is the criticism that what is not elucidated in the materialist framework is the way in which capitalist and patriarchal relations are internalised in men and women and how they might come to challenge these relations.

As Thompson (1992: 210) has argued: 'The problem with constructing a critical psychology from Marxism . . . is that there are no adequate tools for understanding how alienated social relations are subjectively experienced and acted on by the individual.' McNay (2000) has made a similar point: 'The central problem of the Marxist insistence on the primacy of economic structures is that it precludes an account of creative activity and an explanation of the constitutive role played by individuals in the formation and development of human society' (2000: 133).

Leonard (1984) argues that both dominant ideologies and the material relations which they legitimate contain contradictions and are continually struggled against. It is these contradictions and these struggles which provide the space for individual and collective resistance. But where do agency and resistance come from?

Mullaly (1997: 209) says that 'changing social structures will naturally affect individuals, both materially and psychologically'. However, Kovel (1977) argues that changing the oppressive material circumstances of an individual's life will not necessarily alleviate the individual's suffering. We thus need to distinguish between 'the ultimate causes of a phenomenon such as neurosis and its actual manifestations. The harsh truth is that once neurosis sets in . . . the ensuing neurotic structure takes on a life of its own' (Kovel 1977: 326). Thus political action and structural change will not necessarily resolve the activity of neurotic functioning in the present. While Kovel (1977: 332) agrees with the Marxist view that 'neurosis would not exist if the social world did not impose contradictory and destructive demands on individuals', he also believes 'once it does exist, it takes on a life of its own due to repression'. This has led him and others to a Marxist engagement with psychoanalytic theory.

PSYCHOANALYTIC MARXISM AS THE BASIS OF A CRITICAL PSYCHOLOGY

One of the fundamental premises of psychoanalytic theory is the view that the individual inhabits two worlds. 'There is an outer world of the present in which men and women contend with the routines and pressures of daily existence and there is an inner psychic world which refers back to the repressions and frustrated desires of the past' (Golding 1982: 557). How useful is this notion of the unconscious to the project of developing a critical psychology?

Ingleby (1987: 202) argues that 'Freud is useful to a critical view of society because he also offers a detailed explanation of the compulsions and delusions that make people more at home in an oppressive society than they would be in a free one'. The view from the Freudian left is 'that we must understand capitalist society not only in terms of economic and political oppression but also as involving the psychic oppression and emotional impoverishment of the individual . . . who is an active participant in her own subordination' (Leonard 1984: 41). Kovel (1977: 326) argues that 'the neurotic character structure itself impedes people's awareness of the actual nature of domination'. Thus attempts to resolve issues in the 'here and now' may be subverted by unconscious motivation.

Freud's theory of the unconscious has been criticised as a concept essentially detached from reality in which the unconscious is regarded as a reflection of a deep, primitive instinctual drive. It has been argued by a number of critical theorists that traditional psychoanalytic theory fails to locate the unconscious within an historical specific social context. 'It fails to connect to the reality of class relations [and] . . . it is over-determinist in that no fundamental changes in social relations are envisaged as possible' (Leonard 1984: 34).

Can a critical theory of the unconscious be developed which would overcome the limitations of Freud's theory? Leonard (1984) argues that if we see the unconscious as deriving from the material world, not from primitive instinctual drives, it significantly alters our understanding of its progressive potential. By understanding the nature of the unconscious at particular periods in history, it enables us to unmask important aspects of dominant ideology. It also enables us to understand some of the barriers to critical consciousness among oppressed people.

So the theory of the unconscious can be used as a means of explaining how psychic oppression takes place and Freudian theory can be used to understand the means by which patriarchal and capitalist social relations are legitimated and reproduced. The implications for social change are clear. What is required is not only a change in the external world and a change in consciousness but also a transformation of the inner structure of people's unconsciousness.

There have been a number of attempts to develop a dialogue between Marxism and psychoanalytic theory to endeavour to overcome these problems, from Reich (1972), writing in the 1930s, through Marcuse (1962) and Fromm (1971) to Schneider (1975), Kovel (1981) and more recently Wolfenstein (1993). A number of socialist feminists (for example, Mitchell 1975) have also explored the progressive possibilities of psychoanalysis, using it to explain the entrenched resistance to feminist ideas and to challenge the truth status of patriarchal consciousness among both men and women. While these attempts at a Marxist-Freudian synthesis and a feminist engagement with Freud have not been entirely successful, Dowrick (1983: 14) argues that 'such a dialogue provides various means of overcoming the split between inner and outer functioning between emphasis on the individual and emphasis on environmental influences'. Thus it is seen as having something important to contribute to a critical psychology for social work.

Postmodernists raise questions about the validity of the truth claims of psychoanalysis. Foucault (1978) rejected psychoanalytic theory on the grounds that the concept of repression implied a hidden truth or essence to identity. This need not lead to a negation of the contribution of psychoanalytic theory, however. It simply requires that we temper psychoanalytic truth claims with a postmodern scepticism (Flax 1993).

POSTMODERN CRITICAL PSYCHOLOGY

There are numerous postmodern perspectives on the construction of the self. What they have in common is a critique of an essentialist version of the self upon which most social work conceptions of the person are based (Pardeck et al. 1994). Postmodernists argue that the self is socially constructed through the application of language categories and labels. The self is thus a product of what Foucault (1978) calls 'discourse'. It is through discourses that subjectivity is formed.

Discourses make positions available for individuals to take up in relation to other people. The world is then seen from the standpoint of that position, a process which involves, among other things, locating oneself in relation to categories and storylines. It also involves locating oneself as a member of various subclasses of categories distinct from other subclasses, thus developing a sense of oneself 'as belonging to the world in certain ways and thus seeing the world from the perspective of one so positioned' (Davies and Harre 1990: 46–7). Through this process, people can become fixed in a position as they are shaped by 'the range of linguistic practices available to them to make sense' of the world (Potter and Wetherell 1987: 109). The individual is thus constituted and reconstituted through a variety of discursive practices and changing material circumstances.

Postmodernism then promotes the notion of multiple selves that are fragmented and contradictory (Jackson 1990). Multiple subject positions resulting from involvement in different discourses lead to individuals being composed of a set of contradictory positionings or subjectivities. This multiplicity of discourses leads to internal conflict and contradiction.

In acknowledging the power of dominant discourses, it is necessary to avoid discourse determinism, whereby individuals are mechanically positioned in one or more discourses, leaving no room to explore the possibilities for resistance and change. While subjectivity is constructed within discourse, subject positions cannot be predicted as the outcome of specific discourses. Dominant discourses can be resisted and challenged, and this resistance is an important stage in the development of alternative subject positions.

Thus we need to develop ways of encouraging resistance. The possibility of agency is opened up to the subject by 'the very act of making visible the discursive threads through which their experience of themselves as specific beings is woven' (Davies 1993: 12). Some resources must be available, though, for the individual to have agency. These include a definition of oneself as one who makes sense of the meanings within discourses; access to alternative discourses; access to means of bringing about alternative positionings; a belief in one's capacity to reposition oneself; and access to others who will support alternative positionings (Davies 1990).

What are the implications of this view of the self for critical social work practice? Gorman (1993: 250) emphasises 'the transformative power of local narratives . . . ones that tell the collective story of the disempowered'. O'Brien and Penna (1998: 54) argue that 'the precondition for human emancipation is seen to be the recovery of the voices of the oppressed'. This constitutes what Foucault (1978) called 'the insurrection of subjugated knowledge'. Oppressed and marginalised populations challenge the definitions of themselves by powerful experts and tell their own story of their experiences as part of the process of redefining themselves (Hartman 1992).[4]

CONCLUSION

The different critical theoretical perspectives I have reviewed in this chapter emphasise different concepts in developing a critical psychology. Radical humanist approaches emphasise dominant ideology and consciousness. Materialist perspectives stress the importance of material conditions, social practices and lived experience. Marxist and feminist Freudian views emphasise the unconscious and repression. Finally, postmodern perspectives emphasise discourse, subjectivity and subject positions.[5]

I have not attempted to develop a synthesis of these critical theory traditions. While I do not believe that a unified theory of the self is possible, I do believe that all of the critical concepts that I have reviewed in this chapter are necessary to shed light on the relationship between self and society. We thus need to develop a more complex understanding of the relationship between these different traditions. This includes continuing the dialogues between materialism and humanism, rethinking the relations between the material and symbolic structures, and examining the relationship between subjectivity and the unconscious. Furthermore, it will mean that we will have to straddle the modern/postmodern divide. As argued elsewhere in this book, there is no one critical approach to social work and we need to tease out the implications for practice of a number of different critical theoretical orientations.

13

RESPONDING TO THE CHANGING SOCIO-POLITICAL CONTEXT OF PRACTICE

Gary Hough and Linda Briskman

For a time, Australia was widely considered to be a 'lucky country' (Horne 1964), a nation fortunate enough to have experienced a buoyant economy framed by sustainable agriculture and abounding natural resources. Even when that formulation was held to be true Australia, like many other Western countries, had a political economy that privileged economic interests over social goals. Entrenched inequality, alienation and exclusion were always present, but the gap between rich and poor has escalated over the past decade as globalising forces have swept across the old order. Unemployment and insecure employment shape the lives of many Australians and for some groups, including those who had a safe place in the lucky country formulation, life chances are seriously diminished by current trends in public policy.

This chapter seeks to sketch the impact of the current policy climate on contemporary social work, and to explore the prospects and potential for critical social work practitioners to contribute to progressive social change within the contemporary political economy.

THE POLICY CONTEXT

Until the last fifteen years or so, Australia prided itself on the presence of a welfare state that had both universal provision of a range of primary services and targeting of secondary support services to the most vulnerable and disadvantaged. Early provisions of universal child endowment and universal pensions had wide popular support. Under the currently dominant policy of fiscal restraint, universal provision has been gradually eroded, with social programs rationed and targeted to the most needy. However, over the same period, new categories of need continued to emerge. These include single parenthood (as young mothers were no longer adopting out their children), an increasingly ageing population, increased immigration and higher than previously experienced unemployment.

Nowithstanding the recognition of these newly emerging social problems, increasingly restrictive measures have been introduced in many policy fields. These include 'work for the dole' schemes and restrictions on support mechanisms for newly arrived migrants, particularly those seeking refugee status. Jordan (2000: 25) speaks of 'tough love', where service providers must expect more from service users, must test their eligibility for services more strictly, must activate them more rigorously and support them more strongly in any efforts they make to be independent. The eschewing of passive welfare can be argued to have directed attention and resources at the individual, while ignoring or discounting systemic societal inequalities. Active welfare approaches challenge previous conceptions of justice, including both justice as a social right of citizenship and as compensation for 'dis-welfare' (Shaver 2001: 3). In Australia, as in other Western countries, it is now taken as self-evident that the role of the state as the provider of a wide range of public services that promise evening-up the life-chances of people, is drawing to an end (Leonard 1997). Rosanvallon (1988) has argued that the limits of welfare, although expressed in debates about levels of taxation or levels of welfare spending, should not be considered as primarily economic questions but as cultural and political ones that speak to the boundaries of social acceptance.

In recent decades, the postwar consensus on the welfare state has evaporated. A pervasive meta-policy of 'economic fundamentalism' prescribes economic goals as paramount, and this is used to justify the erosion of the welfare state (Ife 2001). Social work has had to assimilate changing notions of security of employment, changing family structures and a diminishing social security safety net. Although there has been a strong continuing stream of radical social work practice (evident in poverty campaigns, for example), the social work profession has been relatively powerless as a change agent. In this context, Miller and Rose (1990) have warned that social work might thrive as an occupation at the same time that it perishes as a caring and liberal profession.

During the past twenty years, the social work profession has had to work within organisational environments saturated with managerialism. Corporate planning processes have been transplanted from the private sector, and the image of the private firm, with its clarity of purpose, its capacity for innovation, its supposed responsiveness to consumers and its pliability in the hands of executive management, is held up as the model for efficient organisation *per se*. In essence, corporate planning processes integrate budgets with goals and objectives, translate missions into realisable action plans, and seek, from the top of the organisation, to apply objective, apolitical criteria of efficiency and effectiveness to performance goals. These dictates, underpinned by economic fundamentalism, affect the working conditions of social workers and may result in their having to limit both the quality and quantity of the services they provide (Ife 2001).

The rise of managerialism has coincided with the decline of professional power and autonomy across nearly all of the professions. Within this context, social work has had to compete with other professional groupings in a de-regulated market place where social work is not always valued as a professional calling.

The lucky country was also built on an eschewing of difference, a mythology of rural living, and on isolationism and protectionism. Schaffer (1990) asserts that 'real Australians' included Australian-born men (heterosexual), Anglo-Irish Australian-born men and women, Australian bush dwellers (but never the Chinese) and naturalised English-speaking migrants without foreign accents. This order has been transformed by the attempt of successive governments over recent decades to portray Australia as a globalised economy. Citizenship theorists have challenged the assumption that citizenship status for all transcends particularity and difference (Young 1994). Social movements of oppressed and excluded groups have constantly made the obvious point that an extension of equal citizenship rights has not led to social justice and equality (Young 1994). For some, recognising and promoting the rights of minority groups constitutes a threat to individual human rights, with a view that group rights create distinctions between citizens (Federal Race Discrimination Commissioner 1995). Cultural identification is not recognised by most liberal theorists as a ground for group-specific rights, but as a purely private matter in which individuals are free to participate (Dodds 1998).

SOCIAL WORK IN AUSTRALIA

In recent decades social work has had to deal with both the challenges of a managerialist environment and the complexities of adapting its practices to meet the needs of diverse constituents. Social workers have always worked within policy and organisational environments not interested in, or sometimes inimical to, social workers' espoused goals and values. For this reason, some critics argue that social workers can be seen as part of the problem rather than as advocates for reform (Wharf 1990b: 145). Social work practitioners are sometimes accused of being complicit with current policy imperatives, seeing their only viable role as softening the impact of harsher policy excesses. This is scarcely surprising, given that all established professions may be seen as having 'struck a bargain with society' in return for their privileged position within the state order. In other words, a degree of technical autonomy may be granted in return for ideological cooptation.

Over time, the social work profession has come under considerable criticism from the most marginalised groups, particularly Aboriginal groups and groups representing children and young people in care. Challenges have been mounted to the 'globalisation of the specific' (Thorpe 1994: 199), the implementation of practice solutions that present universal answers to localised problems. There has been a rejection of the idea that the perspectives of racialist, gendered, differently-abled and aged groups and individuals can be represented in universal discourses of need, identity or role (O'Brien and Penna 1998b). Some of the strongest critiques have come from inside the institutions of social work, with the development of an extensive anti-professional literature from within the profession itself. It can be argued that such a degree of self-critique distinguishes social work from most other professions (Sibeon 1991).

Yet the constant challenges to the profession are not always evident in practice, and social work has never been monolithic, in either its ideology or its practice frameworks (Noble and Briskman 2000). This is both a strength and a weakness. Although social workers do condone isolated, occasional or trivial acts of 'banditry' (Jordan 1990: 67), there is little evidence that there is engagement in a systematic manner in challenging the systems which oppress those most marginalised in society. There are of course exceptions, including smaller collectivities that employ social workers. However, these organisations most often have little relative power and are often struggling for their existence. The stronger their advocacy and contest with the state, the more limited their hold. Social workers and their professional body, the Australian Association of Social Workers, have not engaged consistently in activism targeted at structural change (De Maria 1997; Briskman and Noble 1999). The professional association argues that social workers pursue their goals in part by analysing and challenging social policies (Australian Association of Social Workers n.d.), but this does not alter the fact that social work, like all other human service professions, has been largely complicit with current policy directions, either because of cooptation, complacency or the need for employment security.

MANIFESTATIONS OF FEAR

One of the key challenges facing critical social work is to find a way of working within a society that is fearful of breakdown and disintegration. This fear is evident in fiscal retraction based on concern about a diminishing national resource base, in a fear of difference evident in reactions to ethnic diversity, sexual identity and different family forms, and in moral panic about child abuse, law and order, and drug and alcohol use. The view of Australia as an open democratic society comes under increasing strain as governments and the community struggle with such issues as supervised injecting rooms, compassionate euthanasia, Indigenous land rights and rights for gay partners under the law. There is an emergence of a range of linked issues relating to the position of an impoverished and excluded group of people seen as troublesome, burdensome or threatening (Jordan 2000). Using the example of child protection, Thorpe (1994) argues that the portrayal of emotive images that signify urgency and pity are without context and have no meaning other than one that creates alarm. They offer little to those who require help in managing the contexts of poverty, deprivation and discrimination while managing their children's lives.

The expression of fear is evidenced by measures for those who break the law. In some jurisdictions young people (especially Indigenous) have been incarcerated for trivial offences under mandatory sentencing regimes. Asylum seekers are detained with few rights, and with little recognition of their motivations for escaping repressive regimes. Media commentator Philip Adams suggests that never before have so many people been placed behind bars or electric fences (Adams 2000).

The state plays the major role in enacting legislation, providing funds and establishing targets and goals for the resolution of a range of social problems (O'Brien and Penna 1998b). Beyond this, a wide range of civil institutions operate systems of power which become inculcated into the behaviours, habits and practices of the society, resulting in rules, codes and regulations experienced as normal features of everyday life (O'Brien and Penna 1998b). In a seemingly paradoxical way, as the world is seen as more chaotic and characterised by exponential or discontinuous change, our organisational worlds, like our policy worlds, are currently characterised by a quest for predictability and certainty, with the development of converging monocultures across and within organisations.

As the contemporary organisations in which social workers are employed become more intent on procedural control, professional values are diminished and there is limited scope for the questioning of policies and practices decided at the corporate centre. Critical engagement of social workers with the wider context is in danger of dissipation as social workers, like their teachers, accede to systems antithetical to their training in the interests of acceptance and job security. Theoretical frameworks built on anti-racism or feminism are increasingly absent from the practice frameworks of social workers, who are frequently required to work within a routinised structure of predetermined client pathways within a wider framework of throughput and output based services. At the same time as empiricist paradigms have lost their privileged place in the academies (in the face of feminist, critical and postmodern critiques), they have come to completely dominate the world of practice (Ife 1995b). In the performance culture there is optimism about the credibility and utility of comparative performance information, and especially of performance indicators, which are mostly used for drawing conclusions rather than for asking questions (which is their proper use). This follows from managerialism's embrace of positivist, or sometimes even functionalist, understandings of the social world, and of how performance in it should be planned, described, implemented and measured.

These developments illuminate what has always been the core focus of 'social' work—the well-being of the individual and the collectivity. The crisis of identity for both individuals and the community/ society/nation brings new focus to the helping individuals/social change divide, as systems based models of unitary social work are revealed as increasingly stretched and inadequate. As the outside changes, identity becomes contingent and dislocated, and we have a different understanding of how the subject/object or individual/society constitute each other.

Interrogation of difference has encouraged analysis of the way identities and cultures have been differentiated through the political process (O'Brien and Penna 1998b). Postmodern perspectives have provided new insights into the nature of individuals and what is outside them. In increasingly organisational societies, common beliefs and values give way to more fragmented patterns of belief and practice, and the present market-dominated organisational world is built on crises of identity. As the expansion of services, the globalisation of production and exchange, and the feminisation of the labour force replace the old order of national economies, large-scale manufacturing and male breadwinners, we are faced with recognising the constructed nature of what were once seen as 'natural' entities.

The problem of mutual need, of who needs me, has been highlighted by the comprehensive indifference of contemporary capitalism. This is evident in winner-take-all markets, in the absence of trust in people and institutions, and in the re-engineering of institutions so that people are treated as disposable. We now talk of jobs rather than careers. If we imagine a career, it is unlikely to be within the one organisation or even within the one sector. Organisations are increasingly unlikely to assume any long-term commitment to their workers. The unemployment problem is no longer about access to secure employment, because there is very little employment now that may be assumed to be secure. Rather than a society with certain classes and groups excluded from full participation, we have an economy with an escalating number of 'economic fringe-dwellers'. We are asked to accept that ever larger numbers of people are 'victims of time and place', with no useful state or governmental responses to be made (Sennett 1998: 147), and we are constantly reminded that our lives consist only of personal problems to be solved privately.

PROSPECTS

The discussion to this point has been about the changed circumstances in which social workers have to practice. Our interest is not in naming the different circumstances and bewailing the inability of social workers to carry out our (progressive, critical or traditional) practice in it, as if the practices are always right but the circumstances currently wrong. We know that the institutional alignments (the politics) change and, in changing, periodically reconstitute the practice (Rein and White 1981). A focus on how people are 'made up' in contemporary society promises to bring together the individual/social change divide, and the split between critical and traditional practitioners. For traditional practitioners, direct service will have to be undertaken very differently. And there are direct challenges to the foundations of critical social work practice too, because the promotion of inclusion and greater acceptance for those excluded from full participation as citizens brings a new set of risks as the bonds holding the collectivity together are seen to stretch and weaken.

While modernism generates the cult of the individual, communitarianism may push us back to the prescriptive identities from which we have come. If the antidote to competitive capitalism and competitive individualism is seen in communitarianism, it cannot be a form of communitarianism that equates conflict within a community as a threat to social bonds. On the contrary, strong bonding between people may mean engagement, over time, with fundamental difference (Sennett 1998). In the current era, the search for safety in an insecure world is manifested in the shrinking of the world to our communities and the reduction of the community to the self. Social polarisation rules in a situation where community means sameness, sameness equals absence of the other, and individuals lose the capacity to connect personal problems into public issues.

Sennett (1998) concludes that a regime that provides human beings with no deep reason to care about one another cannot preserve its legitimacy in the longer term, and that social work, of whatever sort, can make a crucial contribution in continuing to assert and build commitments between people, and groups of people, that must endure over time. Reconciling conflict and difference with mutual obligation (between individuals, and within and across groups, communities and work organisations, and at different levels of 'government') becomes the clear mission for critical social work.

EMANCIPATORY CHALLENGES

A number of commentators have challenged the social work profession to find its contemporary place in a combination of resistance to dominant economic paradigms and proactive engagement with the policy context. The widening gulf between policy and management and counselling and support services (Carter 1996) has to be the focus of a redefined social work. Ife (1997) expresses a belief that social workers have the capacity and the obligation to work towards an alternative system not only in the interest of a better world, but also in the interest of their own professional survival. Social work has always lived with contradictions, uncertainty and a changing context and, generally, has been able to adapt, to speak out, to move on and survive. Despite the enormous changes, partly spurred on by global forces, there is no reason to believe that the profession is in any great danger at the present time. What may be at stake is not the institutional survival of the occupation, but its integrity and autonomy. In this sense, one of the greatest threats to social work can be seen to lie inside the profession itself. Despite continuing change confronting the profession, Carter (1996) suggests that there is little evidence of public analysis or angst among social workers about their future role in Australian society. Rather, the prevailing mood has been one of complacency.

As most social workers work 'within the system', in the public services or in organisations funded by the state, there is a need for engagement with those working from the 'outside' to avoid total immersion in the policy imperatives. The current emphasis, in many practice fields, on social workers as case managers assumes the notion of a mutuality of interests between the system and its client group. This notion has obscured the diversity of needs of client groups and has allowed professionals to collude with pathologising of clients rather than addressing broader political issues (Dominelli 1996). Although seldom evident in mainstream policy and practice, postmodern perspectives have legitimised the struggles of various groups to name themselves, to speak for themselves, to claim legitimate access to resources from the vantage point of their own reality, and to insist that any policy-making for the collective reflects the diverse nature of the collective (Ingamells 1994). Postmodern perspectives also draw attention to a number of areas of social transformation, including the growing significance of difference, plurality and awareness of relativities (Parton and Marshall 1998). Postmodernity's suspicion of grand narratives is reflected in social work's continued diversification, with postmodernity feeling comfortable with difference and multiplicity (Howe 1994). Critical social workers need to avoid being drawn into frameworks that adopt universalist assumptions and privilege certain groups over others.

There are numerous examples to show that it is possible to work within the system for change. The question remains about how much it is possible to work on the inside of the state without being coopted and restricted, given that activism can imply the need to work against the system. A related question is whether people can engage in such roles without being seen as betraying their constituents. Nyland (1998) asserts that it is possible to have a link between top-down and bottom-up elements. Using the example of housing reform, she argues that a complementary approach, one that forms a bridge between both forms of reformism, is feasible. She argues that workers in the community sector are sometimes presented with an opportunity to play a part in the policy process from which they were previously excluded, enabling direct participation in the design and formulation of new policy directions. For critical social workers within the system, it is not a great leap from advocating for individual clients to advocating for wider system changes. Freedman and Stark (1995) discuss a model in which they adapted a well-entrenched model of white foster care to meet the needs of Aboriginal communities within an extended-family care framework. This model embraced a 'tripartite agreement' between the state, the community sector and Indigenous communities.

Crawford (1997) challenges 'urbanocentric' models of social work, which interpret rural issues through a modernist lens that presumes a deficit model of understanding. Consistent with Crawford's theorising, there are examples of rural practice that reject solutions from the centre and adopt local, context-specific adaptations. Examples include adopting appropriate understandings for rural women from non-English-speaking backgrounds (Babacan 1999), acknowledging women's work against violence in rural communities (La Nauze and Rutherford 1999) and developing community-embedded rural social care practice (Cheers 1999). These examples go some way towards addressing criticisms of social work as a profession that stands aloof educationally and professionally from the industry in which it is based (Carter 1996). They represent the recognition of practice as a reciprocal construction of meaning, identity and change. Instead of adopting legal and procedural methods, there is an emphasis on creativity and imagination and on making sense of experience, self and relationships (Jordan 2000).

For critical social workers who are hesitant about working for change from the 'inside', there are opportunities to participate in social movements to bring pressure on policy-makers to take heed of alternative visions (Ife 1997). Although there may be organisational constraints against joining visible activist bodies, participation in national and international conferences, and membership of committees and boards, can lead to an engagement with those who are working towards a change agenda. Healy (1999) defines the activist social worker as one who highlights the essentially political nature of social work that remains concealed in orthodox practice theories. For Jordan and Parton (1983), social workers cannot ignore the political dimensions of social work practice if they are to provide a caring, responsive and sensitive service to their clients and the wider community. Dealing with the diverse needs in society can be challenging at a time when policy is becoming more unitary and program driven. But even within such a constrained environment, social workers aligning themselves with a critical perspective can constantly remind management of the specific service-delivery needs of all its constituents.

Ife (1997) proposes that social workers need to come to terms more explicitly with the decline in the welfare state and position social work in other sorts of human service structures. This view is reinforced by Carter (1996), who suggests that social workers can no longer assume that they are there to grease the wheels of the welfare state or to mop up the relatively few disasters of capitalism in an economy of full employment. Unless social workers are more creative in the definitions of their own roles, they are open to the charge that their only option for survival is to join the managerialist orthodoxies of economic rationalism (Ife 1997).

There are many practitioners who believe the role of social work is to make the world a better place (Ife 1997: 1). Outside professional paradigms there are examples of action to achieve this goal, including global protests against the excesses of capitalism and cases mounted for economic human rights. To achieve change from an insider perspective, we need to interrogate the meaning of social justice in social work (Carter 1996). This requires a clear analysis of equality and inequality, and social and economic justice and injustice. For McMahon, A. (1993), the development of an Australian social work means developing bodies of theory and practice that are Indigenous, multicultural, based in social justice, feminist and critical.

CONCLUSION

Social work is being dragged to the marketplace (Aldridge 1996). At the same time it is facing new challenges, with the entry into that marketplace of new and divergent interests. This means that critical social workers must resist changes that destroy their capacity to deliver services consistent with the profession's defined knowledge, skills and value base, particularly in relation to diversity. At the same time, the profession needs to proactively and creatively engage with new possibilities for progressive practice within the dominant policy environment. Leonard (1997: 169) speaks of two intertwined strategies—collective resistance and welfare building. These strategies require confronting the structures of domination in welfare, the economy and culture, as well as placing an emphasis on overcoming oppressive elements of modernity through a process of reconstructing the social policies, programs and discourses in which they are located. Adopting proactive strategies can go some way to dealing with a climate that is seen as problematic.

14

ENACTING CRITICAL SOCIAL WORK IN PUBLIC WELFARE CONTEXTS

Gary Hough

This chapter focuses on the contemporary terrain of public welfare and the new boundaries within which a critical social work practice must be enacted. In the public welfare field, as in other practice arenas of social work, models and frameworks have been built around generalist, therapeutic, transformative or developmental theories of assessment and intervention (McDonald and Jones 2000; Ife 2000). But in addition, practice in public welfare has always been constructed from directions other than the models, frameworks and values that resided in the heads and hearts of the practitioners. Public welfare has a statutory base and involves authoritative interventions by state agents in the lives of certain categories of citizens.

THE ORGANISATIONAL CONTEXT

The policy and organisational context of public welfare has always been a prime determinant of the parameters of practice; this is reflected throughout the public administration and street-level bureaucracy literatures. To some extent, social workers in public welfare have always had to practice within organisational contexts indifferent or even inimical to the core values that they bring to their work. This is scarcely surprising, given that public welfare is the area where overwhelmingly political issues, to do with the state's requirements of its citizens, and its obligations to them, are reformulated and expressed. In any practice in public welfare there are always many actors and stakeholders other than the clients and workers, even if they are not always visible.

Public welfare can be defined as welfare work that is centrally concerned with certain types of regulatory and protective practice, which:

- concentrates on social work's historical involvement with issues of care and control and the enforcement of sometimes contested or contradictory normative standards;
- derives its authority to a large extent from a legislative or statutory mandate; and
- will generally be planned and delivered by one of the social service departments of the state.

However, the question of auspice can be confusing, given the historical role of voluntary agencies in this area of practice, policies fostering the development of community based social support and control, and contemporary moves towards outsourcing and privatisation.

Fields of practice covered by public welfare include corrections, income security, some aspects of child and family welfare, mental health, youth services, aged services and arguably, some sectors of housing, employment, and drug and alcohol services. Of course, in the lives of many citizens, these services may not embody separate phenomena: a particular family subject to a child protection intervention might embrace most or even all of them.

The history of public welfare can be told alongside the history of social work itself, from the settlement house movement to the genesis of institutionalised support services in the depression of the 1930s, the development of the comprehensive support and safety net of the postwar welfare state, the wars on poverty and the rights-based community development approaches of the 1960s and 1970s, and on to the subsequent retreat from the welfare state and the era of managed markets and the customer culture.

There are some significant discontinuities over this period; these relate particularly to very different formulations about what policies public welfare organisations should pursue, and to the ways in which they should be structured and managed in order to pursue them. But there are continuities too, and these relate mostly to actual practice. Practice has remained inherently difficult in its enactment, uncertain and often contradictory in its outcomes, and continually resistant to successful containment within the (succession of) policy and management prescriptions that have sought to re-engineer the public welfare practice systems.

Obviously the policy and organisational contexts cannot be disconnected from the practice level because 'the outside is inside', constructing and 'structurating' (Giddens 1984) the micro-practices of public welfare social workers. However, despite the major changes in macro policy and management ideology that have swept across the field of public welfare and the human services since the middle of the last century, research on public welfare continually throws up some familiar themes from the front line. This chapter will consider some of these themes and their connection to critical practice. But first, it seems sensible to include a brief discussion of the major discontinuities in public welfare policy and management, with the discussion organised under the three headings the street-level bureaucracy thesis; the first wave of managerialism: 'circling the wagons and rationing the supplies' (Considine 1988); and the second wave of managerialism: enacting social work in the customer culture.

Connecting the two waves of managerialism is the transition to the 'risk society' and the advent of protection as the validated state welfare mission. Over the 1980s the discourse of protection came to dominate public welfare practice, and public welfare service delivery has increasingly been structured around protective interventions in a number of fields: mental health, aged services, youth services and, most clearly of all, the field of child welfare.

While the state role of offering protection for the vulnerable and oppressed can be argued to have been central to the early development of social work, the contemporary resurgence of the protective role is proving highly problematical for critical social workers. Indeed, some critics have argued that contemporary social work is being significantly transformed because it is so centrally placed in the contemporary state's collapse of its welfare role to narrowly focused 'protective' interventions.

PUBLIC WELFARE SOCIAL WORKERS AS STREET-LEVEL BUREAUCRATS

Lipsky's (1978) notion of the street-level bureaucrat encapsulates some of the forlorn hopes—both technical and ideological—of social workers (Howe 1986: 149). The street-level bureaucracy thesis comes from the literature on public policy implementation, and recognises the strategic importance of the front line and the way in which front-line workers deal with the formal organisational constraints on their work by exercising discretion in the form of informal coping mechanisms and routines. Although front-line workers, such as field social workers, are formally accountable to publicly funded bodies, the particular circumstances in which they work make their activities difficult to supervise and control, at least as far as the informal, qualitative aspects of the work are concerned. Because of the dual focus of their account-ability—to the agency and to the clients—there must be an inevitable and fundamental conflict, which comes to constitute both the greatest strength and the greatest weakness of the public services (Lipsky 1978). There is extensive debate about the level of this discretion and in whose interests it operates. Lipsky was worried that street-level bureaucrats, in enacting their work, could effectively make policy, some-times buffering out the formal organisational policies and protecting their clients, sometimes seeking recourse to 'strategies of survival' which could lead workers with good intentions to do less for their clients than they might, or sometimes behaving in ways that might be positively damaging (Satyamurti 1981: 82).

In terms of the amount of discretion that workers exercise, it is worth noting that agency records do not necessarily contain accounts of what workers do; indeed, they are often only a formal recitation of what the agency expects (Pithouse 1987). Lipsky contends that public welfare agencies have always taken recourse to formal methods of organisational integration and control, through processes such as policy and procedure manuals and performance audits. However, these have seldom been able to reduce the inherent uncertainty of the work, primarily because unclear or contradictory goals will 'accurately reflect the contradictory impulses and orientations of the society the agencies serve' (Lipsky 1978: 346).

The street-level bureaucracy literature highlights an enduring fea-ture of public welfare work—that attempts by the agency to produce standardised outcomes that can be quantitatively measured are likely to reduce the coping mechanisms that enable the workers to sustain their jobs, under very difficult conditions, in the first place. The workers' sense of responsibility for clients and concerns for the qualitative aspects of their work (for its content and meaning) are continually eroded in a work-world of time-and-motion studies, evaluation research,

quantitative measures of client contact, case-load management techniques, priority scaling, workload formulae, review forms and practice
manuals.

Administrators faced with the dilemmas of statutory social work are
likely to understand the environment in a particular way in order to
reduce anxiety and manage the work. Social workers, on the other
hand, have always known that there is a very high amount of indeter-
minacy and uncertainty confronting occupations which practise in the
spheres of moral behaviour, social problems and human conduct (Howe
1986). Public welfare agencies will always provide a fertile breeding
ground for organisational uncertainty (Brannon 1985).

THE FIRST WAVE OF MANAGERIALISM: CIRCLING THE WAGONS

Managerialism involves not just a management ideology and a set of
managerial techniques. It should also be viewed 'as an element of a
political program and campaign to curtail the role of the state in
society' (Jones and May 1992: 386). Managerialists tend to view
management as a generic, purely instrumental activity, embodying a set
of principles that can be applied to the public business as well as
private business.

The reconfiguration of the state (Fabricant and Burghardt 1992)
needs to be understood and contextualised locally, because it is manifested differently in different cultural contexts (Deetz 1992). But it is
also argued to be expressive of a larger phenomenon, with the key
developments having been shared across national boundaries. The program of restructuring and globalisation, which Australian governments
have been pursuing for two decades now (with the major political
parties seemingly differing only about the rate of change), is familiar
enough. What is particularly important to the field of public welfare is
the organisational expression of this broad set of changes.

To the extent that a different constellation of interests, technologies
and modes of rationality has achieved generalised dominance in the
wider culture, and in the management of public sector organisation,
the formal work of the social services has been transformed and re-
directed. This has profound implications for the scope and perceived
legitimacy of state welfare provision and for critical or progressive
social work. Dale (1989, 1990) has characterised the reconstruction project (in the United Kingdom) as one of 'conservative modernisation',

with the rationale for this broad movement being to free individuals economically while seeking to control them socially. This conservative modernisation has been configured in a number of overlapping discursive and institutional changes, namely, from collectivism to individualism; from egalitarianism to hierarchies; from public interest to national interest; from progressivism to modernisation; and from conjunctural to structural political rationality.

This last concept was articulated by Offe (1984) and essentially means that policies are now shaped by resources available rather than by identifiable need. We have moved from a demand to a supply-driven economy. Jones and Novak (1993) saw the development of supply-led welfare in the clearer emergence of friction between workers and clients, in an era where gatekeeping and rationing have become significant activities for social workers in public welfare, associated with operational principles of exclusion, restrictiveness and client control. Jordan (1988) has noted a greater antagonism, with the increased use of compulsory measures by social workers against their clients. As clients have come more and more to identify social workers with agencies that do not meet their needs, we can expect to find reduced cooperation, more punitive practice ideologies among workers, and more social distance as workers stress decision-making over sharing or partnership.

In these processes Jones and Novak (1993) feared that the progressive and humanitarian characteristics of social work could be stripped away, leaving behind those authoritarian and controlling dimensions that have always been held in uneasy tension in state social work. For all the espoused goals of caring for families and communities, or of mutual obligation, one can easily conjure up images of the work of state departments of human services, or the Commonwealth service delivery agency Centrelink, when thinking about the issues raised above.

In Australia, as in the United States and United Kingdom, policies directed to human service work in the first wave of managerialism relied on the reduction of expenditures, the targeting of resources and activity to particular areas of social anxiety (where more judgmental, individualising and punitive responses have their genesis not so much in formal policy as in administrative practice), and the introduction of market forms of technical-instrumental rationality and technologies of control. In so doing these policies sought to resolve some of the problems at the core of the street-level bureaucracy syndrome. In practice, they have mostly exacerbated them.

As I have argued above, state public welfare provision has always been directed in ways that obstructed and compromised the service ideals that practitioners initially brought to the work. Social workers are compelled to carry out a highly ambiguous role in attempting to speak on behalf of those they are regulating (Parton 1991). To do this success-fully would require a degree of autonomy and discretion that few other professional groups and interests would be willing to grant them. The space occupied by social work has become increasingly contested over the last two decades; social workers have been the subject of particular scrutiny and criticism in public welfare, which can be argued to be the field where they have mostly lost control of the overall design of their own practice. The field of public welfare, particularly in the areas of child protection and income security, has seen the most vigorous and radical managerial re-engineering of the policy and practice systems.

There have always been substantial dissonances between pro-fessional understandings that reflect social work technologies and values, and managerially constructed practice systems where the 'product' is changed, by higher design, from a complex one to one that is readily assessed and created. Elements of service work like empowerment, problem resolution, utilisation of all available options, confidentiality, advocacy and social change may be eliminated from the record-keeping, and even from the practice, of social workers. Quality practice may be redefined as quality control and a non-routinised form of work forced into a standardised framework. Where this happens there will be a reduced need for skilled workers, as in the crucial areas of practice the worker loses control of her own work and a de-skilling cycle ensues (Cousins 1987). Of course, non-programmed responses too have gener-ally failed to bring people and their situations under control, and in some ways many areas of public welfare work remain uncontrollable. Child abuse and other areas of inter-personal and intra-familial violence, emblematic in many ways of contemporary public welfare practice, may be seen as 'wicked problems' which will continue to be charac-terised by uncertainty and volatility.

While managerial technologies are likely to emphasise ahistorical and short-term perspectives, they do have strategic effectiveness in managing austerity and, due to social work's inability to control its own practices, the scandals that excite media interest have tended to be labelled as social work rather than management failures—externally at least. The internal response has most frequently been the throwing of an even heavier blanket of administrative law over welfare practice.

THE SECOND WAVE OF MANAGERIALISM: THE CUSTOMER CULTURE

The changes described above constituted the first wave of managerialism. Over the 1990s we can discern a second wave, which again reflects developments in the wider culture. The idea of the market has come to dominate over this period and public welfare agencies have been transformed once again to fit the prescriptions of the customer culture. This has entailed the prescription of new modes of behaviour and practice, and new norms of relating for the state to its citizens, citizens to the state, workers to their employing agency, agencies to each other and workers to clients.

Du Gay (1996) has written about the construction of new identities in the customer culture, and of how traditional separations between production and consumption identities have collapsed. If organisational life is dominated by the customer culture, then people are encouraged to conflate their identities as consumer and worker, or as customer and claimant. Every individual is positioned as a self-seeking entrepreneur and 'win–win' solutions are promised for the organisation and for each of the self-seeking and self-creating individuals in it. The idea of clients as customers, who should make wise choices in order to maximise their self-interest, is but the latest example of the syndrome where the needs of clients do not originate with the clients themselves. They are formulated and prescribed by the service providers. This has always been the case. De Montigny (1995: 39) talks about how people subject to social work learn how to think through their lives, employing the terms of an institutional reality. People come to see themselves as particular kinds of cases and so, for instance, former psychiatric patients describe themselves as schizophrenic, manic or depressive. This problem—of inscribing messy and inherently multifaceted daily life into institutional categories—is the core practice problematic that will be considered below, but the continuing struggle by the workers to throw off, ameliorate, humanise or find ways around the organisational prescription of their practice is what has characterised public welfare practice under the very different policy and organisational regimes of the last four or five decades.

The link between the first and second waves of managerialism (or between modernist/Fordist modes of organisation and postmodern organisations) is the continued privileging of the managerial principle. A fundamental clash is said to exist between the 'managerial' principle and the 'occupational' principle (Ingersoll and Adams 1986).

221

The managerial principle lays stress on the organisation of tasks (and the people performing them) beyond the bounds of a single occupational specialism and into a total productive system, whereas the occupational principle emphasises intrinsic standards of work or service. So while practitioners will stress, rhetorically at least, values like flexibility, difference and individualisation, managers are likely to privilege predictability, sameness and regularisation.

One significant development in public welfare over the last fifteen or so years is the use of software programs that standardise operational procedures (SIMS). It is possible for a very large corporation to see what all of the cells in its institutional honeycomb are producing by using SIMS software. With the introduction of SIMS systems, the practitioners (after the 'business process' rules have prescribed) will be marginalised as more peripheral actors, because any context-bound knowledge will be devalued.

Public welfare has been, within the human services field, the site of the greatest investment in information technologies to reorganise the practice systems. The managerial reconstruction of state statutory welfare systems has been significantly built around new IT-based management information systems (Hough 1996), and the prime structuring force in workers' practice is now the software programs within which they enact and record their work.

Clegg (1996: 10) asserts that the 'postmodern organisation' operates on a decentralised, distributed model, which means that activities that were once central are now distributed through a network of sub-units that are linked electronically. There will be a number of mechanisms for coordinating action, including groupware, and the size of the organisation becomes meaningless as these organisations can be both big and small at the same time. In remembering Pithouse's (1987) observation that the agency records are often only a recitation of agency expectations, we should also note that these systems are not primarily about record-keeping; they represent the latest frontier of control in the struggle to structure and define public welfare practice.

THE FAMILIAR THEMES FROM THE FRONT LINE

Attempts to make sense of the system 'must center around the misfocus of child protective services, the bureaucratization of workers' relationships with clients, and the creation of work contexts that value the development of helping relationships between workers and clients'

(McMahon, T. 1993: 234). These same issues continually surface in research on front-line public welfare work.

Ethnographic studies of front-line work (McMahon, T. 1993; Hough 1994; De Montigny 1995) all stress that good social work is not marked by confident pronouncements, certain decisions and resolute action, but by openness to dialogue, self-reflection, self-doubt and humility. Although workers will often refer to the 'bureaucracy' or the 'system', what they are frequently denoting is the problematic of the 'everyday world'. This refers to the translation of daily life into institutional realities, which happens everywhere in public welfare in the process of making people's lives understandable and manageable. Parton (1991: 9–10) refers to discourse as 'the technology of thought' whereby the particular technical devices of writing, listing, numbering and computing render an issue as a knowable, calculable and administrative object. Knowing an object requires the invention of notational procedures, methods of gathering and presenting information, and the use of these so that calculations and judgments can be made. A critical practice will be attuned to the practices of the social workers in producing cases and the social relations through which these practices are accomplished. In the process of workers turning situated and local activities into coordinated professional accounts, events are reconceptualised into institutional reality and people's lives are inscribed into institutional categories. Through their documentary practices (reading and writing) social workers construct an institutional reality and clients' daily lives become organisationally actionable.

So, for instance, the initial activities of a child protection worker are structured through an institutional question: Is this a case of child abuse or neglect? In this process, the validity and incorrigibility of child abuse as a category describing the 'real world' is always taken for granted (De Montigny 1995: 26).

For front-line workers, sense-making and accounting practices relate to the demand to manage, order and account for the lives of others. A greater self-reflexiveness about this process will attune us to 'hegemony [which] directs our attention to the multiform separations, differential locations, and class divisions effected between those who administer the lives of others and those who are subject to this administration' (De Montigny 1995: 18). Wherever this problematic is recognised, there must also be spaces and forms of resistance. Front-line workers will often refer to the disjunction between their desires and the actual forms of practice. For example, a common story about the removal of children is a regret about not wanting to apprehend them, but not having the material resources to keep them at home. The intervention/non-intervention question may represent a false dichotomy, with the more crucial issue being the type of intervention that is possible in a particular situation. The familiar street-level bureaucrats problem resurfaces: how to reconcile actual situated activities and experiences with extra-local forms of authority and discursively organised power. Workers in my study of a front-line child protection agency (Hough 1994) would often lament their inability to protect the service users from the organisation's interventions, which not only frequently failed to help but often made their lives, on balance, worse.

The second theme from the front line is the need to redefine protection. The current policy construction of child protection in Australia presents child abuse as an individual, classless, gender-blind, culturally inclusive, individually caused phenomenon, which can be responded to within an after-the-fact 'investigative' paradigm. Parton (1991, 1996, 1999) has written about the role of social anxiety in contributing to the recognition of social problems, and the role of the media and child death enquiries in contributing to the development of this particular policy response.

At the practice level, the atmosphere of social anxiety around child protection has been inimical to professional reflectiveness. McMahon reflects the views of most progressive social workers when he laments that 'the hijacking of child welfare into a reactive, punitive service and the subsequent application of technical skills to passive, acquiescent clients has resulted in practice that is narrowly focused, biased against women . . . and counterproductive' (McMahon, T. 1993: 234).

The workers in my study (Hough 1994) displayed at least ambivalence, and in most cases strongly negative feelings, about what the organisation actually does with clients, in terms of both the focus and the quality of the work. The work was, at its worst, presented as a disconnected series of abuse-assessment episodes. One worker reported the case of a family that was 'reported' four times within a twelve-month period. Assessments indicated that the family, and to differing degrees its individual members, were experiencing substantial difficulties with day-to-day living, but there was not seen to be evidence of abuse (within the definitions). No help or support was offered until, on the fourth assessment after the fourth different notification, defined evidence of abuse was found.

The third consistent theme is the need to reinvent relationships

224

and to continue to struggle and insist on the importance of relating to individuals as subjects, not as objects of administrative action. Workers will need to do this for themselves as well as for the service users, because failure to remain engaged will entail alienation and estrangement from their own practice. A deeper conception of democracy requires a focus on the production of personal identity and joint decisions within state organisations. We need to have organisational forms that recognise and legitimate peoples' experiences (Weick 1995). Such relationships need to centre on empowerment and collaboration rather than on control, and to reflect the necessity for social workers to play out their democratic ideals in all of their social interactions.

The major cause of the divide between the managers and the workers lies with the organisation having adopted a set of managerial imperatives and values that make it almost impossible for it to mobilise the antecedent values and commitments of participants. Social workers need to find and explore degrees of discretion that are relative and conditional but allow them to engage with clients in an authentic way. The present emphasis on narrow role-based individualism is inimical to critical practice, to the exchange of knowledge and information, and to the 'knowhow trading and transmission' (Considine 1992) that is necessary to build a practice culture and to retain staff. These points come together in indicating the need to return to the front line as the central locus for generating policy and practice. Significant learning can only take place if we understand what the front-line workers commonly do, how the work is experienced by them, and the meaning they draw from that experience.

Given that practice is an active, intervening process that has its reality in action, a progressive practice system would draw on that experience to influence policy-making and management. The command model does not allow any mechanisms to learn from the day-to-day sources of information (available only at the front line), and does not allow a learning environment that can deliver a complex program of care. The command model assumes that events and decisions mean the same whenever and wherever they are located, hence the tendency to practise from the top down. In contrast, a critical approach to practice requires an emphasis on the phenomenological (events have their meaning in how they are experienced), and so individuals, teams and facilities have their unique characteristics. They define themselves by difference, whereas corporate managerialism defines them by similarity.

In many ways, the practice parameters for critical practice in public welfare are even more constrained now. But a critical practice has always been possible and remains so. Firstly, there remains the continuing 'disconnect' between the inscriptions of the formal organisation and their informal enactment by the workers. My research with public welfare social workers (Hough 1994) confirmed a long-held contention: that the system by and large works in spite of its formal rationality, not because of it. The resistance of professional staff to bureaucratic authority has been at the centre of formulations about the nature of the agency in social work practice, as has the street-level bureaucracy thesis (Lipsky 1980; Reisch and Ephros 1983). Research on front-line child protection practice (Hough 1994) confirms that the (predominantly female) front-line staff in public welfare are likely, in all of their micro practices, to find (mostly passive or deviant) ways to resist what they regard as inappropriate agency expectations, and to find opportunities to work in their own ways in concert with colleagues and clients. The workers report a continuing attempt to develop non-instrumental and non-contract based relationships with clients and with workers in other agencies, and to use non-official discourses with clients and other workers, although this activity remains invisible in the formal practice records. Although there has traditionally been a 'loose-coupling' within public welfare organisations, which may have tolerated or tacitly acknowledged the front-line workers' needs for authenticity in their actions, the new public-sector managers' efforts to narrow the boundaries and scope for such semi-autonomous action have, not surprisingly, nourished the deviant unofficial culture at the front line.

CONCLUSION

As this chapter has demonstrated, workers are constantly engaged in making sense of an organisational world that should never be seen as fixed or immutable. These intentional or interpretive activities (whether conscious or unconscious) are central to the production or reproduction of social arrangements, and while they may be 'structurated' (Giddens 1984), they can never be simply determined by formal organisational (and inter-organisational) structures, policies and procedures. They are better seen as conditions of social action that are produced, reproduced, and sometimes contested and transformed, by different social actors.

The issue is not about the need for organisational control *per se*, but about which forms of control and social relationships, which technologies and which kinds of work relations are morally, politically and technically appropriate to public welfare work. The claim for critical social workers to be able to articulate and pursue their practice goals should be put forward as a claim for the nature of the work itself rather than as a professionalising strategy for social workers or the privileging of a particular political position.

15

GLOBALISING PRACTICE IN THE INTERNATIONAL CONTEXT

Jacques Boulet

This chapter offers one participant's reflections on what it feels like to try and 'act/think/local/global' as a social worker and a human being. Using my personal trajectory in the context of international development and solidarity work over the last four decades, the first section attempts to set the historical context. The following sections briefly examine more specific aspects of globalisation and international social development and their relation to critical social work. I discuss the notions of 'development' and human rights, and their relevance for social work and for the lives of those the profession touches, especially in a globalising but diverse context. Some final thoughts are spent on the role of social work education in the context of globalisation and internationalisation.

A GLOBAL PERSPECTIVE

This chapter rather consciously lacks many direct references to social work 'practice'. On the other hand, it has everything to do with social work practice and its theory, and with the changing context in which it occurs. As well, attempting to fully comprehend the processes, events and facts associated with the 'global' in their interrelated objective and subjective dimensions would necessarily require much more space as well as an additional dose of analytical complexity. If the personal is political, as posited in the critical tradition of social work espoused by this collection, and if one tries to apply it to the domestic, the known and familiar sphere of, say, interpersonal social work with victims of domestic abuse, one already faces a complex task in sorting out the above-mentioned linkages and causalities. Add that other commonplace exhortation to 'simultaneously think/act both globally and locally', and the complexity becomes truly overwhelming. Think about issues like post- and neo-colonialism; international money markets; the World Bank and structural adjustment policies; aid; famine and drought; international water and resource politics; other variables associated with disciplines like economics, international politics, ecology, anthropology, comparative religion, cultural studies, to name a few, and you will start to appreciate what it means to write about 'globalisation' and 'international social development' and what they may have to do with critical social work practice and theory. This is probably why there is often only passing attention to such matters in professional social work, in social work education (see, for example, Boulet 2001) and in the everyday contexts in which we live our lives.

And yet, the destruction of the World Trade Centre towers and part of the Pentagon on 11 September 2001, and the associated loss of life— capturing so much media space, so much of our emotional energy and our conversations—have certainly brought 'home' the global in a rather unsubtle and urgent way. Suddenly, things and events usually occurring in well-defined places 'out there', in places referred to as 'under-developed', 'third world', 'uncivilised', at best located in 'our backyard' but generally well away from 'our doorstep', have now 'come home to roost', as some of the lesser-heard commentators think. Attempts by our 'civilised' political, economic and journalistic leaderships to call these events 'terrorism', and simply get on with the business of eradicating it and of exterminating the perpetrators, do not sound entirely convincing. This is especially so for those of us who try to be reflective and think about things and people with empathy—in other words, those of us who try to apply the knowledge, skills, attitudes and ethics of critical social work.

How can one come to grips with the fact that across the world all our pasts, presents and futures are inseparably bound together:

- when we're sheltering from United States missiles in a drought-stricken Afghan mountainside, not knowing where our next meal will come from or whether we will still be around when it comes?
- when we're refusing entry into Australia to those who flee from

those missiles, and instead detaining them as 'illegal asylum seekers' in other poverty-stricken Pacific islands, whose governments badly need the cash we pay them to do that job?

- when we remember that many of those arriving in this country 200 years ago, often rejects themselves and refugees-of-sorts from societies which denied them a present and a future, justified taking it from its original inhabitants by calling it *terra nullius*, 'nobody's land'?

- when, as Australian volunteers, we're erecting shelter against the blazing sun and the bitter winter cold for Afghanis, whether or not we do it out of a Christian motivation?

- when we're contributing towards supporting these volunteers, our tax-deductible donations derived from salaries made or shares invested in the manufacture or sale of the above missiles now raining on said Afghanis?

- when we, exhausted social workers in Melbourne, Australia, are spending our Sunday afternoon recuperating with a bit of retail therapy, probably at the global-Swedish furniture store IKEA, sipping a cappuccino, before throwing ourselves into the throngs to select another lounge suite to replace the out-of-fashion one, barely three years old, which will soon end up in the opportunity shop frequented by—finally legal—Afghani refugees?

- or finally, when our community, educational and other public services are cut because our Western government decides that economic rationalism demands their privatisation and marketisation, or because our (southern) government is forced by the International Monetary Fund to use our meagre economic resources to repay the national debt (plus interest), into the pockets of those among us who already have too much anyway?

Such are the challenges to inserting a global perspective into a reflective framework for critical social work practice and theory!

This chapter can only present a collection of fragments towards a framework for 'global-local praxis'; of more or less systematic responses to a constant state of personal bafflement in the face of so much contradiction and human capacity for destruction, but also of continuing hope in the human capacity to see it through. It is derived from my own past learning, as I was involved in social and community practice and education of many kinds, within all manner of contexts and relating to a great variety of people, places and issues. The spirit of this chapter, therefore, leans more towards the 'sharing of wisdom' than towards the development of a 'body of knowledge'. It also is written in a spirit of humility and deep gratitude to all those who invited me to share in their wisdom and knowledge and friendship.

SOCIAL AND COMMUNITY WORK IN AN INTERNATIONAL CONTEXT

The following reflections derive from my participation in the international solidarity movements over the past nearly 40 years while working and living across four continents, first as a volunteer 'development worker' in the 1960s; as part of the 'ex-volunteers international' critical network in the 1970s; as an engaged academic (social work and community development) and participant in various international networks for the last 30 years; and, generally, as someone who is baffled by the contradictions one gets into when trying to 'do' something about global inequalities and injustices, and even more baffled when not trying to do anything about them.

Work in the field of international 'development' has seen some remarkable transformations over this period. From the mid- to late 1960s, the term 'development cooperation' still captured reasonably well the attitude and motivation of those of us who wanted to do something about the increasing evidence of past and ongoing ravages imposed on the 'developing' world. For a while, 'development' and 'co-operation' seemed to provide converging points for governments, non-governmental organisations and activists, strongly emphasising community development, education and rapid industrialisation, all under the benevolent aegis of the fledgling United Nations and its various sub-systems (including, rather timidly then, the World Bank and the International Monetary Fund).

That convergence, however, quickly shattered during the late 1960s and the 1970s; 'neo-colonialism' and 'imperialism' became standard concepts in the verbal repertoire of those of us in the developed West who were critical of the underside of such development aid. Cast in the context of the Cold War, the emergence of new social movements and a vigorous critique of globalising capitalism, our support for national liberation struggles in the dependent countries started to take shape, with initial traces of a critique of the development enterprise itself.

By the end of the 1970s, nagging doubts about the universal applicability of our analyses of the dependency syndrome began to seep in. Some of the features of the socialist project became rather suspect, especially as the global roles of the USSR and China became more ambiguous. Our 'modernist' certitude about the rightfulness and inevitability of the violence used by some of the liberation movements was shaken and we were appalled at some of the 'petit bourgeois' excesses of their leaders and by the systems they set up after the victorious outcomes of their struggles. In tune with emerging postmodernist thought, we became aware of how much we had projected our own desires, frustrations and impotent rages into our support for the liberation struggles in the dependent countries. We started to understand how much we, as Western Marxists, humanists, feminists, environmentalists, had homogenised and appropriated people's struggles against their very specific local oppressions. It seemed that 'we' had expected 'them' to fight 'our' struggles, as if by proxy, against global oppression and alienation—struggles which we had found ourselves unable to win in our own societies.

And then, initially only faintly, from the late 1970s onwards came the onslaught of the neo-liberal, economic-rationalist reconstruction of the 'global order' under the ideological-political command of capitalism and the military-political powers which sustain it and which are sustained by it. While those of us on the left were having great deductive arguments about the best course of action to solve not only the global inequalities, but the locally derived problems as well, the logic and real-life practices of the political economy of capitalism were inexorably determining the world-wide course of events. Aided and abetted by the operations of global bodies (the World Bank and the IMF), facilitated by the demise of the once-dominant power of the 'second' world (the USSR and its associates), the imposition of a renewed Western hegemony on the rest of the world took its course virtually unopposed. Or so it seemed . . .

The last decade of the second millennium has somewhat sobered the triumphalism of US President George Bush (the first), who declared in 1989 the coming of a New World Order, bringing 'wealth and solidarity' on the basis of 'market-oriented policies, democratic polities and individual rights', which would lead to the 'well-being of billions of people' (Lechner and Boli 2000: 7). Indeed, the litany of events and processes which have questioned many of the assumptions underlying the positive globalisation mantra does not need repeating here. One should probably have suspected what the notions of 'solidarity, democracy and rights' were intended to convey. When Bush-the-first enunciated, just three years later, at the occasion of the 1992 Earth Summit, that 'the lifestyle of the United States would not be up for discussion at

Rio' (in Sachs 1995), the provisos attached to the New World Order were immediately clarified.

Remembering Bush senior's remark also helps us to understand, depending on where one is positioned on the continua of political ideology and of factual wealth and poverty, how the global policies and politics of his son, about ten years later, are really bringing home the point. The results of these politics are very much a part of the news we are fed daily via print and other media. Just to name a few and without any particular order: Palestine; Kuwait and Iraq; Rwanda and Burundi; the former Yugoslavia; Chechnya; East Timor and Indonesia; wars and oppression world-wide; the explosion of poverty and destitution in parts of the former USSR; the increasing gap between rich and poor everywhere; ill-health. Also, witness HIV-AIDS; depression; hunger, malnutrition, anorexia; the lack of shelter and of subsistence/income-generating work; the abuses of social justice and human rights; inequality everywhere. A truly depressing list, inexorably leading to the following question, so central to social work in any critical name: how long will it take for Western moral indignation to tip the balance towards exercising pressure and/or intervening towards establishing the mere conditions for livelihood for all, and away from short-term, self-interested economic and ideological calculation?

On the other hand, there are the recent successes scored by alliances of activist groups around the world, including the obstruction and eventual blocking in 1999 of the implementation of the OECD's Multilateral Agreement in Investment and, even more recently, a string of attempts at blocking the further entrenchment of the World Trade Organization's policies geared at maintaining the existing inequalities and palpably contributing to the further deterioration of the environment. Seattle, Prague, Washington DC, Melbourne, Quebec and Porto Alegre will probably (hopefully) become historical markers on the road to a more accountable and just world. As well, given the nature of the hybrid communities now established across the world and reaching deep into the centres of global power, it is now more likely that whatever goes on anywhere in the world will be transported across the globe right into the heart of the Western capitals, thus making it less likely that the divide-and-rule strategy of those in power can succeed without challenge.

And then, on 11 September 2001, the terrorist attacks on the symbols of Western hegemonial power brought the challenge violently and destructively right across the doorsteps previously thought to keep 'us' immune from 'them'. The precariousness of our global 'arrangements' was suddenly brought 'home'. Given the power of the 'guardians of public learning', this will most likely intensify domestic repression inside the Western nations and cast the pall of suspicion and of complicity on all those who ask for more complex thinking about these events. It will probably also bring more devastation to those groups, peoples and nations who are already suffering most from the present inequalities and exploitative relationships on a world scale.

These events happened at a time when the previously mentioned multi-faceted and multifaced resistance against the negative aspects of the overall process of globalisation—usually demonised, criminalised, ridiculed and patronisingly referred to as 'infantile' by the serious press and those in the know—had started to receive some affirmation, however grudgingly that may have been. Witness Amartya Sen (Nobel Prize in economics!) speaking in Melbourne (in *The Age*, 16/5/2001: 17):

> The world in which we live is both remarkably comfortable and thoroughly miserable. Faced with this dual recognition, we can go in one of several directions. One line of thinking says the combination of processes that has led to the prosperity of some will lead to similar prosperity for all. This advocacy comes from obdurate optimists, who see the doubters as soft in the head, whether or not they are kind in heart. In contrast, the stubborn pessimists acknowledge—indeed emphasise—the continuing misery in the world but are pessimistic about our ability to change the world significantly. This can—and often does—lead to a quiet acceptance of a great many ills.
>
> There is, thus, a partial but effective congruence between the stubborn optimist and the incorrigible pessimist. The optimist finds resistance unnecessary, whereas the pessimist finds it useless. The opposing views unite in resignation. Global passiveness is fed not just by apathy, but by a conservative unity of radical opposites. One effect is to divorce our lives from any kind of global ethics.
>
> The global doubts, of which we see many different expressions, can be viewed as a rejection of this comforting conservatism. The protest movements against the global economy are often ungainly, ill-tempered, simplistic, frenzied and frantic, and yet they do serve the function of questioning and disputing the complacency about the world in which we live. The global doubts can help to broaden our attention and extend the reach of policy debates, by contesting global resignation and acquiescence. The global doubts are, in this sense, a way to global solutions.

SOME REFLECTIONS ON THE NOTION OF DEVELOPMENT

Despite his aesthetic qualms, Sen (2001) does suggest that interrogating the context of globalisation is a necessary task today, in the face of the stark realities of the human condition. And that has to start with the very terminology we use to critically understand and express the complex paradoxes and contradictions involved in, and often hidden behind, everyday phenomena associated with such contexts.

'Development' is one such term, and we use it in a variety of social work contexts (think of 'child development', 'life-span development' or 'organisational development'); it is often applied as a comparative marker of and for the assessment of the levels of economic prowess, well-being and welfare, across nations and groups of people. Our understanding of the use of the word in the latter context has to start with US President Truman's speech to Congress, on 20 January 1949, at the beginning of the so-called Development Era. Coining the poorer countries as 'underdeveloped areas', he projected a vision splendid about lifting the 'underdeveloped' countries to the levels of democracy and economic productivity so obviously on display in the industrialised societies—above all, in Truman's own country (Sachs 1995).

The Western view of development seems to suggest, rather arrogantly, that it represents the most successful of all past and present models of and for human existence, and that it is unproblematic overall, in spite of some minor, and largely unavoidable, side-effects. In addition, its semantic field does not easily allow shadings of meaning, let alone alternative or competing ones, to be accepted as viable purposes for human effort, either individually or collectively. As Esteva points out (in Sachs 1992):

> Development occupies the centre of an incredibly powerful semantic constellation. There is nothing in modern mentality comparable to it as a force guiding thought and behaviour . . . It converted history into a programme: a necessary and inevitable destiny . . . [It] gave global hegemony to a purely Western genealogy of history, robbing peoples of different cultures of the opportunity to define the forms of their social life (Esteva in Sachs 1992: 8–9).

Critiques of Western modes and understandings of development have meanwhile gathered pace and depth, with contributions by Korten (1990, 1995), Verhelst (1990), Ndione (1992, 1994), Sachs (1992), Latouche (1993), Crush (1995) and Escobar (1995); the work associated with the notion of Human Scale Development and 'real-life economics'

(Max-Neef et al. 1991); by the post-colonial (Said 1993) and feminist discourses (Mies and Shiva 1993), and others. My own examination of the hegemonial syndrome of Western development thinking, especially informed by some of the post-colonial discourses, has crystallised into a framework which may prove useful for reflecting on how the suggestive-ideological power of the development belief system closes off our own minds (Boulet 1996). This framework is dialectically supported by, and in turn supports, the existing 'objective' societal and global structural arrangements from which we (Westerners), seem to benefit most. It may also help us explain a great deal of our own psycho-social predicaments. I offer it here for reflection, in the knowledge that many may read it as unduly negative and pessimistic, but with the hope that it may encourage dialogue and action.

I distinguish within the Western development syndrome six 'thought-and-practice' or 'praxis' clusters (praxis understood as a dialectically related set of ideological, normative and philosophical moments, and associated and often distorted life-practices) around which we organise our daily lives as well as the structures of our society. They are discursive constructs for generating reflection and debate and therefore also carry the risk of being suspected of 'reverse bias'. As 'development' is primarily about values, however, bias should be explicit and expected. As well, the clusters are not meant to be exclusive nor exhaustive and the overlap between them is not only unavoidable, but intended. It should also be noted that they are not exclusive to the 'West', a notion which is fluid itself and best kept that way. I have presented them elsewhere (Boulet 1996), but I offer them here for wider consideration.

1 The economistic bias and the focus on paid work as the main and central meaning-giving human activity

This includes the assumption of the centrality of economic processes and relationships to both society and individual; the assumption of the market as the central principle organising human relationships and the constitution of the individual, autonomous actor entering contractual market relations; the resultant commodification of all human endeavours; the focus on ownership-as-possession when defining and comprehending relationships between humans and 'things', including life-sustaining resources; finally (but not exhaustively), the focus on and the absolutising of growth and accumulation as necessary ingredients and prerequisites for economic—and therewith human—survival.

2 The political bias towards 'formal' representation and the focus on democracy as 'abstract' delegation, rather than 'participation'

This includes the belief in the necessity of centralism and delegation as the proper and only way to cope with issues of scale (catchword: globalisation); it also posits the possibility of the separation of issues of rights and freedoms from social and economic inequalities and differentials of power; it justifies existing forms of domination; it relies on instruments and mechanisms of decision-making, which are often highly inadequate for the task and the nature of the decision—for example, parties, parliaments, separation of powers, 'leadership', etcetera; it assumes an exclusivity of formal political process that ignores, omits or disempowers many other relevant forms of relationships among human beings; it relies overwhelmingly on the construct of the nation-state that increasingly proves to be as irrelevant for global processes as it has historically been unresponsive to and oppressive of local concerns.

3 The Judaeo–Christian (monotheistic?) bias towards and focus on 'humans' as the species central to the rest of the universe

Anthropocentrism is endemic to our Western conception of the self, both individually and collectively; human salvation and survival interests supersede the rights of existence of all other species and things (now, paradoxically, ever more likely to be leading to the demise of the species); it is often combined with Darwinist and racist assumptions; species supremacy is specifically justified on the basis of our presumed adaptability and our rational/cognitive capabilities; focus on redemption and future salvation is leading to a loss of spirituality-of-the-present.

4 The socio-cultural bias towards the primary if not exclusive focus on the individual

The category of the 'social' is being reduced to a contractual arrangement or to an abstract political construct; a strong tendency towards the commodification of the cultural; a reductive focus on the individual as the only relevant consideration and as an autonomous ontological–existential category and as the only seat of morality; increasing atomisation (or 'nuclearisation') of social reproduction, of satisfaction of need, of both consumptive and productive activity; the utilitarian reduction of the 'social' to its utility for the individual(s); conception of the social as the simple aggregate of individual units, rather than as a category *sui generis* (in its own right); the generic understanding of white/Western culture as the most advanced and therefore the benchmark for all cultures.

5 The masculine–patriarchal bias

The 'myth' and the reality of male domination across time and space; the de-gendering of the economy and the body politic; 'counting for nothing' (Waring 1998)—the systematic devaluing of women's work and actions (and of all non-commodified work); the artificial and arbitrary nature/nurture distinction and what it means for welfare, development, social relationships; patriarchy and its correlates of intersecting class and race based power structures and rationales; masculinity, aggression and violence, or, of hunters and territorial imperatives; (nuclear) family and other social and biological reproductive constructs—the imposition of an inadequate model.

6 The systematic reversal of the material and spiritual dimensions of our social–individual reproduction or recreation

The West, as a merchant in commodities and artefacts and as a merchant in spiritual systems, dogmas and beliefs; materialism, commodity fetishism and the moral life—reconciling the irreconcilable; the various 'crises' of meaning and the various responses—New Age and old habits; the desperate importation of surplus meaning, or, borrowing spirituality from the subjected (and possibly making money out of it); the loss of 'connectivity' with other humans and with the non-human as reason for the loss of spirituality.

HUMAN RIGHTS AND SOCIAL WORK

Over the past decade or so, Ife (1995a, 1997, 2001) has relentlessly attempted to establish and affirm social work as a 'human rights profession' in Australia. What he has been able to express across three books, numerous articles and speeches, as well as in his practice, cannot possibly be dealt with in the few pages available for this chapter. He summarises his approach thus: '[human] rights not only provide a universal moral framework for the legitimation of a social justice perspective, but they also are relevant for a model of empowerment-based practice' (Ife 1995a: 72).

For Ife (1995a: 181), 'many of the ideals of the Universal Declaration [of Human Rights] are only imperfectly realised in the Australian context' and he lists a series of domestic issues—Aboriginal people's rights, ecology, the social vs. the individual (and their associated rights), public vs. private, needs vs. rights-based policies, laws and interventions —which show the contradictory and potentially unresolvable tensions which emerge when dealing with 'rights-based' approaches to policy and practice. He nevertheless takes a firm stand on the side of the 'universality' of rights, as it provides a moral and a legal basis for the pursuit of social justice (1995a: 70), while warning against 'a too ready acceptance of a relativist position', as the latter is all too easily misused to excuse oppressive practices in the political and economic realms.

In subsequent written work, Ife (2001) further provides analyses as to the nature of human rights and refers to the tensions existing between what is commonly referred to as the 'three human rights generations': the 'negative rights', dealing with individual liberties; the 'positive rights', dealing with social justice, participation and freedom of want; and the 'collective rights' on regional, national and international levels (United Nations and Centre for Human Rights 1992: 6; see also Berting et al. 1990). But, unfortunately, we are not really given much help in dealing with the dichotomy in the debates between the human rights 'universalists' and the 'relativists'. Such dichotomising often leads to the creation of 'I-know-where-you-come-from' pigeonholing, based more on assumption than on understanding, which prevents us from establishing a really creative tension between the universality and the specificity (which I prefer to relativity) of rights, something this debate shares with other welfare-related debates about, for example, needs, claims and interests of the various groups social workers deal with in their daily practice.

Some further reflection on this tension is particularly important when one considers some of the issues we have been exploring before, and which relate to the imposition of the Western modes of thinking and behaving on all other people(s) in the world. Take, for example, the Western belief in the centrality and primordial nature of the pursuit of one's self-interest, which, so it is assumed, will almost automatically lead to optimal social arrangements as well as to a proper relationship with the non-human world of 'resources', and which is now rapidly becom-ing the universal quasi-ethical blueprint for how we are to live and run our affairs. This belief, quite obviously, provides the philosophical basis for the various human rights of the 'first generation' and it certainly ignores, if not denies, the relevance of other more socio-centred and less anthropocentric modes of living.

On the following pages I provide a glimpse into the ongoing and very fertile discourse about rights and needs, especially focusing on their application in welfare contexts. In this section I will let others do the talking so as to provide readers with a sense of the participants and actors in those debates.

The massive United States-initiated and supported human rights campaigns of the late 1970s, the years of the presidency of Jimmy Carter, were often denounced as a political instrument of both the 'rich' Western nation states and the various capital interests which made (and still make) up global capitalism. Jouve (1979), for example, said:

> So when the capitalist world, and especially its richest countries, are faced with the real problems of their survival, the diplomacy of human rights is quickly forgotten, for it is in fact a luxury for the rich countries. And the United States only accept to pay themselves this luxury as there are no more fundamental emergencies which solicit their attention (1979: 91).

If human rights are indivisible, as is often claimed, why is it, then that the right to a life without poverty, the right to development and to work, are not recognised, let alone pursued, with much less vigour, if at all, by those same countries? The successive summits organised by the UN, especially the Social Development Summit (Copenhagen 1995) and Environment Summit (Rio 1992), have incisively demonstrated the double standards applied by many of the protagonists of the human rights paradigm. This is especially so when viewed against the background of the monetary crisis (even if some deny the existence of that crisis: Weiss 1998) of the nation-state, the traditional *bête-noire* against which the human rights of the 'individual' were to be established and maintained ever since the bourgeois revolutions in France and the United States in the late eighteenth century. It is also, and somewhat paradoxically, demonstrated when one realises that it is other UN agencies (the IMF, the World Bank and their instrumentalities, like the World Trade Organization) which are doing quite a lot of the damage.

Kilby (1994) makes pretty much the same point when he indicates that the human rights abuses which are being detected and discussed seem solely to refer to civil and political rights and the various Conventions which enshrine them. By contrast, rights of the 'second generation', those relating to social, economic and cultural matters (for example, the right to development) are 'largely ignored and often openly flouted by donor and recipient countries'. Kilby refers to the fact that some of the 'small script' which comes together with structural adjustment programs (the infamous SAPs) 'directly contravenes the Conventions' relating to these rights; the 'right to a free elementary education is fast disappearing, freedom from hunger and the equitable distribution of the world's food resources are not happening, and access for all to medical services is declining' (Kilby 1994: 20).

Addressing the tension between universality and specificity, Brown (1995: 134) attempts to confront a set of paradoxes about rights, 'the central one of which is . . . the question of the liberatory or egalitarian force of rights [which] is always historically and culturally circumscribed'. She maintains that 'rights have no inherent political semiotic, no innate capacity either to advance or impede radical democratic ideals'. On the other hand, they 'operate in and as an a-historical, a-cultural, a-contextual idiom . . . and they necessarily participate in a discourse of enduring universality rather than provisionality or partiality' (Brown 1995: 97). Further, she warns against making rights too 'specific' and against 'attaching them' to the 'current constitutive injuries' of certain groups of people. She fears that such strong specificity (for example, focusing rights on 'the hungry', 'the poor', 'the disabled') 'may draw on our least expansive, least public, and hence least democratic sentiments'. She advocates for inserting rights within the context of 'an egalitarian political community' so that—'in the abstraction from the particulars of our lives'—they can be made valuable in the 'democratic transformation of these particulars' (1995: 134).

Brown's is a useful contribution, but in many ways as inconclusive as many others when it comes to how practical applications and systematic translations from the universal to the culturally, geographically, socially and gender specific are to be made. Critically evaluating Brown's hopes attached to the universalising of human rights, let us again include a reality check and listen to Wallerstein (1995) urging us to understand the present and future of Human Rights as part and parcel of the 'insurmountable contradictions of liberalism':

> Liberalism today is cornered by its own logic. It continues to assert the legitimacy of human rights and, a bit less loudly, the rights of peoples.

It still doesn't mean it. These rights are asserted in order to avoid their full implementation. But this is getting more difficult to avoid. And liberals, caught, as they say, between a rock and a hard place, are showing their true colors by transforming themselves into conservatives, even occasionally into radicals.

The self-contradiction of the liberal ideology is total. If all humans have equal rights, and all peoples have equal rights, then we cannot maintain the kind of inegalitarian system that the capitalist world-economy has been and always will be. But if this is openly admitted, then the capitalist world-economy will have no legitimacy in the eyes of the 'dangerous' (i.e. the dispossessed) classes. And if this system has no legitimacy, it will not survive (Wallerstein 1995: 1175–7).

This is probably a useful reminder in the aftermath of the terrorist attacks and in the context of the 'eradication of terrorism' euphoria which seemingly has engulfed the free (and rich) part of the world.

Looking more specifically at the area of social work and welfare policy, there is a re-emerging debate around the universality of needs, claims and rights and it is worth allowing in voices which in my view are somewhat absent from the local social work discourse. Drover and Kerans (1993: 11), reporting on a Canadian conference in the early 1990s, are critical of an unqualified adherence to and promotion of universal rights, as they are based on 'respect due to an abstract, generalised, disembedded and disembodied other'. They see such universalism as 'substitutionalist' rather than 'interactive' and, with Benhabib (1989), suggest that it rests on a 'paradigmatic' assumption of the human as (generally) white, male, propertied adults and 'people who define themselves or are socially defined in other ways are understood as lacking'. And, the authors conclude: 'A reflection on welfare cannot rest content with the received distinction between the right and the good, nor that between public and private' (Drover and Kerans 1993: 11).

Further, in the context of the welfare discourse, various attempts have been made during the last decade or so to reconceptualise the relationship between 'basic/universal' and 'relative' understandings of need, especially those deriving from the feminist debates surrounding the ambiguity of the concept. Fraser (1989), borrowing from Geertz's (1973) characterisation of ethnography as the 'thick description' of reality, proposed to distinguish between 'thin' and 'thick' needs as two ends of a spectrum, especially aiming to avoid the oppositional dichotomisation inherent in the universal-relative conceptual pair:

242

[The]'thin' notion of need is abstract, objective and universal . . . developed to show that need has 'moral weight', that it implies an obligation on the part of others to meet it, hence it provides the moral foundation for the non-market allocation of resources [while the] 'thick' understanding of need is rooted in an attempt to understand the cultural context in which people name their needs . . . The purpose of a thick, interpretive approach is critical rather than prescriptive, i.e. to point to the ideological limits of universalistic discourse—the unthought, the unseen and the unheard in such theories (Fraser 1989: 415–6).

This can only happen within a framework which is dialogical, where those without power are heard out as carefully as any other (Fraser 1989):

. . . [it] focuses on the politics of need interpretation, since it foresees that claims arising from the particularities of everyday experiences, hence incommensurate with other claims, will be contested (Drover and Kerans 1993: 11).

What I am suggesting here is the possibility that 'universal-thin' descriptions of rights, while having their usefulness as 'benchmarks' for minimum conditions and claims across the spectrum of cultures and social specificities, should be complemented by 'specific-thick' negotiated understandings of what they indeed mean for the locally concrete situation within which they are to be implemented, with the aim of improving people's lives and of responding to their fundamental yet specific needs.

What much of these debates do suggest is the need for 'important postmodernist investigations [which] will not be rejecting modernist assumptions [for example, those expressed in universalist or essentialist terms] as such but rather problematising them in some "positive" rather than "negative" way' (McLennan 1994: 120). Enlarging on Brown's suggestion to insert the rights–needs discourse into a discourse about democracy and equality, New (1996), in discussing eco-feminism, proposes that such theoretical work

would encourage the creative critique of current political forms and methods. It would require the extension of the practical critique of dualism to the overlapping dimensions of class, ethnicity and so on. It would offer . . . alongside irreducibly real sectional interests, the ethical vision of grounded human solidarity, of human interests in reversing the current destructive trend' (New 1996: 94).

As the 'needs debate' already has a strong presence in the critical social work discourse, the above suggested integration of the discourses would provide the 'rights debate' with a quite useful beginning framework, to which the work of Max-Neef and his colleagues (1991) would contribute equally powerfully. The latter provides a strong ontological, epistemological and methodological foundation to not only begin the necessary self-reflection I have been suggesting in this chapter, but to also start and 'dream' better presents and therewith futures for humanity and the cosmos it is part of.

CONCLUSION

Let me conclude these reflections with a call to those involved in critical social work education to take the task of 'globalising' their respective curricula seriously and comprehensively. I am offering the following four broad philosophical-practical grounds as a possible guide to reflecting on the present curricula and the associated teaching and learning formats and practices and the learning content associated with them:

- The global–local futures of all of us, North–South and East–West, are all bound up together; from our factual interconnectedness through communications to the inexorability of the ecological and social consequences of our individual and collective acts;
- We, in the dominant North or West, have a responsibility to recognise and redress past injustices to the peoples of the non-West/North and especially address the ongoing consequences of these injustices;
- Social work and welfare thinking has traditionally and generally (although not always and not by all those who did the thinking and the acting) assumed, and continues to assume, that the need to fundamentally change the unequal distribution of resources is tempered by the belief in the ever-expanding availability of resources. The finiteness of resources and, therefore, of 'growth', inexorably forces us to shift our focus to global–local political and economic mechanisms and relationships of redistribution;
- Finally, looking at the decay of ethical/moral grounding increasingly revealed throughout the Western/Northern ways of living, acting

and thinking and our apparent inability to properly understand our common predicament, learning from the wisdom and practices of those who are 'differently civilised' is becoming an essential necessity for our common survival. And for social workers, that would definitely include the need to learn from colleagues from other places and cultures (Boulet 2001).

ENDNOTES

Preface

1   See Chapter 2 by Jennifer Martin for a history of these approaches.

Chapter 1

1   See Fraser (1991) for an attempt to integrate feminist perspectives with critical theory.

Chapter 3

1   The notion of social structure as the primary source of oppression sits within a conflict perspective of society and social problems. Underpinning this perspective is the belief that society comprises opposing groups who compete for resources and power. Those who win out exercise control and power by establishing an ideological climate that favours them, through the development of social institutions and laws, and the distribution of ideas beneficial to their group. From this perspective, structural inequality reflects the power of particular individuals and groups who are dominant, with social institutions serving private rather than public interests (Mullaly 1997).

Chapter 4

1   'Self-actualisation' refers to the identification and satisfactory fulfilment of human wishes and needs, enabling personal growth and fulfilment (Payne 1998: 125-6).

2   These practices include providing information to individuals on how to obtain the services of agencies, falsifying and altering statistics, turning a

blind eye to violation of policies and working to change organisational rules, regulations or practice (Moreau and Leonard 1989:151–85).

Chapter 6

1   In keeping with current convention, the term 'Indigenous' is used to refer to the Aboriginal and Torres Strait Islander peoples of Australia.

Chapter 7

1   This research was supported by a small grant from the Australian Research Council. See also Weeks (1998, 2001) and Kostecki (2000). Robyn Mason is writing up women's services' response to rural women's issues from this research for a doctoral dissertation, University of Melbourne.

2   The 1993 study was published in Weeks, W. (1994) *Women Working Together: Lessons From Feminist Women's Services*, (Longman Cheshire, Melbourne).

Chapter 8

1   The emphasis in this chapter is on what men can contribute to ending sexism. Following Pringle (1997: 63), I do not believe it is appropriate for a man to suggest what women should do to challenge patriarchal gender relations. Furthermore, a number of feminist commentators have already proposed feminist strategies for working with men. See, for example, Cavanagh and Cree (1996) and Dominelli (1999).

2   See Pringle (1998b: 629) also on this point.

3   See Pease (in press: a) for a more detailed discussion of these practices.

4   In this chapter I have commented upon issues of class, race and culture and sexuality. Of course the same analysis applies to ageing and disability. See Thompson (1994) and Solomon and Szabo (1994) for analyses of the issues facing men in later life. For the implications of a gender analysis for disabled men, see Gerschick and Miller (1995) and Shakespeare (1999).

5   See Pease (1999) for a detailed account of a men's anti-sexist consciousness-raising group.

6   See Pease (in press: b) for an analysis of the limitations and potential of men's groups.

Chapter 11

1   In a recent Australian sociological study examining the place of the cemetery within concepts of grief, Bachelor (2001) reveals that, annually, over 33 million visits are made to Australia's 2300 cemeteries.

2   We Al-Li is the Wonpaburra term for 'Fire and Water', the ceremonial,

cleansing and life-giving elements which are essential for life and which balance each other (Atkinson and Ober 1995: 208).

3   Holocaust survivors from Europe, people fleeing regimes in which ethnic cleansing has been practised (for example, Cambodia) and, more recently, those fleeing highly repressive regimes such as those in Afghanistan, are examples of these migrations.

4   For a useful account of the patterns of care in traditional, modern, late modern and postmodern societies, refer to Walter (1999: 185–7).

5   The term 'mutual help group' is preferred to 'self-help group' because of the mutual process inferred, where help is given as well as received (Silverman 1986, cited in Walter 1999: 187).

Chapter 12

1   See Pease (1991) for a more detailed analysis of the ecological approach.

2   See Pease (2000) for an exploration of this question in relation to men and gender equality.

3   Rather than representing feminist psychology as a separate theoretical strand, I believe that feminist contributions to a critical psychology are best discussed in the context of these four theoretical frameworks. For the implications of these frameworks for working with women and men in the human services see Chapters 7 and 8 of this book.

4   See Chapters 3 and 4 for an elaboration of these ideas in relation to critical social work practice.

5   Another aspect of experience relevant to the development of a critical psychology of the self is the spiritual dimension. A number of writers have commented that the critical contradiction of capitalism 'is not the economic but rather the spiritual and ethical impoverishment caused by the prevailing organization of society' (Lerner 1996: 38). Kovel (1991: 6) refers to this process as 'despiritualisation': 'the process or tendency in social institutions to devalue the spiritual dimension'. Spiritual perspectives on the self challenge social workers to broaden their conception of the relationship between self and society. The social context goes beyond the ideological and material conditions of people's lives to include global harmony for the entire planet. However, an 'emancipatory spirituality' does not just address the internal lives of individuals, it addresses 'the spiritual healing of the entire society' (Lerner 2000: 168). See Canda and Furman (1999) for an application of these issues to social work practice.

REFERENCES

Abetz, E. (2001) *Our Strongest Defence Against the Drug Problem . . .* , Commonwealth Government, Canberra.

Abramovitz, M. (1996) *Under Attack, Fighting Back: Women and Welfare in the United States*, Monthly Review Press, New York.

ABS (1998) *Labour Force 1998*, cat. no. 6203.0 (January), Australian Bureau of Statistics, Canberra.

Acoca, L. (1998) 'Defusing the time bomb: Understanding and meeting the growing health care needs of women in America', *Crime and Delinquency*, vol. 44, no. 1, pp. 49–69.

Adams, P. (2000) *Weekend Australian*, 20–21 October.

Albert, M., Cagan, L., Chomsky, N., Hahnel, R., King, M., Sargent, L. and Sklar, H. (1986) *Liberating Theory*, South End Press, Boston.

Alder, C. (1997) 'Theories of female delinquency', *Juvenile Crime, Justice and Corrections*, eds A. Borowski and I. O'Connor, Addison-Wesley Longman, Melbourne, pp. 43–59.

Aldridge, M. (1996) 'Dragged to the market: Being a profession in the post-modern world', *British Journal of Social Work*, vol. 26, no. 2, pp. 177–94.

Allen, J. and Gordon, S. (1990) 'Creating a framework for change', *Men in Therapy*, eds R. Meth and R. Pasick, Guilford Press, New York.

Alston, M. and McKinnon, J. eds (2001) *Social Work: Fields of Practice*, Oxford University Press, Melbourne.

Alvesson, M. and Willmott, H. (1996) *Making Sense of Management: A Critical Introduction*, Sage, London.

Alway, J. (1995) *Critical Theory and Political Possibilities*, Greenwood Press, Westport, Connecticut.

Andronico, P. (1999) 'Introduction', *Men in Groups: Insights, Interventions and*

Psychoeducational Work, ed. P. Andronico, American Psychological Association, Washington DC.

Argyris, C. and Schon, D. (1976) *Theory in Practice: Increasing Professional Effectiveness*, Jossey-Bass, San Francisco.

Asia Partnership for Human Development (1991) *Draft Framework for Cultural Analysis*, Unpublished manuscript.

Astrachan, A. (1989) 'Men and the new economy', *Men's Lives*, eds M. Kimmel and M. Messner, Macmillan, New York.

Atkinson, G. and Pease, B. (2001) 'The changing role of Indigenous men in community and family life: A conversation between Graham Atkinson and Bob Pease', *Working with Men in the Human Services*, eds B. Pease and P. Camilleri, Allen & Unwin, Sydney.

Atkinson, G., Weeks, W., Hoatson, L. and Briskman, L. (1997) Long Overdue: Collaboration Between the Indigenous Community and Social Work Education in Victoria. Paper presented at AASW National Conference, Canberra, September.

Atkinson, J. and Ober, C. (1995) 'We Al-Li "Fire and Water": A process of healing', *Popular Justice and Community Regeneration: Pathways of Indigenous Reform*, ed. K. Hazelhurst, Praeger Press, Westport, Connecticut.

Attig, T. (1996) *How We Grieve: Relearning the World*, Oxford University Press, New York.

Attwood, B. and Marcus, A. (1997) *The 1967 Referendum or When Aborigines Didn't Get the Vote*, Australian Institute of Aboriginal and Islander Studies, Canberra.

Australian Association of Social Workers (1999) *Code of Ethics*, AASW, Canberra.
—— (nd) *About AASW*, <http://www.aasw.asn.au/about/index.html> [accessed 12 August 2001].

Australian Institute of Health and Welfare (1997–1998) *Child Protection Australia*, AIHW, Canberra.

Babacan, H. (1999) 'Do I belong here?: An exploration of the issues facing rural women of NESB', *Challenging Rural Practice: Human Services in Australia*, eds L. Briskman and M. Lynn with H. La Nauze, Deakin University Press, Geelong.

Bachelor, P. (2001) 'Beyond the funeral', *Grief Matters*, Summer, pp. 43–6.

Bailey, R. and Brake, M. eds (1975) *Radical Social Work,* Edward Arnold, London.

Bainbridge, L. (1999) 'Mental health practice and education', *Transforming Social Work Practice*, eds B. Pease and J. Fook, Allen & Unwin, Sydney.

Baines, C., Evans, P. and Neysmith, S. eds (1991) *Women's Caring: Feminist Perspectives on Social Welfare*, McClelland & Stewart, Toronto.

Balswick, J. (1982) 'Male inexpressiveness: Psychological and social aspects', *Men in Transition*, eds K. Solomon and N. Levy, Plenum Press, New York.

Banton, R., Clifford, P., Frosh, S., Lousada, J. and Rosenthal, J. (1985) *The Politics of Mental Health*, Macmillan, London.

Barbalet, J. M. (1996) 'Developments in citizenship theory and issues of Australian citizenship', *Australian Journal of Social Issues*, vol. 31, no. 3, pp. 55–72.

Barrett, L. (2001) Personal communication, 24 October.

Barrett, M. and McIntosh, M. (1982) *The Anti-Social Family*, Verso, London.

Bartky, S. (1975) 'Toward a phenomenology of feminist consciousness', *Social Theory and Practice*, vol. 3, no. 4, pp. 425–39.

Belknap, J. (1996) *Access to Programs and Health Care for Incarcerated Women*, Division of Criminal Justice, Cincinnati.

Benhabib, S. (1989) 'Liberal dialogue versus a critical theory of discursive legitimation', *Liberalism and the Moral Life*, ed. N. Rosenblum, Harvard University Press, Cambridge.

Benjamin, J., Bessant, J. and Watts, R. (1997) *Making Groups Work: Rethinking Practice*, Allen & Unwin, Sydney.

Benn, C. (1976) 'A new developmental model for social work', *Social Work in Australia: Responses to a Changing Context*, eds P. Boas and J. Crawley, Australian International Press, ACT.

—— (1981) *Attacking Poverty Through Participation: A Community Approach*, PIT Publishing, Bundoora, Victoria.

Benveniste, E. (1966) *Problems of General Linguistics*, tr. Mary E. Meek, Miami University Press, Miami, 1971.

Bertha Capen Reynolds Society (1990) Call to join the Bertha Capen Reynolds Society, Columbus Circle Station, New York.

Berting, J., Baehr, P., Burgers, H., Flinterman, C., de Klerk, B., Kroes, R., van Minnen, C. and Vander, W. eds (1990) *Human Rights in a Pluralist World: Individuals and Collectivities* Unesco (Neth.), Roosevelt Study Centre and Meckler, The Hague and Westport.

Bessant, J. and Watts, R. (1999) *Sociology Australia*, Allen & Unwin, Sydney.

Bessarab, D. (2000) 'Working with Aboriginal families: A cultural approach', *Issues Facing Australian Families: Human Services Respond*, eds W. Weeks and M. Quinn, 3rd edn, Longman, Sydney.

Best, S. and Kellner, D. (1991) *Postmodern Theory: Critical Interrogations*, The Macmillan Press, London.

Bhavnani, K. and Coulson, M. (1986) 'Transforming socialist-feminism: The challenge of racism', *Feminist Review*, vol. 23, pp. 811–92.

Biddulph, S. (1994) *Manhood*, Finch, Sydney.

REFERENCES

Bird, C. (1998) *The Stolen Children: Their Stories*, Random House, Sydney.

Bittman, M. and Pixley, P. (1997) *The Double Life of the Family*, Allen & Unwin, Sydney.

Bocock, R. (1992) 'The cultural formations of modern society', *Formations of Modernity*, eds S. Hall and B. Gieben, Polity Press in association with the Open University, Cambridge.

Bograd, M. (1984) 'Family systems approaches to family violence: A feminist critique', *Australian Journal of Orthopsychiatry*, vol. 54, no. 1, pp. 132–5.

Bolger, A. (1991) *Aboriginal Women and Violence*, Australian National University, Darwin.

Bordo, S. (1993) *Unbearable Weight: Feminism, Western Culture, and the Body*, University of California Press, Berkeley.

Boulet, J. (1996) 'Learning and Teaching International Social Development', *Advances in Social Work and Welfare Education*, eds J. Ife, S. Leitmann and P. Murphy, School of Social Work, University of Western Australia, Perth, pp. 100–9.

—— (2001) *International Content in Victorian Social Work Courses: Report of a Research Project*, AASW and Borderlands Cooperative, Melbourne.

Brannon, D. (1985) 'Decision making in public welfare: Scientific management meets organized anarchy', *Administration in Social Work*, vol. 9, pp. 23–33.

Bricker-Jenkins, M. and Hooyman, N. eds (1986) *Not for Women Only: Social Work Practice for a Feminist Future*, National Association of Social Workers, Washington DC.

Bricker-Jenkins, M., Hooyman, N. and Gottlieb, N. eds (1991) *Feminist Practice in Clinical Settings*, Sage, Newbury Park, CA.

Brieland, D. (1990) 'The Hull-House traditions and the contemporary social workers: Was Jane Addams really a social worker?', *Social Work*, vol. 35, no. 2, pp. 134–8.

Briskman, L. (1996) 'Justice for Aboriginal people off the political agenda', *Forum*, Centre for Citizenship and Human Rights, Deakin University, Geelong, pp. 2–3.

—— (2001) 'A moral crisis for social work', *Critical Social Work*, vol. 2, no. 1, <http://www.criticalsocialwork.com/CSW_2001_1.html> [accessed 15 July 2001].

Briskman, L. and Noble, C. (1999) 'Social work ethics: Embracing diversity', *Transforming Social Work Practice: Postmodern Critical Perspectives*, eds B. Pease and J. Fook, Allen & Unwin, Sydney.

Brittan, A. and Maynard, M. (1984) *Sexism, Racism and Oppression*, Basil Blackwell, Oxford.

Broadbent, A. and Bentley, R. (1997) *Children on Care and Protection Orders*

Australia 1995-96, Australian Institute of Health and Welfare, Canberra.

Brooks, G. (1998) *A New Psychotherapy for Traditional Men*, Jossey-Bass Publishers, San Francisco.

Brower, A. (1988) 'Can the ecological model guide social work practice?', *Social Service Review*, September, pp. 411-29.

Brown, A. (1992) *Groupwork*, 3rd edn, Ashgate, Aldershot.

Brown, A. and Mistry, T. (1994) 'Groupwork with "mixed" membership groups: Issues of race and gender', *Social Work with Groups*, vol. 17, no. 3, pp. 5-21.

Brown, C. (2001) 'Grief—an Indigenous view', *Loss and Grief: Our Stories*, ed. G. McLean, Rose Education, Narellan, NSW.

Brown, W. (1995) *States of Injury: Power and Freedom in Late Modernity*, Princeton University Press, Princeton.

—— (2000) 'Family, state, market and citizenship', *Issues Facing Australian Families*, 3rd edn, eds W. Weeks and M. Quinn, Longman, Sydney.

Burdekin, B. (1993) *Human Rights and Mental Illness: Report of the National Inquiry into the Human Rights of People with a Mental Illness*, vols. 1 and 2, AGPS, Canberra.

Busfield, J. (1996) *Men, Women and Madness*, Hutchinson, London.

Butler, B. (1993) 'Aboriginal children: Back to origins', *Family Matters*, no. 35, pp. 7-11.

Byrnes, J. (2000) 'A comparison of Aboriginal and non-Aboriginal values', *Dissent*, Spring, pp. 6-11.

Camilleri, P. (1999) 'Social work and its search for meaning: Theories, narratives and practices', *Transforming Social Work Practice*, eds B. Pease and J. Fook, Allen & Unwin, Sydney.

Camilleri, P. and Jones, P. (2001) 'Doing "women's work"?: Men, masculinity and caring', *Working with Men in the Human Services*, eds B. Pease and P. Camilleri, Allen & Unwin, Sydney.

Campbell, D., Moore, G. and Small, D. (2000) 'Death and Australian cultural diversity', *Death and Dying in Australia*, ed. A. Kellehear, Oxford University Press, Melbourne.

Campbell, W. (1993) Personal Communication.

Canda, E. and Furman, L. (1999) *Spiritual Diversity in Social Work Practice*, The Free Press, New York.

Caplan, P. (1995) *They Say You're Crazy: How the World's Most Powerful Psychiatrists Decide Who's Normal*, Addison-Wesley, New York.

Carby, H. (1982) 'White woman listen! Black feminism and the boundaries of sisterhood', *The Empire Strikes Back*, ed. Centre for Contemporary Cultural Studies, Hutchinson, London.

Carmody, M. (1990) 'Midnight companions: Social work involvement in sexual assault services in New South Wales', *Australian Social Work*, vol. 43, no. 4, pp. 9–16.

Carnaby, H. (1998) *Road to Nowhere: A Report of Women's Housing and Support Needs When Leaving Prison in Victoria*, Flat Out, Melbourne.

Carniol, B. (1990) *Case Critical: Challenging Social Work in Canada*, 2nd edn, Between The Lines, Toronto.

Carter, B. and McGoldrick, M. (1999) *The Expanded Family Life Cycle: Individual, Family, and Social Perspectives*, 3rd edn, Allyn & Bacon, Needham Heights.

Carter, J. (1996) The Future of Social Work. Paper presented to the Faculty Association of the University of Queensland Faculty of Social Work and the AASW Queensland Branch, 23 October.

Carter, R. (1997) 'Is white a race? Expressions of white racial identity', *Off White: Readings on Race, Power and Society*, eds M. Fine, L. Weis, L. Powell and L. Mun Wong, Routledge, New York.

CASA House (1995) *Breaking the Silence: A Guide to Supporting Adult Victim/Survivors of Sexual Assault*, 2nd edn, CASA House, Royal Women's Hospital, Carlton.

Cass, B., Cappo, D., Edgar, D., George, J., and Setches, K. (1994) The Heart of the Matter: Families at the Centre of Public Policy. Discussion paper prepared for the National Committee for the International Year of the Family, AGPS, Canberra.

Cavanagh, K. and Cree, V. eds (1996) *Working With Men: Feminism and Social Work*, Routledge, London.

Cemlyn, S. and Briskman, L. (2002) 'Social (dys) welfare in a hostile state', *British Journal of Social Work Education*, vol. 21, no. 1, pp. 49–69.

Chambers, B. and Pettman, J. (1986) *Anti-Racism: A Handbook for Educators*, Human Rights Commission Series No. 1, AGPS, Canberra.

Chambers, D. (1989) Contemporary Problems in the Study of Masculinities: A Comparison between Australia and Britain. Paper presented at the Australian Sociological Association Conference, La Trobe University, Melbourne.

Cheek, J., Shoebridge, J., Willis, E. and Zadoroznyj, M. (1996) *Society and Health: Social Theory for Health Workers*, Longman, Melbourne.

Cheers, B. (1999) 'Community-embedded rural social care practice', *Challenging Rural Practice: Human Services in Australia*, eds L. Briskman and M. Lynn with H. La Nauze, Deakin University Press, Geelong.

Chesler, P. (1972) *Women and Madness*, Doubleday, New York.

Chesterman, J. and Galligan, B. (1997) *Citizens Without Rights: Aborigines and Australian Citizenship*, Cambridge University Press, Melbourne.

Choo, C. (1990) *Aboriginal Child Poverty*, Brotherhood of St Laurence, Melbourne.

Christie, A. (1998) 'Is social work a non-traditional occupation for men?', *British Journal of Social Work*, vol. 28, pp. 491–510.

—— (2001) 'Gendered discourses on welfare, men and social work', *Men and Social Work: Theories and Practice*, ed. A. Christie, Palgrave, London.

—— ed. (2001) *Men and Social Work: Theories and Practices*, Palgrave, London.

Cixous, H. (1994) '(With) or the art of innocence' (tr. S. Flood), *The Hélène Cicoux Reader*, ed. S. Sellers, Routledge, New York.

Clarke, J. (1979) 'Critical sociology and radical social work: Problems of theory and practice', *Social Work, Welfare and the State,* eds N. Parry, M. Rustin and C. Satyamurti, Edward Arnold, London.

Clegg, S. (1996) 'The rhythm of the saints', *The Electronic Journal of Radical Organisation Theory*, vol. 1, no. 1.

Cline, S. (1996) *Lifting the Taboo: Women, Death and Dying*, Abacus, London.

Collinson, D. (1992) *Managing the Shopfloor: Subjectivity, Masculinity and Workplace Culture*, de Gruyter, Berlin.

Collinson, D. and Hearn, J. (1994) 'Naming men as men: Implications for work, organization and management', *Gender, Work and Organization*, vol. 1, no. 1, pp. 2–22.

Coltrane, S. (1996) *Family Man: Fatherhood, Housework and Gender Equity*, Oxford University Press, New York.

Connell, R.W. (1982) 'Men and Socialism', *Labour Essays 1982*, eds G. Evans and J. Reeves, Drummond, Melbourne.

—— (1987) *Gender and Power: Society, the Person and Sexual Politics*, Polity Press, Cambridge

—— (1995) *Masculinities*, Allen & Unwin, Sydney.

Considine, M. (1988) 'The costs of increased control: Corporate management and Australian community organisations', *Australian Social Work*, vol. 41, no. 7, September, pp. 17–25.

—— (1992) 'Alternatives to hierarchy: The role and performance of lateral structures inside bureaucracy', *Australian Journal of Public Administration*, vol. 51, no. 3, pp. 309–20.

Coombs, H. C. (1978) 'A decade of progress?', *Kulinma: Listening to Aboriginal Australians*, ANU Press, Canberra.

Coppock, V. and Hopton, J. (2000) *Critical Perspectives on Mental Health*, Routledge, London.

Corrigan P. and Leonard, P. (1978) *Social Work Practice Under Capitalism: A Marxist Approach*, Macmillan, London.

Costello, S. (1997) What About the Women? The Views of Women Whose Partners Attend Groups for Violent Men. Unpublished Master of Social Policy thesis, RMIT University, Melbourne.

Cousins, C. (1987) *Controlling Social Welfare*, Wheatsheaf, Sussex.

Cowburn, M. and Pengell, H. (1999) 'Values and processes in groupwork with men', *Working With Men For Change*, ed. J. Wild, UCL Press, London.

Cox, D. (1987) *Migration and Welfare: An Australian Perspective*, Prentice Hall, Sydney.

—— (1989) *Welfare Practice in a Multicultural Society*, Prentice Hall, Sydney.

Cox, M. (1994) *Good Practices in Women's Mental Health*, Healthsharing Women, Melbourne.

Cracknell, R. (2000) *Journey From Venice: A Memoir*, Viking, Melbourne.

Crawford, F. (1997) 'No continuing city: A postmodern story of social work', *Australian Social Work*, vol. 50, no. 1, pp. 23-30.

Cree, V. (2001) 'Men and masculinities in social work education', *Men and Social Work: Theories and Practice*, ed. A. Christie, Palgrave, London.

Crush, J. ed. (1995) *Power of Development*, Routledge, London.

Cullen, Y. (n.d.) An Alternative Tradition in Social Work: Bertha Capen Reynolds 1885-1978. Unpublished paper, University of Sydney.

Cuneen, C. (1997) 'Address to SNAICC', *Proceedings of Second Aboriginal and Torres Strait Islander Child Survival Conference*, Townsville, June.

D'Souza, N. (1993) 'Aboriginal child welfare: Framework for a national policy', *Family Matters*, no. 35, pp. 40-5.

—— (1994) 'The Secretariat of the National Aboriginal and Islander Child Care', *Aboriginal and Islander Health Worker Journal*, vol. 18, no. 1, p. 18.

Dale, R. (1989/90) 'The Thatcherite project in education', *Critical Social Policy*, vol. 27, pp. 4-19.

Dalrymple, J. and Burke, B. (1995) *Anti-Oppressive Practice: Social Care and the Law*, Open University Press, Buckingham.

Damousi, J. (2000) 'The politics of grief', *The Age*, 25 November, p. 9.

Davies, B. (1990) 'Agency as a form of discursive practice', *British Journal of Sociology of Education*, vol. 11, no. 3, pp. 341-61.

Davies, B. (1993) *Shards of Glass*, Allen & Unwin, Sydney.

Davies, B. and Harré, R. (1990) 'Positioning: The discursive production of selves', *Journal for the Theory of Social Behaviour*, vol. 20, no. 1, pp. 43-63.

Davis, C. (2001) 'The tormented and the transformed: Understanding responses to loss and trauma', *Meaning Reconstruction and the Experience of Loss*, ed. R. Neimeyer, American Psychological Association, Washington DC.

Davis, L. ed. (1994) *Building on Women's Strengths: A Social Work Agenda for the Twenty-first Century*, Haworth Press, New York.

de Jong, P. and Berg, I. (2002) *Interviewing for Solutions*, 2nd edn, Wadsworth, Pacific Grove.

de Maria, W. (1993a) 'Critical pedagogy and the forgotten social work student: The return of radical practice', *Australian Social Work*, vol. 46, no. 1, pp. 9-21.

—— (1993b) 'Exploring radical social work teaching in Australia', *Journal of Progressive Human Services*, vol. 4, no. 2, pp. 45-63.

—— (1997) 'Flapping on clipped wings: Social work ethics in an age of activism', *Australian Social Work*, vol. 50, no. 4, pp. 3-19.

de Montigny, G. (1995) *Social Working: An Ethnography of Front-Line Practice*, University of Toronto Press, Toronto.

de Shazer, S. (1985) *Keys to Solutions in Brief Therapy*, Norton, New York.

Deetz, S. (1992) *Democracy in an Age of Corporate Colonization*, State University of New York Press, New York.

Dempsey, K. (1997) *Inequalities in Marriage: Australia and Beyond*, Oxford University Press, Melbourne.

Denborough, D. (1996) *Beyond the Prison: Gathering Dreams of Freedom*, Dulwich Centre Press, Adelaide.

Dennis, J. (1995) 'Local indigenous rights in a global environment', *Forum*, no. 4, Centre for Citizenship and Human Rights, Deakin University, Geelong, pp. 9-10.

Department of Community Services (2001) *Stronger Families and Communities Strategy*, Department of Family and Community Services, AGPS, Canberra.

Devore, W. and Schlesinger, E. G. (1996) *Ethnic-Sensitive Social Work Practice*, Allyn & Bacon, Needham Heights.

Dienhart, A. (1998) *Reshaping Fatherhood: The Social Construction of Shared Parenting*, Sage, Thousand Oaks, CA.

Dixon, J. (1993) 'Feminist community work's ambivalence with politics', *Australian Social Work*, vol. 46, no. 1, pp. 37-44.

Dodds, S. (1998) 'Citizenship, justice and group-specific rights: Citizenship and Indigenous Australians', *Citizenship Studies*, vol. 2, no. 1, pp. 105-19.

Dodson, M. (1996) 'First fleets and citizenship', *Citizenship in Australia: Democracy, Law and Society*, ed. S.R. Davis, Constitutional Confederacy Foundation, Melbourne.

—— (1997) in *Bringing Them Home* (video), HREOC, Sydney.

Doka, K. (1995) 'Recognising hidden sorrow: Disenfranchised grief', *The Path Ahead: Readings in Death and Dying*, eds L. DeSpelder and A. Strickland, Mayfield, Mountain View, CA.

—— (1999) 'Disenfranchised grief', *Bereavement Care*, vol. 18, no. 3, pp. 37-9.

Doka, K. and Martin, T. (1998) 'Masculine responses to loss: Clinical implications', *Journal of Family Studies*, vol. 4, no. 2, pp. 143-58.

Dominelli, L. (1988) *Anti-Racist Social Work: A Challenge for White Practitioners and Educators*, Macmillan, Hampshire.

—— (1990) *Women and Community Action*, Venture Press, Birmingham.

—— (1996) 'Deprofessionalizing social work: Anti-oppressive practice, competencies and postmodernism', *British Journal of Social Work*, vol. 26, no. 2, pp. 153–75.

—— (1997) *Sociology for Social Work*, Macmillan, Basingstoke.

—— (1998) 'Anti-oppressive practice in context', *Social Work: Themes, Issues and Critical Debates*, eds R. Adams, L. Dominelli and M. Payne, Macmillan, London.

—— (1999) 'Working with men from a feminist perspective', *Working With Men For Change*, ed. J. Wild, UCL Press, London.

Dominelli, L. and McLeod E. (1989) *Feminist Social Work*, Macmillan, London.

Douglas, P. (1993) Men = Violence: A Profeminist Perspective on Dis- mantling the Masculine Equation. Paper presented at the Second National Conference on Violence, Canberra, Australian Institute of Criminology.

Dowrick, C. (1983) 'Strange meeting: Marxism, psychoanalysis and social work', *British Journal of Social Work*, vol. 13, pp. 1–18.

Drewery, W. and Winslade, J. (1997) 'The theoretical story of narrative therapy', *The Archeology of Hope*, eds G. Monk, J. Winslade, K. Crocket and D. Epston, Jossey-Bass, San Francisco.

Drover, G. and Kerans, P. eds (1993) *New Approaches to Welfare Theory*, Edward Elgar, Aldershot.

Drugs and Crime Prevention Committee (2001) *Inquiry into Public Drunkenness: Final Report*, Parliament of Victoria, Melbourne.

Du Gay, P. (1996) *Consumption and Identity at Work*, Sage, London.

Dulwich Centre Newsletter (1990) 'Social Justice and Family Therapy', *Dulwich Centre Newsletter*, no. 1, Dulwich Centre Publications, Adelaide.

Easteal, P. (1992) 'Women and crime: Imprisonment issues', *Trends and Issues in Crime and Criminal Justice*, vol. 35, Australian Institute of Criminology, Canberra.

Edgar, D. (1998) 'Reclaiming care for men: Family and work futures', *National Forum on Men and Family Relationships*, Commonwealth Department of Family and Community Services, Canberra.

—— (2000) 'Families and the social reconstruction of marriage and parenthood in Australia', *Issues Facing Australian Families*, 3rd edn, eds W. Weeks and M. Quinn, Pearson Education Australia, Sydney.

Edley, N. and Wetherell, M. (1995) *Men in Perspective: Power, Practice and Identity*, Prentice Hall, London.

Edwards, C. and Read, P. (1992) *The Lost Children*, Doubleday, Sydney.

Eisler, R. (1987) *The Chalice and the Blade*, Harper & Row, San Francisco.

—— (1996) *Sacred Pleasure*, Doubleday, New York.

Eisler, R. and Loye, D. (1990) *The Partnership Way*, Harper, San Francisco.

Elliott, B., Mulroney, L. and O'Neil, D. (2000) *Promoting Family Change: The Optimism Factor*, Allen & Unwin, Sydney.

Ely, P. and Denny, D. (1987) *Social Work in a Multi-Racial Society*, Gower Publishing, Aldershot.

Epstein, M. and Wadsworth, Y. (1994) *Understanding and Involvement: Consumer Evaluation of an Acute Psychiatric Hospital; A Project's Beginnings*, Victorian Mental Illness Awareness Council, Brunswick, Victoria, February.

Escobar, A. (1995) *Encountering Development*, Princeton University Press, Princeton.

Ettore, E. and Riska, E. (1993) 'Psychotropics, sociology and women', *Sociology of Health and Illness*, vol. 15, pp. 503–24.

Fabricant, M. and Burghardt, S. (1992) *The Welfare State Crisis and the Transformation of Social Service Work*, M. E. Sharpe, Armonk, New York.

Fanon, F. (1978) *The Wretched of the Earth*, Penguin, Middlesex.

Fawcett, B., Featherstone, B., Fook, J. and Rossiter, A. eds (2000) *Practice and Research in Social Work*, Routledge, London.

Fay, B. (1987) *Critical Social Science*, Polity Press in association with Basil Blackwell, Oxford.

Federal Race Discrimination Commissioner (1995) *Alcohol Report*, AGPS, Canberra.

Fernando, S. (1991) *Mental Health, Race and Culture*, Macmillan, London.

Fine, M. and Turner, J. (1991) 'Tyranny and freedom: Looking at ideas in the practice of family therapy', *Family Process*, vol. 30, no. 3, September, p. 317.

Fine, M. (1997) 'Witnessing Whiteness', *Off White: Readings on Race, Power and Society*, Fine, M., Weis, L., Powel, C. and Won L. Mun, Routledge, New York.

Fisher, R. and Karger, H. (1997) *Social Work and Community in a Private World*, Longman, New York.

FitzRoy, L. (1999) 'Offending mothers: theorising in a feminist minefield', *Transforming Social Work Practice: Postmodern Critical Perspectives*, eds B. Pease and J. Fook, Routledge, London.

Flax, J. (1990) *Thinking Fragments: Psychoanalysis, Feminism and Postmodernism in the Contemporary West*, University of California Press, Berkeley.

—— (1993) *Disputed Subjects: Psychoanalysis, Politics and Philosophy*, Routledge, London.

Fletcher, R. (1997) *Australian Men and Boys: A Picture of Health?*, University of Newcastle, NSW.

Flynn, S. (1986) 'Issues for Aboriginal men', *Linking Men's Services*, Noarlunga Health Services, Adelaide.

Fook, J. (1993) *Radical Casework: A Theory of Practice*, Allen & Unwin, Sydney.

—— (1999) 'Critical reflectivity in education and practice', *Transforming Social Work Practice*, eds B. Pease and J. Fook, Allen & Unwin, Sydney.

—— (2000a) 'Deconstructing and reconstructing professional expertise', *Practice and Research in Social Work*, eds B. Fawcett, B. Featherstone, J. Fook and A. Rossiter, Routledge, London.

—— (2000b) 'Critical perspectives on social work practice', *Contemporary Perspectives on Social Work and the Human Services: Challenges and Change*, eds I. O'Connor, P. Smyth and J. Warburton, Pearson Education Australia, Sydney.

Foote, C. and Frank, A. (2000) 'Foucault and therapy: the disciplining of grief', *Reading Foucault for Social Work*, eds A. Chambon, A. Irving and L. Epstein, Columbia University Press, New York.

Foucault, M. (1967) *Madness and Civilisation: A History of Insanity in the Age of Reason*, Tavistock, London.

—— (1969) *The Archaeology of Knowledge*, Tavistock, London.

—— (1977) *Discipline and Punish: The Birth of the Prison*, Allen Lane, London.

—— (1978) *The History of Sexuality, Volume 1: An Introduction*, tr. R. Hurley, Penguin, London.

—— (1980) *Power/Knowledge: Selected Interviews and Other Writings 1972-1977*, ed. C. Gordon, Pantheon, New York.

Fox, D. and Prilleltensky, I. (1997) 'Introducing critical psychology: Values, assumptions and the status quo', *Critical Psychology: An Introduction*, eds D. Fox and I. Prilleltensky, Sage, London.

Frankenberg, R. (1993) *White Women, Race Matters: The Social Construction of Whiteness*, Routledge, London.

Fraser, N. (1989) *Unruly Practices: Power, Discourse and Gender in Contemporary Social Theory*, University of Minnesota Press, Minneapolis.

—— (1991) 'The uses and abuses of French discourse theory for feminist politics', *Critical Theory Now*, ed. P. Wexler, Falmer, London.

Fraser, N. and Nicholson, L. (1990) 'Social criticism without philosophy: An encounter between feminism and postmodernism', *Feminism/Postmodernism*, ed. L. Nicholson, Routledge, New York.

Fredericks, B. (1995) 'Recreating the circle with We Al-Li: A program for sharing and regeneration', *Aboriginal and Islander Health Worker Journal*, vol. 19, no. 2, pp. 22-3.

Freedman, L. (1989) The Pursuit of Aboriginal Control of Child Welfare. Unpublished Master of Social Work thesis, University of Melbourne, 1989.

Freedman, L. and Stark, L. (1995) 'When the white system doesn't work', *Issues Facing Australian Families: Human Services Respond*, 2nd edn, eds W. Weeks and J. Wilson, Longman Australia, Melbourne.

Freire, P. (1972) *Pedagogy of the Oppressed*, Penguin, Harmondsworth.

Freire, P. and Faundez, A. (1990) *Learning to Question: A Pedagogy of Liberation*, WCC Publications, Geneva.

Fromm, E. (1971) *The Crisis of Psychoanalysis*, Jonathan Cape, London.

Frow, J. (1998) 'A politics of stolen time', *Meanjin*, vol. 57, no. 2, pp. 351–67.

Fukuyama, M. and Sevig, T. (1999) *Integrating Spirituality into Multicultural Counseling*, Sage, Thousand Oaks, CA.

Funk, E. (1993) *Stopping Rape: A Challenge for Men*, New Society Publishers, Philadelphia.

Furlong, M. (2001) 'Neither colluding nor colliding: Practical ideas for engaging men', *Working with Men in the Human Services,* eds B. Pease and P. Camilleri, Allen & Unwin, Sydney.

Gale, F. (1973) *Urban Aborigines*, ANU Press, Canberra.

Galper, J. (1975) *The Politics of Social Services*, Prentice Hall, Englewood Cliffs, New Jersey.

Gatens, M. (1992) 'Power, bodies and difference', *Destabilising Theory: Contemporary Feminist Debates*, eds M. Barrett and A. Phillips, Stanford University Press, Stanford.

Gee, T. (2001) 'The grieving process in separation and divorce', *Grief Matters*, vol. 4, no. 1, pp. 6–9.

Geertz, C. (1973) *The Interpretation of Cultures*, Basic Books, New York.

—— (1995) *After the Fact: Two Countries, Four Decades, One Anthropologist*, Harvard University Press, Cambridge, Mass.

Genugten, W. and Perez-Bustillo, C. (2001) *The Poverty of Rights: Human Rights and the Eradication of Poverty*, United Nations Document E/CN.4/1995/101:19, Zed Books, London.

Germain, C. and Gitterman, A. (1980) *The Life Model of Social Work Practice*, Columbia University Press, New York.

Gerrand, V. (1993) *The Patient Majority: Mental Health Policy and Services for Women*, Centre for Applied Social Research, Deakin University, Geelong.

Giddens, A. (1984) *The Constitution of Society*, University of California Press, Berkeley.

Gil, D. (1998) *Confronting Injustice and Oppression: Concepts and Strategies for Social Workers*, Columbia University Press, New York.

Gilbert, S. (2001) 'Social work with Indigenous Australians', *Social Work: Fields of Practice*, eds M. Alston and J. McKinnon, Oxford University Press, Melbourne.

Gilding, M. (1997) *Australian Families: A Comparative Perspective*, Longman, Melbourne.

Gilley, T. (1990) *Empowering Poor People*, Brotherhood of St Laurence, Melbourne.

—— (1995) *Responding to Service Users*, Brotherhood of St Laurence, Melbourne.

Ginsburg, N. (1979) *Class, Capital and Social Policy: Critical Texts in Social Work and the Welfare State*, Macmillan, London.

Giroux, H. (1990) *Curriculum Discourse as Postmodernist Practice*, Deakin University Press, Geelong, Victoria.

Goffman, E. (1961) *Asylums*, Pelican, Harmondsworth.

Golden, T. (1997) *Swallowed by a Snake: The Gift of the Masculine Side of Healing*, Golden Healing, USA.

—— (1999) Masculine Grief. Seminar presentation, Melbourne, 5 July.

Golding, R. (1982) 'Freud, psychoanalysis and sociology: Some observations on the sociological analysis of the individual', *British Journal of Sociology*, vol 33, no. 4, pp. 545-62.

Gondolf, E. (1987) 'Changing men who batter: A developmental model for integrated interventions', *Journal of Family Violence*, vol. 2, no. 4, pp. 335-49.

Goodnow, J. and Bowles, J. (1994) *Men, Women and Household Work*, Oxford University Press, Melbourne.

Gorman, J. (1993) 'Postmodernism and the conduct of inquiry in social work', *Affilia*, vol. 8, no. 3, pp. 247-64.

Gould, K. (1987) 'Life model versus conflict model: A feminist perspective', *Social Work*, May-June, pp. 346-51.

Green, R. (1999a) 'Human behaviour theory, person-in-environment and social work method', *Human Behaviour Theory and Social Work Practice*, ed. R. Greene, Aldine De Gruyter, New York.

—— (1999b) 'Human behaviour theory and professional social work practice', *Human Behaviour Theory and Social Work Practice*, ed. R. Greene, Aldine De Gruyter, New York.

—— (1999c) 'General systems theory', *Human Behaviour Theory and Social Work Practice*, ed. R. Greene, Aldine De Gruyter, New York.

Griffin, G. (2000) 'Defining Australian death: Religion and the state', *Death and Dying in Australia*, ed. A. Kellehear, Oxford University Press, Melbourne.

Grimshaw, P., Lake, M., McGrath, A. and Quartly, M. (1994) *Creating a Nation*, McPhee Gribble, Melbourne.

Grosz, E. (1994) *Volatile Bodies: Towards a Corporeal Feminism*, Allen & Unwin, Sydney.

Gunzburg, J. and Stewart, W. (1994) *The Grief Counselling Handbook: A Student's Guide to Unresolved Grief*, Chapman & Hall, London.

Gupta, L. (1999) 'Bereavement recovery following the Rwandan genocide', *Bereavement Care*, vol. 18, no. 3, pp. 40–2.

Gutiérrez, L., Parsons, R. and Cox, E. (1998) *Empowerment in Social Work Practice: A Sourcebook*, Brooks/Cole, Pacific Grove, CA.

Hage, G. (1998) *White Nation: Fantasies of White Supremacy in a Multicultural Society*, Pluto Press, Sydney.

Hagman, G. (2001) 'Beyond decathexis: Toward a new psychoanalytic understanding and treatment of mourning', *Meaning Reconstruction and the Experience of Loss*, ed. R. Neimeyer, American Psychological Association, Washington DC.

Hancock, P. and Taylor, M. (2001) *Work, Postmodernism and Organization: A Critical Introduction*, Sage, London.

Hanmer, J. and Statham, D. (1988) *Women and Social Work: Towards a Woman-Centred Practice*, Macmillan, London.

Harris, J. (1994) *One Blood: 200 years of Aboriginal Encounter with Christianity, a Story of Hope*, 2nd edn, Albatross Books, Sydney.

Hartley, R. ed. (1995) *Families and Cultural Diversity in Australia*, Allen & Unwin, Sydney.

Hartman, A. (1992) 'In search of subjugated knowledge', *Social Work*, vol. 37, no. 6, pp. 483–4.

Harvey, J. (2000) *Give Sorrow Words: Perspectives on Loss and Trauma*, Brunner/Mazel, Philadelphia.

Hayes, G. (1996) 'The psychology of everyday life', *Psychology and Society: Radical Theory and Practice*, eds I. Parker and R. Spears, Pluto Press, London.

Haynes, K. (1998) 'The one-hundred year debate: Social reform versus individual treatment', *Social Work*, vol. 53, no. 6, pp. 501–8.

Hayward, R. (2000) Needed: A New Model of Masculinity to Stop Violence Against Women and Girls. Paper presented at WHO Global Symposium on Violence and Health, Kobe, Japan.

Healy, K. (1999) 'Power and activist social work', *Transforming Social Work Practice*, eds B. Pease and J. Fook, Allen & Unwin, Sydney.

—— (2000) *Social Work Practices: Contemporary Perspectives on Change*, Sage, London.

—— (2001) 'Reinventing critical social work: Challenges from practice, context and postmodernism', *Critical Social Work*, vol. 2, no. 1, <http://www.criticalsocialwork.com/CSW_2001_1.html> [accessed 23 August 2001].

Healy, K., Foley, D. and Walsh, K. (2001) 'Families affected by the imprisonment of a parent', *Children Australia*, vol. 26, no.1, pp. 12-19.

Hearn, J. (1996) 'Is masculinity dead? A critique of the concept of masculinity/masculinities', *Understanding Masculinities*, ed. M. Mac an Ghaill, Open University Press, Buckingham.

—— (1998) 'The welfare of men?' *Men, Gender Divisions and Welfare* eds J. Popay, J. Hearn and J. Edwards, Routledge, London.

—— (2001) 'Men, social work and men's violence towards women', *Men and Social Work: Theories and Practice*, ed. A. Christie, Palgrave, London.

Hekman, S. (1999) *The Future of Differences: Truth and Method in Feminist Theory*, Polity Press, Cambridge.

Held, D. (1980) *Introduction to Critical Theory: Horkheimer to Habermas*, Hutchinson, London.

Henning, T. (1995) 'Psychological explanations in sentencing women in Tasmania', *Australian and New Zealand Journal of Criminology*, vol. 28, no. 3, pp. 298-322.

Herberg, D.C. (1993) *Frameworks for Cultural and Racial Diversity: Teaching and Learning for Practitioners*, Canadian Scholars Press, Toronto.

Hester, M. (1984) 'Anti-sexist men: A case of cloak and dagger chauvinism', *Women's Studies International Forum*, vol. 17, no. 1, pp. 33-7.

Hite, S. (1987) *Women and Love*, Penguin, London.

Hochschild, A. (1989) *The Second Shift: Working Parents and the Revolution at Home*, Platkus, London.

Hocking, B. J. and Hocking, B. A. (1998) 'A comparative view of Indigenous citizenship issues', *Citizenship Studies*, vol. 2, no. 1, pp. 121-31.

Hollingsworth, D. (1997) 'The work of anti-racism', *The Resurgence of Racism: Howard, Hanson and the Race Debate*, eds G. Gray and C. Winter, Monash Publications in History, Melbourne.

Hollis, F. (1964) *Casework: A Psychosocial Therapy*, Random House, New York.

Holst-Warhaft, G. (2000) *The Cue For Passion: Grief and Its Political Uses*, Harvard University Press, Cambridge.

Hood, M. (2001) 'Men and child protection: Developing new kinds of relationships between men and children', *Working with Men in the Human Services*, eds B. Pease and P. Camilleri, Allen & Unwin, Sydney.

hooks, b. (1984) *Feminist Theory: From Margin to Centre,* South End Press, Boston.

—— (2000) *All About Love: New Visions*, William Morrow & Company, New York.

Horne, D. (1964) *The Lucky Country*, Penguin Books, Melbourne.

Hough, G. (1994) The Re-direction of State Welfare: A Case Study of the Labour Process in Child Protection in Victoria. Unpublished PhD thesis, La Trobe University, Melbourne.

—— (1996) 'Information technology in the human services: Whose dreams, whose realities?', *Dreams and Realities*, Papers from the HUSITA 4 Conference, ed. B. Glastonbury, National Research and Development Centre for Welfare and Health, Helsinki, pp. 161–73.

House, Y. and Stalwick, H. (1990) 'Social work and the First Nation movement: "Our children, our culture"', *Social Work and Social Change in Canada*, ed. B. Wharf, McClelland & Stewart, Toronto.

Howard, J. (2001) *Mothers and Sons: Bringing up Boys as a Sole Parent*, Lothian, Melbourne

Howarth, G. (2000) 'Australian funerals', *Death and Dying in Australia*, ed. A. Kellehear, Oxford University Press, Melbourne.

Howe, D. (1986) *Social Workers and Their Practice in Welfare Bureaucracies*, Aldershot, Gower, United Kingdom.

—— (1987) *An Introduction to Social Work Theory*, Aldershot, Gower.

—— (1993) *On Being a Client: Understanding the Process of Counselling and Psychotherapy*, Sage, London.

—— (1994) 'Postmodernity and social work', *British Journal of Social Work*, vol. 24, pp. 513–32.

Howson, R., Graham, T., Hall, R. and Jenkins, A. (1994) Certificate in Narrative Therapy for Aboriginal People. A project of the Social Health and Counselling Team of the Aboriginal Community Recreation and Health Services Centre of SA Inc.

Hull, C. (2001) 'Lynne's story', *Loss and Grief: Our Stories*, ed. G. McLean, Rose Education, Narellan NSW.

Human Rights and Equal Opportunity Commission (HREOC) (1997) *Bringing Them Home: Report of the National Inquiry into the Separation of Aboriginal and Islander Children from their Families*, HREOC, Sydney.

Human Rights and Equal Opportunity Commission and Australian Law Reform Commission (1996) *Speaking for Ourselves: Children and the Legal Process*, Issues paper 18, AGPS, Canberra.

Ife, J. (1995a) *Community Development*, Longman, Melbourne.

—— (1995b) Paradigms Lost: The Disjunction Between Analysis and Practice. Paper presented at the AASW National Conference, Launceston, July.

—— (1997) *Rethinking Social Work: Towards Critical Practice*, Longman, Melbourne.

—— (1999) 'Postmodernism, critical theory and social work', *Transforming Social Work Practice*, eds B. Pease and J. Fook, Allen & Unwin, Sydney.

—— (2001) *Human Rights and Social Work: Towards Rights-Based Practice*, Cambridge University Press, Cambridge.

Ingamells, A. (1994) 'Practice and the post modern', *Advances in Social Work and Welfare Education*, University of Western Australia, Perth.

Ingersoll, V. and Adams, G. (1986) 'Beyond organizational boundaries: Exploring the managerial metamyth', *Administration and Society*, no.18, pp. 360-81.

Ingleby, D. (1987) 'Psychoanalysis and ideology', *Critical Theories of Psychological Development*, ed. J. Boughton, Plenum Press, New York.

Ingram-Fogel, C. (1991) 'Health problems and needs of incarcerated women', *Journal of Prison and Jail Health*, vol. 10, no. 1, pp. 43-57.

International Federation of Social Work (2000) *International Policy on Women*, IFSW, Berne, Switzerland.

Jackson, D. (1990) *Unmasking Masculinity: A Critical Autobiography*, Unwin & Hyman, London.

Jackson, S. (2001) 'Working more and enjoying it less: "No logo" and family therapy', *Victorian Association of Family Therapists VAFT News*, vol. 23, no. 5, pp. 29-35.

Janmohamed, A. (1994) 'Some implication of Paulo Freire's border pedagogy', *Between Borders: Pedagogy and the Politics of Cultural Studies*, eds H. Giroux and P. McLaren, Routledge, New York.

Jessup, H. and Rogerson, S. (1999) 'Postmodernism and the teaching and practice of interpersonal skills', *Transforming Social Work Practice*, eds B. Pease and J. Fook, Allen & Unwin, Sydney.

Jones, A. and May, J. (1992) *Working in Human Service Organisations: A Critical Introduction*, Longman, Melbourne.

Jones, C. and Novak, T. (1993) 'Social work today', *British Journal of Social Work*, vol. 23, no. 3, pp. 195-212.

Jonker, G. (1997) 'Death, gender and memory: Remembering loss and burial as a migrant', *Death, Gender and Ethnicity*, eds D. Field, J. Hockey and N. Small, Routledge, London.

Jordan, B. (1988) 'Poverty, social work and the state', *Public Issues, Private Pain: Poverty, Social Work and Social Policy*, eds S. Becker and S. McPherson, Insight, London.

—— (1990) *Social Work in an Unjust Society*, Harvester Wheatsheaf, Hemel Hampstead.

—— (1997) 'Partnership with service users in child protection and family support', *Child Protection and Family Support: Tensions, Contradictions and Possibilities*, ed. N. Parton, Routledge, London.

Jordan, B. (with Jordan, C.) (2000) *Social Work and the Third Way: Tough Love and Social Policy*, Sage, London.

Jordan, B. and Parton, N. (1983) 'Introduction', *The Political Dimensions of Social Work*, eds B. Jordan and N. Parton, Basil Blackwell, Oxford.

Jordan, K., Schlenger, W., Fairbank, J. and Caddell, J. (1996) 'Prevalence of psychiatric disorders among incarcerated women', *Archives of General Psychiatry*, vol 53, pp. 513-19.

Jouve, E. (1979) 'The ideology of human rights', *Ecumenical Institute for the Development of Peoples Trilateral Commission*, National Security, Human Rights INDEP, Paris, pp. 83–92.

Joy, M. (2001) 'Shame on who? Consulting with children who have experienced sexual abuse', *Once Upon a Time . . . Narrative Therapies with Children and Their Families*, ed. A. Morgan, Dulwich Centre Publications, Adelaide.

Kagawa-Singer, M. (1998) 'The cultural context of death rituals and mourning practices', *Oncology Nursing Forum*, vol. 25, pp. 1752–6.

Kasiya, H. (1996) 'Recultivating community: an interview with Howard Kasiya', *Dulwich Centre Newsletter*, no. 3, pp. 17–22.

Katz, J. (1978) *White Awareness*, University of Oklahoma Press, Oklahoma.

Kaufman, M. (1993) *Cracking the Armour: Power, Pain and the Lives of Men*, Viking, Toronto.

Kellehear, A. ed. (2000a) *Death and Dying in Australia*, Oxford University Press, Melbourne.

—— (2000b) 'The Australian way of death: formative historical and social influences', *Death and Dying in Australia*, ed. A. Kellehear, Oxford University Press, Melbourne.

Khisty, K. (2001) 'Transcultural differentiation: A model for therapy with ethno-culturally diverse families', *Australian and New Zealand Journal of Family Therapy*, vol. 22, no. 1, pp. 17–24.

Kilby, P. (1994) 'Human Rights and participatory development: Stemming the rise of the "new anarchy"', *Development Bulletin*, vol. 32, October, pp. 20–2.

Kimmel, M. (2000) *The Gendered Society*, Oxford University Press, New York.

Kinsman, G. (1987) 'Men loving men: The challenge of gay liberation', *Beyond Patriarchy*, ed. M. Kaufman, Oxford University Press, Toronto.

Klass, D. and Walter, T. (2001) 'Processes of grieving: how bonds are continued', *Handbook of Bereavement Research: Consequences, Coping, and Care*, eds M. Stroebe, R. Hansson, W. Stroebe and H. Schut, American Psychological Association, Washington DC.

Klass, D., Silverman, P., and Nickman, S. eds (1996) *Continuing Bonds: New Understandings of Grief*, Taylor & Francis, Philadelphia.

Klein, E., Campbell, J., Soler, E. and Ghez, M. (1997) *Ending Domestic Violence: Changing Public Perceptions/Halting the Epidemic*, Sage, Thousand Oaks, CA.

Kondrat, M. (1999) 'Who is the "self" in self-aware: Professional self-awareness from a critical theory perspective', *Social Service Review,* December, pp. 451–78.

Korten, D. (1990) *Getting to the 21st Century*, Kumarian Press, West Hartford.

—— (1995) *When Corporations Rule the World*, Kumarian Press, West Hartford.

Kostecki, K. (2000) Policy Activism in the Field Against Sexual Assault in Victoria during the 1990s. Unpublished Master of Social Work thesis, University of Melbourne, Melbourne.

Kovel, J. (1977) *A Complete Guide to Therapy*, Penguin, New York.

—— (1991) *History and Spirit: An Inquiry into the Philosophy of Liberation*, Beacon Press, Boston.

Kübler-Ross, E. (1970) *On Death and Dying,* Tavistock, London.

Laing, R. D. (1961) *Self and Others*, Penguin, Harmondsworth.

—— (1965) *The Divided Self*, Penguin, Harmondsworth.

—— (1967) *The Politics of Experience and the Bird of Paradise*, Penguin, Harmondsworth.

La Nauze, H. and Rutherford, S. (1999) 'Women's work against violence: Community responses in a rural setting', *Challenging Rural Practice: Human Services in Australia*, eds L. Briskman and M. Lynn with H. La Nauze, Deakin University Press, Geelong.

Langan, M. (1985) 'The unitary approach: A feminist critique', *Women, the Family and Social Work*, eds E. Brook and A. Davis, Tavistock, London.

Latouche, S. (1993) *In the Wake of the Affluent Society*, Zed Books, London.

Law, I. (1994) 'A conversation with Kiwi Tamasase and Charles Waldegrave', *Dulwich Centre Newsletter*, no.1, pp. 20-7.

Lawrence, R. J. (1965) *Professional Social Work in Australia*, The Australian National University, Canberra.

Leach, M. (1993) 'Hard Yakkin', *XY: Men, Sex, Politics*, vol. 3, no. 3, pp. 14-17.

Lechner, F. and Boli, J. eds (2000) *The Globalization Reader*, Blackwell, Oxford.

Lecomte, R. (1990) 'Connecting private troubles and public issues in social work education', *Social Work and Social Change in Canada*, ed. B. Wharf, McLelland & Stuart, Toronto.

Lendrum, S. and Syme, G. (1992) *Gift of Tears: A Practical Approach to Loss and Bereavement Counselling*, Routledge, London.

Leonard, P. (1975) 'Towards a paradigm for radical practice', *Radical Social Work*, eds R. Bailey and M. Brake, Edward Arnold, London.

—— (1984) *Personality and Ideology: Towards a Materialist Understanding of the Individual*, Macmillan, London.

—— (1995) 'Postmodernism, socialism and social welfare', *Journal of Progressive Human Services*, vol. 6, no. 2, pp. 3-19.

—— (1997) *Postmodern Welfare: Reconstructing an Emancipatory Project*, Sage, London.

—— (2001) 'The future of critical social work in uncertain conditions', *Critical Social Work*, vol. 2, no. 1, <http://www.criticalsocialworkcom/CSW_2001_1.html> [accessed 23 August 2001].

Lerner, M. (1996) *The Politics of Meaning*, Addison-Wesley, Reading, MA.

—— (2000) *Spirit Matters*, Hampton Roads, Charlottesville, VA.

Lichtenberg, P. (1988) *Getting Equal: The Equalising Law of Relationship*, University Press of America, Lanham.

Liffman, M. (1978) *Power for the Poor: The Family Centre Project, an Experiment in Self-Help*, Allen & Unwin, Sydney.

Lipsky, M. (1978) 'The assault on human services: Street-level bureaucrats, accountability and the fiscal crisis', *Accountability in Urban Society: Public Agencies under Fire*, eds S. Greer, R. Hedlund and J. Gibson, Sage, Beverly Hills.

—— (1980) *Street Level Bureaucracy*, Russell Sage Foundation, New York.

Lisak, D. (1991) 'Sexual aggression, masculinity and fathers', *Signs: Journal of Women, Culture and Society*, vol. 16, no. 2, pp. 239–63.

Lister, R. (1997) *Citizenship: Feminist Perspectives*, Macmillan Press, London.

Little, G. (1999) *The Public Emotions: From Mourning to Hope*, ABC Books, Sydney.

Litwin, J. (1997) 'Child protection interventions with Indigenous communities: An "anthropological" perspective', *Australian Journal of Social Issues*, vol. 32, no. 4, pp. 317–40.

Locke, D.C. (1992) *Increasing Multi-Cultural Understanding: A Comprehensive Model*, Multi-Cultural Aspects of Counselling, Series 1, Sage, New York.

London-Edinburgh Weekend Return Group (1980) *In and Against the State*, Pluto Press, London.

Longres, J. and Bailey, R. (1979) 'Men's issues and sexism: A journal review', *Social Work*, January, pp. 26–32.

Macey, D. (2000) *The Penguin Dictionary of Critical Theory*, Penguin Books, London.

Macy, J. (1998) *Coming Back to Life: Practices to Reconnect Our Lives, Our World*, New Society Publishers, Gabriola Island, BC.

Maden, T., Swinton, M. and Gunn, J. (1994) 'Psychiatric disorder in women serving a prison sentence', *British Journal of Psychiatry*, vol. 164, pp. 44–54.

Manne, R. (1999) 'Stolen lives', *The Age Saturday Extra*, 27 February, p. 3.

Marchant, H. and Wearing, B. eds (1986) *Gender Reclaimed: Women in Social Work*, Hale & Iremonger, Sydney.

Marcuse, H. (1962) *Eros and Civilisation*, Vintage Books, New York.

Marris, P. (1996) *The Politics of Uncertainty: Attachment in Private and Public Life*, Routledge, London.

Martin, E. and Healy, J. (1993) 'Social work as women's work: Census data 1976–1986', *Australian Journal of Social Work*, vol. 46, no. 4, pp. 13–18.

Martin, J. (1999) *In-Patient Mental Health Program for Women: An Issues Paper*, Victorian Institute of Forensic Mental Health, Melbourne.

—— (2001) 'Social work direct practice with women prisoners', *Australian Social Work*, vol. 54, no. 2, pp. 37–47.

Martin, S. (2001) 'Grief and suffering: separation and divorce and the family court', *Grief Matters*, vol. 4, no. 1, pp. 10–12.

Mason, J. (2001) 'Social Work with Families', *Social Work: Fields of Practice*, eds M. Alston and J. McKinnon, Oxford University Press, South Melbourne.

Max-Neef, M., Elizalde, A. and Hopenhayn, M. (1991) *Human Scale Development: Conception, Application and Further Reflections*, The Apex Press, New York.

Mayo, M. (1977) *Women in the Community*, Routledge & Kegan Paul, London.

McBride, J. (1995) *War, Battering and Other Sports*, Humanities Press, New Jersey.

McCain, M. and Mustard, J. F. (1999) *Reversing the Real Brain Drain: Early Years Study Final Report*, Canadian Institute for Advanced Research, Toronto.

McCormack, J. (2001) 'How many social workers now? A review of census and other data', *Australian Social Work*, vol. 54, no. 3, pp. 63–72.

McDonald, C. and Jones, A. (2000) 'Reconstructing and reconceptualizing social work in the contemporary milieu', *Australian Social Work*, vol. 53, no. 3, pp. 3–11.

McDonald, H. (1998) What's in a Name? Definitions and Domestic Violence. Discussion Paper No. 1, Domestic Violence and Incest Resource Centre, Melbourne.

McDonald, P. (1994) 'What are the Issues?', *Family Matters*, no. 37, pp. 4–5.

McGoldrick, M. ed. (1998) *Re-Visioning Family Therapy: Race, Culture and Gender in Clinical Practice*, The Guildford Press, New York.

McGoldrick, M., Broken Nose, M. and Potenza, M. (1999) 'Violence and the family life cycle', *The Expanded Family Life Cycle: Individual, Family, and Social Perspectives*, 3rd edn, eds B. Carter and M. McGoldrick, Allyn & Bacon, Needham Heights.

McGuiness, M. and Wadsworth, Y. (1992) *Understanding Anytime: A Consumer Evaluation of an Acute Psychiatric Hospital*, Victorian Mental Illness Awareness Council, Melbourne.

McGurk, H. (1996) 'Child care in a caring society', *Family Matters*, no. 46, pp. 12–17.

McIntosh, P. (1998) 'White privilege: Unpacking the invisible knapsack', *Re-Visioning Family Therapy: Race, Culture and Gender in Clinical Practice*, ed. M. McGoldrick, The Guildford Press, New York.

McKendrick, J. and Thorpe, M. (1998) 'The legacy of colonisation: Trauma, loss and psychological distress amongst Aboriginal people', *Grief Matters*, September, pp. 4–8.

McLean, G. ed. (2001) *Loss and Grief: Our Stories*, Rose Education, Narellan NSW.

McLean, L. (1996) 'Forced removal of children: An Australian holocaust', *The Age*, 28 May, p. 4.

McLennan, G. (1994) 'Feminism, epistemology and postmodernism: Reflections on current ambivalence', *Sites 28*, Autumn, pp. 98–124.

McLeod, J. (2000) *Beginning Postcolonialism*, Manchester University Press, Manchester.

McMahon, A. (1993) Who'll come a Waltzing Matilda?: Developing an Australian Social Work. Paper presented at the Asian Pacific Association of Social Work Educators, Bombay, November.

—— (1999) *Taking Care of Men: Sexual Politics in the Public Mind*, Cambridge University Press, Melbourne.

McMahon, T. (1993) It's No Bed of Roses: Working in Child Welfare. Unpublished PhD thesis, University of Illinois at Urbana-Champaign.

McMaster, K. (2000) 'Working with male social work students', *Fieldwork in the Human Services*, eds L. Cooper and L. Briggs, Allen & Unwin, Sydney.

McNay, L. (2000) *Gender and Agency: Reconfiguring the Subject in Feminist and Social Theory*, Polity Press, Cambridge.

Meemeduma, P. (1994) 'Cross-cultural social work: New models of teaching for new practices', *Advances in Social Work Education*, AASWE, Melbourne, pp. 86–94.

Mendes, P. (2001) 'Getting tough on the war on drugs', *Arena Magazine*, no. 53, pp. 34–6.

Mental Health Act 1986, including amendments 1 July 1997, Victoria.

Mercia, K. and Julien, I. (1988) 'Race, sexual politics and black masculinity: A dossier', *Male Order: Unwrapping Masculinity*, eds R. Chapman and J. Rutherford, Lawrence & Wishart, London.

Messner, M. (1997) *Politics of Masculinities: Men in Movements*, Sage, Thousand Oaks, CA.

Mickler, S. (1998) *The Myth of Privilege*, Fremantle Arts Press, South Fremantle.

Middleman, R. and Goldberg, G. (1974) *Social Service Delivery: A Structural Approach to Social Work Practice*, Columbia University Press, New York.

Mies, M. and Shiva, V. (1993) *Ecofeminism*, Zed Books, London.

Miley, K., O'Melia, M. and DuBois, B. (1998) *Generalist Social Work Practice: An Empowering Approach,* 2nd edn, Allyn & Bacon, Needham Heights.

Miller, E. and Omarzu, J. (1998) 'New directions in loss research', *Perspectives on Loss: A Sourcebook*, ed. J. Harvey, Brunner/Mazel, Philadelphia.

REFERENCES

Miller, P. and Rose, N. (1990) 'Governing economic life', *Economy and Society*, vol. 19, no. 1, pp. 1–31.

Minajalku Aboriginal Corporation (1997) *Home Still Waiting*, Minajalku, Melbourne.

Mitchell, P. (2000) *Valuing Young Lives: Evaluation of the National Youth Suicide Prevention Strategy*, Australian Institute of Family Studies, Melbourne.

Monk, G., Winslade, J., Crocket, K. and Epston, D. (1997) *The Archaeology of Hope*, Jossey-Bass, San Francisco.

Moreau, M. (1977) A Structural Approach to Social Work. Unpublished paper, School of Social Work, Carleton University, Ottawa.

—— (1979) 'A structural approach to social work practice', *Canadian Journal of Social Work Education*, vol. 5, no. 1, pp. 78–94.

—— (1990) 'Empowerment through advocacy and consciousness raising: Implications of a structural approach to social work', *Journal of Sociology and Social Welfare*, vol. 17, no. 2, pp. 78–94.

Moreau, M. in collaboration with L. Leonard (1989) *Empowerment Through a Structural Approach to Social Work: A Report from Practice*, École de service sociale, Université de Montreal and Carleton University School of Social Work and Health and Welfare, Canada, Montreal and Ottawa, May.

Moreau, M., Frosst, S., Frayne, G., Hlywa, M., Leonard, L. and Rowell, M. (1993) *Empowerment II: Snapshots of the Structural Approach in Action*, Carleton University Press, Ottawa, September.

Moreton-Robinson, A. (2000) *Talkin' Up to the White Woman: Indigenous Women and Feminism*, University of Queensland Press, St Lucia.

Morgan, A. ed. (1999) *Once Upon a Time ... Narrative Therapies with Children and Their Families*, Dulwich Centre Publications, Adelaide.

Morgan, J. (2000) 'Boxes and remembering in the time of AIDS', *Dulwich Centre Journal*, no. 4, pp. 45–8.

Mullaly, R. (1993) *Structural Social Work: Ideology, Theory, and Practice*, McLelland & Stewart, Toronto.

—— (1997) *Structural Social Work: Ideology, Theory, and Practice*, 2nd edn, Oxford University Press, Toronto.

Mullaly, R. and Keating, E. (1991) 'Similarities, differences and dialectics of radical social work', *Journal of Progressive Human Services*, vol. 2, no. 2, pp. 49–78.

Mullender, A. and Ward, D. (1991) *Self-Directed Groupwork: Users Take Action for Empowerment*, Whiting & Birch, London.

Murkitt, I. (1991) *Social Selves: Theories of the Social Formation of Identity*, Sage, London.

Murphy, B. (1999) *Transforming Ourselves, Transforming the World*, Zed Books, London.

Murphy, P. (2001) 'Police review on domestic violence', *The Age*, 5 October, p. 3.

National Association of Services Against Sexual Violence (2001) *Cultural Diversity and Services Against Sexual Violence*, CASA House, Melbourne.

National Association of Services Against Sexual Violence, Hardiman, A. and Dean, C. (1998) *National Standards of Practice for Services Against Sexual Assault Manual*, CASA House, Melbourne.

Ndione, E. (1992) *Le Don et le Recours*, Enda Eds, Dakar.

—— ed. (1994) *Réinventer le Présent*, Enda Graf Sahel, Dakar.

Neimeyer, R. (2000) *Lessons of Loss: A Guide to Coping*, PsychoEducational Resources, Keystone Heights.

—— ed. (2001) *Meaning Reconstruction and the Experience of Loss*, American Psychological Association, Washington DC.

New South Wales Law Reform Commission (1997) *The Aboriginal Child Placement Principle*, Research Report 7, Sydney.

New, C. (1996) 'Man bad, woman good? Essentialisms and ecofeminisms', *New Left Review*, no. 216, March/April, pp. 79–94.

Nguyen, T. and Bowles, R. (1998) 'Counselling Vietnamese refugee survivors of trauma: points of entry for developing trust and rapport', *Australian Social Work*, vol. 51, no. 2, pp. 41–7.

Nicholson, A. (2001) 'Why our children need a new and powerful champion', *The Age*, 15 June, p. 15.

Nicholson, L. and Seidman, S. eds (1995) *Social Postmodernism: Beyond Identity Politics*, Cambridge University Press, Cambridge.

Nierenberg, J. (1987) 'Misogyny: Gay and straight', *New Men, New Minds*, ed. F. Abbott, Crossing Press, Freedom, CA.

Nightingale, D. and Neilands, T. (1997) 'Understanding and practising critical psychology', *Critical Psychology: An Introduction*, ed. D. Fox and I. Prilleltensky, Sage, London.

Noble, C. and Briskman, L. (1996) 'Social work ethics: The challenge to moral consensus', *New Zealand Social Work Review*, vol. 8, no. 3, pp. 2–8.

—— (2000) 'AASW code of ethics: The impact of progressive theory on moral and ethical assumptions', *Advances in Social Work and Welfare Education*, vol. 3, no. 1, pp. 89–103.

Norman, E. and Mancuso, A. (1980) *Women's Issues and Social Work Practice*, F. E. Peacock, Itasca, IL.

Nyland, J. (1998) 'Activists in the woodwork: Policy activism and the housing reform movement in New South Wales', *Activism and the Policy Process*, ed. A. Yeatman, Allen & Unwin, Sydney.

O'Brien, M. and Penna, S. (1998a) 'Oppositional postmodern theory and welfare analysis: Anti-oppressive practice in a postmodern frame', *Postmodernity and the Fragmentation of Welfare*, ed. J. Carter, Routledge, New York.

—— (1998b) *Theorising Welfare: Enlightenment and Modern Society*, Sage, London.

O'Connor, I., Wilson, J. and Setterlund, D. (1995) *Social Work and Welfare Practice*, 2nd edn, Addison Wesley Longman, Melbourne.

Offe, C. (1984) *Contradictions of the Welfare State*, Polity Press, Oxford.

Orme, J. (1998) 'Feminist Social Work', *Social Work: Themes, Issues and Critical Debates*, eds R. Adams, L. Dominelli, and M. Payne, Macmillan, London.

Orr, L. (1997) The Development of Services Against Sexual Assault in the State of Victoria 1970–1991. Unpublished Master of Arts Thesis, La Trobe University, Melbourne.

Pardeck, J., Murphey, J. and Sik Chung, W. (1994) 'Social work and postmodernism', *Social Work and Social Services Review*, vol. 5, no. 2, pp. 113–23.

Parker, S., Fook, J. and Pease, B. (1999) 'Empowerment: The modern social work concept *par excellence*', *Transforming Social Work Practice*, eds B. Pease and J. Fook, Allen & Unwin, Sydney.

Parkes, C. Murray (1996) *Bereavement: Studies of Grief in Adult Life*, 3rd edn, Routledge, New York.

Parsons, R., Gutierrez, L. and Cox, E. (1998) 'A Model for Empowerment Practice', *Empowerment in Social Work Practice: A Sourcebook*, eds L. Gutierrez, R. Parsons, E. Cox, Brooks/Cole, Pacific Grove, CA.

—— (1998) 'Traditional models and theories of grief', *Bereavement Care*, vol. 17, no. 2, pp. 21–3.

Parton, N. (1991) *Governing the Family: Child Care, Child Protection and the State*, Macmillan, London.

—— (1996) 'Social work, risk and "the blaming system"', *Social Theory, Social Change and Social Work*, ed. N. Parton, Routledge, London.

—— (1999) 'Reconfiguring child welfare practices: Risk, advanced liberalism, and the government of freedom', *Reading Foucault for Social Work*, eds A. Chambon, A. Irving and L. Epstein, Columbia University Press, New York.

Parton, N. and Marshall, W. (1998) 'Postmodernism and discourse approaches to social work', *Social Work: Themes, Issues and Critical Debates*, eds R. Adams, L. Dominelli and M. Payne, Macmillan, London.

Parton, N. and O'Byrne, P. (2000a) *Constructive Social Work: Towards a New Practice*, Macmillan, Houndmills.

—— (2000b) 'What do we mean by constructive social work', *Critical Social Work*, vol. 1, no. 2, <http://www.criticalsocialwork.com/CSW_2001_1.html> [accessed 23 August 2001].

Patton, P. (1995) 'Post-structuralism and the Mabo debate: Difference, society and justice', *Justice and Identity: Antipodean Practices*, eds M. Wilson and A. Yeatman, Allen & Unwin, Sydney.

Payne, M. (1997) *Modern Social Work Theory*, 2nd edn, Macmillan, London.

—— (1998) 'Social work theories and reflective practice', *Social Work: Themes, Issues and Critical Debates*, eds R. Adams, L. Dominelli and M. Payne, Macmillan, Houndmills, Hampshire.

Pease, B. (1991) 'Dialectical models versus ecological models in social work practice', *Proceedings of the 11th Pacific Regional Seminar on Social Work*, Hong Kong International Federation of Social Workers.

—— (1997) *Men and Sexual Politics: Towards a Profeminist Practice*, Dulwich Centre Publications, Adelaide.

—— (2000a) 'Beyond the father wound: Memory-work and the deconstruction of father-son relationships', *Australian and New Zealand Journal of Family Therapy*, vol. 21, no. 1, pp. 9-15.

—— (2000b) *Recreating Men: Postmodern Masculinity Politics*, Sage, London.

—— (2001) 'Theoretical issues and political dilemmas in working with men', *Working with Men in the Human Services*, eds B. Pease and P. Camilleri, Allen & Unwin, Sydney.

Pease, B. and Camilleri, P. eds (2001) *Working with Men in the Human Services*, Allen & Unwin, Sydney.

Pease, B. and Fook, J. eds (1999) *Transforming Social Work Practice: Postmodern Critical Perspectives*, Allen & Unwin, St Leonards, NSW.

Pemberton, A. and Locke, R. (1975) 'Knowledge, order and power in social work and social welfare', *Social Work: Radical Essays*, ed. H. Throssell, University of Queensland Press, St Lucia.

Peterson, N. and Sanders, W. eds (1998) *Citizenship and Indigenous Australians: Changing Conceptions and Possibilities*, Cambridge University Press, Melbourne.

Pettman, J. (1992) *Living in the Margins*, Allen & Unwin, Sydney.

Pheterson, G (1986) 'Alliances between women: Overcoming internalised oppression and internalised domination', *Signs: Journal of Women in Culture and Society*, vol. 12, no. 1, pp. 146-60.

Pithouse, A. (1987) *Social Work: The Social Organisation of an Invisible Trade*, Avebury, Aldershot.

Potter, J. and Wetterall, M. (1987) *Discourse and Social Psychology*, Sage, London.

Pozzuto, R. (2000) 'Notes on a possible critical social work', *Critical Social Work*, vol. 1, no. 1, <http://www.criticalsocialwork.com/CSW_2001_1.html> [accessed 23 August 2001].

Pringle, K. (1995) *Men, Masculinities and Welfare*, UCL Press, London.

—— (1998a) 'Current profeminist debates regarding men and social welfare: Some national and transnational perspectives', *British Journal of Social Work*, vol. 28, pp. 623–33.

—— (1998b) 'Men and child care: Policy and practice', *Men, Gender Divisions and Welfare*, eds J. Popay, J. Hearn and J. Edwards, Routledge, London.

—— (2001) 'Men in social work: The double edge', *Men and Social Work: Theories and Practice*, ed. A. Christie, Palgrave, London.

—— (1997) 'Men challenging gender oppression on social work programmes in higher education: A framework for action', *Social Work Education*, vol. 16, no. 4, pp. 55–69.

Probert, B. (2001) 'Grateful Slaves' or 'Self Made Women': A Matter of Choice or Policy?, Clare Burton Memorial Lecture, RMIT University, Melbourne, 2 August.

Pyke, K. (1996) 'Class-based masculinities: The interdependence of gender, class and interpersonal power', *Gender and Society*, vol. 10, no. 5, pp. 527–49.

Quadrelli, C. (1997) 'Women in prison', *Themis*, vol. 2, no. 2, pp. 15–22.

Rabin, C. (1996) *Equal Partners—Good Friends*, Routledge, New York.

Raeside, C. (1995) Post Traumatic Stress Disorders in a Female Prison Population. Examination for Membership, Dissertation for Part 2, Royal Australian and New Zealand College of Psychiatrists.

Ramanathan, C. and Link, R. (1999) *All Our Futures: Principles and Resources for Social Work Practice in a Global Era*, Brooks Cole, Belmont, CA.

Rando, T. (1993) *Treatment of Complicated Mourning*, Research Press, Champaign, Illinois.

Raphael, B. (2000) 'Grief and loss in Australian society', *Death and Dying in Australia*, ed. A. Kellehear, Oxford University Press, Melbourne.

Reamer, F. (1987) 'Values and ethics', *Encyclopaedia of Social Work: Vol. 2*, 18th edn, ed. A. Minahan, National Association of Social Workers, Silver Spring, MD, pp. 801–9.

Rees, S. (1991) *Achieving Power: Practice and Policy in Social Welfare*, Allen & Unwin, Sydney.

Reich, W. (1972) *Sex-Pol Essays: 1929–1934*, Vintage Books, New York.

Reid, J. and Lupton, D. (1991) 'Introduction', *The Health of Aboriginal Australia*, eds J. Reid and P. Trompf, Harcourt Brace Jovanovich, Sydney.

Rein, M. (1970) *Social Policy: Issues of Choice and Change*, Random House, New York.

Rein, M. and White, S. (1981) 'Knowledge for practice', *Social Service Review*, vol. 55, no. 1, pp. 1–41.

Reisch, M., and Ephros, P. (1983) 'Worker and agency in textbooks: Images of which reality?', *Social Casework*, vol. 64, no. 7, pp. 294–405.

Reynolds, B. (1963) *An Uncharted Journey*, NASW Press, Silver Spring, MD.

Reynolds, H. (1993) *The Whispering in Our Hearts*, Allen & Unwin, Sydney.

—— (1997) 'Racism and other discourses', *The Resurgence of Racism: Howard, Hanson and the Race Debate*, eds G. Gray and C. Winter, Monash Publications in History, Melbourne.

Richards, T. (2001) 'Spiritual resources following a partner's death from AIDS', *Meaning Reconstruction and the Experience of Loss*, ed. R. Neimeyer, American Psychological Association, Washington DC.

Ritzer, G. (1997) *Postmodern Social Theory*, McGraw-Hill, New York.

Roberts, D., Jeffery, H. and Roberts J. (2001) Stronger Families. Paper presented at the 27th Australian Association of Social Workers National Conference, Melbourne 23–26 September.

Rogers, R. (2001) Submission to Victoria's Homelessness Strategy: SAAP and Accompanying Children. Centre for Community Health, Royal Children's Hospital, Melbourne.

Rojek, C., Peacock, G. and Collins, S. (1988) *Social Work and Received Ideas*, Routledge, London.

Rosanvallon, P. (1988) 'Beyond the welfare state', *Politics and Society*, vol. 16, no. 4, 533–554.

Rose, D. B. (1997) 'Dark times and excluded bodies', *The Resurgence of Racism: Howard, Hanson and the Race Debate*, eds G. Gray and C. Winter, Monash Publications in History, Melbourne.

Rosenau, P. (1992) *Post-Modernism and the Social Sciences*, Princeton University Press, Princeton.

—— (1995) 'Affirmatives and skeptics', *The Truth About the Truth: De Confusing and Re-Constructing the Postmodern World*, ed. W. Anderson, Jeremy P. Tarcher/Putnam, New York.

Rosenblatt, P. (1997) 'Grief in small scale societies', *Death and Bereavement Across Cultures*, eds C. Parkes, P. Launganii and B. Young, Routledge, London.

Rosenblatt, P. and Tubbs, C. (1998) 'Loss in the experience of multiracial couples', *Perspectives on Loss: A Sourcebook*, ed. J. Harvey, Brunner/Mazel, Philadelphia.

Rossiter, A. (1996) 'A perspective on critical social work', *Journal of Progressive Human Services*, vol 7, no 2, pp. 23–41.

Rowan, J. (1997) *Healing the Male Psyche: Therapy as Initiation*, Routledge, London.

Rowley, C. D. (1970) *The Destruction of Aboriginal Society: Aboriginal Policy and Practice*, vol. 1, ANU Press, Canberra.

Russell, G. (1998) 'Reaching fathers through the corporate world', *National Forum on Men and Family Relationships*, Commonwealth Department of Family and Community Services, Canberra.

Russell, M. (1995) *Confronting Abusive Beliefs: Group Treatment for Abusive Men*, Sage, Thousand Oaks, CA.

Rutherford, A. (1997) 'Women, sentencing and prisons', *New Law Journal*, vol. 21, pp. 424-5.

Ryan, A. (2000) *A Silent Love: Personal Stories of Coming to Terms with Miscarriage*, Penguin Books, Ringwood.

Sachs, W. ed. (1992) *The Development Dictionary: A Guide to Knowledge as Power*, Zed Books, London.

—— (1995) 'Global Ecology and the Shadow of "Development" ', *Deep Ecology for the 21st Century*, ed. G. Sessions, Shambala, Boston.

Sadowski, C. (2001) Working Collaboratively to Develop Strategies to Address the Parenting and Family Needs of Newly Emerging Communities in Melbourne. Paper presented at the 27th Australian Association of Social Worker National Conference, Melbourne, 23-26 September.

Said, E. (1993) *Culture and Imperialism,* Vintage, London.

Sainsbury, D. ed. (1994) *Gendering Welfare States*, Sage, London.

—— (1996) *Gender, Equality and Welfare States*, Cambridge University Press, Cambridge.

—— ed. (1999) *Gender and Welfare State Regimes*, Oxford University Press, Oxford.

Saleebey, D. (1997) *The Strengths Perspective in Social Work Practice*, 2nd edn, Longman, New York.

Saltau, C. (2001) 'Most mothers favour home life for infants', *The Age*, 1 October, p. 1.

Sam, M. (1992) *Through Black Eyes: A Handbook of Family Violence in Aboriginal and Torres Strait Islander Communities*, 2nd edn, SNAICC, Melbourne.

Sattel, J. (1976) 'The inexpressive male: Tragedy or sexual politics', *Men's Lives*, eds M. Kimmel and M. Messner, Macmillan, New York.

Sattem, L., Savells, J. and Murray, E. (1984) 'Sex role stereotypes and commitment to rape', *Sex Roles*, vol. 11, nos. 9/10, pp. 849-60.

Satyamurti, C. (1981) *Occupational Survival*, Basil Blackwell, Oxford.

Saxon, R. and Emslie, A. (1998) *Women's Health Consultation: Final Report*, The Health Development Group, Melbourne.

Schacht, S. and Atkinson, P. (1992) 'Heterosexual instrumentalism: Past and future directions', *Feminism and Psychology*, vol. 2, no. 3, pp. 37-53.

Schaffer, K. (1990) *Women and the Bush: Forces of Desire in the Australian Cultural Tradition*, Cambridge University Press, Cambridge.

Scheff, T. J. (1966) *Being Mentally Ill: A Sociological Theory*, Aldine, Chicago.

Scheyvens, R. and Leslie, H. (2000) 'Gender, ethics and empowerment: Dilemmas of development fieldwork', *Women's Studies International Forum*, vol. 23, no. 1, pp. 119-30.

Schut, H., Stroebe, M., van den Bout, J. and de Keijser, J. (1997) 'Gender differences in the efficacy of grief counselling', *British Journal of Clinical Psychology*, vol. 36, pp. 63-72.

Scull, A. (1979) *Museums of Madness: The Social Organisation of Insanity in Nineteenth Century England*, Allen Lane, London.

Secretariat of National Aboriginal and Islander Child Care (2001) *Newsletter*, August.

Segal, L. (1990) *Slow Motion: Changing Masculinities, Changing Men*, Virago, London.

Seidman, S. (1994) *Contested Knowledge: Social Theory in the Postmodern Era,* Blackwell, Cambridge, Mass.

Sen, A. (2001) 'A global gaze declares free markets "not the enemy" ', *The Age*, 16 May, p. 17.

Sennett, R. (1998) *The Corrosion of Character*, W. W. Norton & Company, New York.

Seve, L. (1978) *Man in Marxist Theory and the Psychology of Personality*, Harvester Press, Brighton.

Shapiro, E. (1994) *Grief as a Family Process: A Developmental Approach to Clinical Practice*, Guilford Press, New York.

—— (1996) 'Family bereavement and cultural diversity: A social developmental model', *Family Process*, vol. 35, no. 4, pp. 313-32.

Shaver, S. (2001) 'From the Director', *Social Policy Research Centre Newsletter*, no. 79, May, SPRC, University of New South Wales, Sydney.

Sheppard, M. (1991) 'General practice, social work and mental health sections: The social control of women', *British Journal of Social Work*, vol. 21, pp. 663-83.

Shor, I. (1980) *Critical Teaching and Everyday Life*, Southend Press, Boston.

Showalter, E. (1987) *The Female Malady: Women, Madness and English Culture, 1838-1980*, Virago, London.

Sibeon, R. (1991) *Towards a New Sociology of Social Work*, Avebury, Aldershot.

Silverman, P. (1986) *Widow-to-Widow*, Springer, New York.

Silverman, P. and Klass, D. (1996) 'Introduction: What's the problem?', *Continuing Bonds: New Understandings of Grief*, eds D. Klass, P. Silverman and S. Nickman, Taylor & Francis, Philadelphia.

Silverstein, O. and Rashbaum, B. (1994) *The Courage to Raise Good Men*, Viking, New York.

Singer, M., Bussey, J., Song, L. and Lunghofer, L. (1995) 'The psychosocial issues of women serving time in jail', *Social Work*, vol. 40, no.1, pp. 103-13.

Sisters Inside (1994) 'Supporting the women behind the walls', *Inside Out*, Brisbane, December.

Sloan, T. (1996) *Damaged Life: The Crisis of the Modern Psyche*, Routledge, London.

—— (1997) 'Theories of personality: Ideology and beyond', *Critical Psychology: An Introduction*, eds D. Fox and I. Prilleltensky, Sage, London.

Small, N. (2001) 'Theories of grief: A critical review', *Grief, Mourning and Death Ritual*, eds J. Hockey, J. Katz and N. Small, Open University Press, Buckingham.

Smith, L. T. (1999) *Decolonizing Methodologies: Research and Indigenous Peoples*, Zed Books, London.

Spears, R. and Parker, I. (1996) 'Marxist theses and psychological themes', *Psychology and Society: Radical Theory and Practice*, eds I. Parker and R. Spears, Pluto Press, London.

Specht, H. and Courtney, M. (1994) *Unfaithful Angels: How Social Work has Abandoned its Mission*, The Free Press, New York.

Speedy, J. (2001) 'Making ourselves up as we go along', *Dulwich Centre Journal*, vol. 1, pp. 43-4.

Stanley, J. and Goddard, C. (1993) 'The effects of child abuse and other family violence in the child protection worker and case management', *Australian Social Work*, vol. 46, no. 3, pp. 3-10.

Staples, R. (1989) 'Masculinity and race: The dual dilemma of black men', *Men's Lives*, eds M. Kimmel and M. Messner, Macmillan, New York.

Statham, D. (1978) *Radicals in Social Work*, Routledge & Kegan Paul, London.

Stevenson, O. (1992) 'Social work intervention to protect children: Aspects of research and practice', *Child Abuse Review*, no. 1, pp. 19-32.

Stoppard, J. M. (1997) 'Women's bodies, women's lives and depression: Towards a reconciliation of material and discursive accounts', *Body Talk: The Material and Discursive Regulation of Sexuality, Madness and Reproduction*, ed. J. M. Ussher, Routledge, London.

Stroebe, M. and Schut, H. (1999) 'The dual process model of coping with bereavement: Rationale and description', *Death Studies*, vol. 23, no. 3, pp. 197-224.

Stroebe, M., Schut, H. and Stroebe, W. (1998) 'Trauma and grief: a comparative analysis', *Perspectives on Loss: A Sourcebook*, ed. J. Harvey, Brunner/Mazel, Philadelphia.

Sturgess, G. (2001) 'Beating the bureaucracy: Humanising modern government',

The Enabling State: People Before Bureaucracy, eds P. Botsman and M. Latham, Pluto Press, Sydney.

Summers, J. (1975) 'Aboriginal policy', *Debate and Decision*, eds D. Gibb and A. Hannan, Heinemann Educational, Melbourne.

Sung Sil Lee Songh (1998) 'Research as an empowerment strategy', *Empowerment in Social Work Practice:A Sourcebook*, eds L. Gutiérrez, R. Parsons and E. Cox, Brooks/Cole, Pacific Grove, CA.

Sutherland, C. (1986) 'Feminist research: A voice of our own', *Gender Reclaimed:Women in Social Work*, eds H. Marchant and B. Wearing, Hale & Iremonger, Sydney.

Szasz, T. S. (1961) *The Myth of Mental Illness*, Hoeber-Rowe, New York.

—— (1963) *Law, Liberty and Psychiatry*, Macmillan, New York.

Taffel, R. (2001) 'The wall of silence', *Psychotherapy Networker*, vol. 25, no. 3, pp. 52–64.

Tatz, C. M. (1979) *Race Politics in Australia*, University of New England Publishing Company, Armidale.

Taylor, J. (1990) *Giving Women Voice*, Brotherhood of St Laurence, Melbourne.

Taylor-Gooby, P. (1993) *Postmodernism and Social Policy: A Great Leap Backwards*, Social Policy Research Centre Discussion Paper No. 45, University of New South Wales, Sydney.

Teplin, L., Abram, K. and McClelland, G. (1996) 'Prevalence of psychiatric disorders among incarcerated women', *Archives of General Psychiatry*, vol. 53, pp. 505–19.

—— (1997) 'Mentally disordered women in jail: who receives services?', *American Journal of Public Health*, vol. 87, pp. 604–9.

Thompson, N. (1992) *Existentialism and Social Work*, Avebury, Aldershot.

—— (1995) 'Men and anti-sexism', *British Journal of Social Work*, vol. 25, pp. 459–75.

—— (1997) *Anti-Discriminatory Practice*, Macmillan, London.

—— (1998) *Promoting Equality: Challenging Discrimination and Oppression in the Human Services*, Macmillan, London.

—— (2000) *Theory and Practice in Human Services*, Open University Press, Buckingham.

Thorne-Finch, R. (1992) *Ending the Silence: The Origins and Treatment of Male Violence Against Women*, University of Toronto Press, Toronto.

Thorpe, D. (1994) *Evaluating Child Protection*, Open University Press, Buckingham.

Throssell, H. ed. (1975) *Social Work: Radical Essays*, University of Queensland Press, St Lucia.

Tolman, R., Mowry, D., Jones, L. and Brekke, J. (1986) 'Developing a profeminist commitment among men in social work', *Feminist Visions for Social Work*, eds N. Van Den Bergh and L. Cooper, National Association of Social Workers, New York.

Tolson, A. (1977) *The Limits of Masculinity*, Tavistock, London.

Turner, A. (1994) 'Genetic and hormonal influences on male violence', *Male Violence*, ed. J. Archer, Routledge, London.

United Nations and Centre for Human Rights and IFSW and IASSW (1992) *Teaching and Learning about Human Rights*, UN Centre for Human Rights, Geneva and New York.

Ussher, J. M. ed. (1997) *Body Talk: The Material and Discursive Regulation of Sexuality, Madness and Reproduction*, Routledge, London.

Van Den Burgh, N. (1995) *Feminist Practice in the Twenty-First Century*, NASW Press, Washington, DC.

Van Den Burgh, N. and Cooper, L. eds (1986) *Feminist Visions for Social Work*, NASW, Silver Springs, MD.

Van Krieken, R. (1992) *Children and the State: Social Control and the Formation of Australian Child Welfare*, Allen & Unwin, Sydney.

Vasta, E. and Castles, S. (1996) *The Teeth are Smiling: The Persistence of Racism in Multicultural Australia*, Allen & Unwin, Sydney.

Verhelst, T. (1990) *No Life Without Roots*, Zed Books, London.

Wadsworth, Y. (2001) *The Essential U & I*, Vic Health, Melbourne.

Wagner, D. (1989) 'Radical movements in the social services: A theoretical framework', *Social Service Review*, June, pp. 264–84.

Walby, S. (1992) 'Post-post-modernism? Theorising social complexity', *Destabilising Theory: Contemporary Feminist Debates*, eds M. Barrett and A. Phillips, Stanford University Press, Stanford, CA.

Waldegrave, C. (1990) 'Just Therapy', *Dulwich Centre Newsletter*, no. 1, pp. 5–47.

Waldegrave, C. and Stephens, B. (2000) Poverty: The Litmus Test of Social and Economic Policy Failure. Paper presented at the Second Biennial Aotearoa New Zealand International Development Studies Network (DEVNET) Conference, 18 November.

Walker, G. (1990) *Family Violence and the Women's Movement: The Conceptual Politics of Struggle*, University of Toronto Press, Toronto.

Wallerstein, I. (1995) 'The insurmountable contradictions of liberalism: Human rights and the rights of peoples in the geoculture of the modern world-system', *The South Atlantic Quarterly*, vol. 94, no. 4, pp. 1161–78.

Walter, T. (1996) 'A new model of grief: Bereavement and biography', *Mortality*, vol. 1, no. 1, pp. 7–25.

—— (1999) *On Bereavement: The Culture of Grief*, Open University Press, Buckingham.

Ward, J. (2000) 'Queer sexism: Rethinking gay men and masculinity', *Gay Masculinities*, ed. P. Nardi, Sage, Thousand Oaks, CA.

Waring, M. (1988) *If Women hunted: A New Feminist Economics*, Harper Collins, New York.

Wearing, B. (1986) 'Feminist theory in social work', *Gender Reclaimed: Women in Social Work*, eds H. Marchant and B. Wearing, Hale & Iremonger, Sydney.

Webb, D. (1985) 'Social work and critical consciousness: Rebuilding orthodoxy', *Issues in Social Work Education*, vol. 5, no. 2, pp 124-39.

Webster, M. (2001) Personal communication. Good Shepherd Youth and Family Services, Collingwood, Melbourne, 20 September.

Weeks, W. (1994) *Women Working Together: Lessons From Feminist Women's Services*, Longman Cheshire, Melbourne.

—— (1998) 'Sites of women's citizenship? Australian women-specific services', *Women Against Violence: An Australian Feminist Journal*, no. 5, pp. 4-14.

—— (2000) 'Reflections on social work and human service theory and practice with families and communities', *Issues Facing Australian Families*, 3rd edn, eds W. Weeks and M. Quinn, Longman, Sydney.

—— (2001) 'Hard-won survival: Women-specific services in Victoria', *Just Policy*, no. 21, March, pp. 37-45.

Weick, K. E. (1995) *Sensemaking in Organisations*, Sage, Thousand Oaks, CA.

Weiss, L. (1998) *The Myth of the Powerless State*, Polity Press, Cambridge.

Were, T. (1998) 'Huon men's health project: Health promotion in the workplace', *Conference Proceedings: Second National Men's Health Conference 1997*, ed. A. Huggins, Commonwealth Department of Health and Community Services, Canberra.

Wharf, B. (1990a) 'Introduction', *Social Work and Social Change in Canada*, ed. B. Wharf, McClelland & Stuart, Toronto.

—— (1990b) 'Lessons from the social movements', *Social Work and Social Change in Canada*, ed. B. Wharf, McClelland & Stuart, Toronto.

White, M. (1988) 'Saying hullo again: The incorporation of the lost relationship in the resolution of grief', *Dulwich Centre Newsletter*, Spring, pp. 7-11.

—— (1992) 'Deconstruction and therapy', *Experience, Contradictions, Narratives and Imagination*, eds D. Epston and M. White, Dulwich Centre Publications, Adelaide.

—— (1993) 'Deconstruction and therapy', *Therapeutic Conversations*, eds S. Gilligan and R. Price, Norton, New York.

White, M. and Epston, D. (1989) *Literate Means to Therapeutic Ends*, Dulwich Centre Publications, Adelaide.

—— (1990) *Narrative Means to Therapeutic Ends*, Norton, New York.

Williams, F. (1996) 'Postmodernism, feminism and the question of difference',

Social Theory, Social Change and Social Work, ed. N. Parton, Routledge, London.

Wilson, E. (1977) *Women and the Welfare State*, Tavistock, London.

Wilson, J. and Leasure, R. (1991) 'Cruel and unusual punishment: The health care of women in prison', *Health Care Issues*, vol. 16, no. 2, pp. 32–8.

Wineman, S. (1984) *The Politics of Human Services*, South End Press, Boston.

Wingard, B. (2001a) 'Finding our own ways to grieve, to remember and to heal', *Telling Our Stories in Ways that Make Us Stronger*, eds B. Wingard and J. Lester, Dulwich Centre, Adelaide.

—— (2001b) 'Grief: Remember, reflect, reveal', *Telling Our Stories in Ways that Make Us Stronger*, eds B. Wingard and J. Lester, Dulwich Centre, Adelaide.

Wingard, B. and Lester, J. eds (2001) *Telling Our Stories in Ways that Make Us Stronger*, Dulwich Centre, Adelaide.

Wolfenstein, V. (1993) *Psychoanalytic Marxism: Groundwork*, Guildford Press, New York.

Wood, A. (1996) 'The origins of family work: The theory and practice of family social work since 1880', *Australian and New Zealand Journal of Family Therapy*, vol. 17, no. 1, pp. 19-32.

—— (2001) 'The origins of family systems work: Social workers' contributions to the development of family theory and practice', *Australian Social Work*, vol. 54, no. 3, pp. 15-30.

Woodroofe, K. (1974) *From Charity to Social Work in England and the United States,* Routledge & Kegan Paul, London.

Worden, W. (1991) *Grief Counselling and Grief Therapy*, 2nd edn, Springer, New York.

Wortman, C. and Silver, R. (1989) 'The myths of coping with loss', *Journal of Consulting and Clinical Psychology*, vol. 57, no. 3, pp. 349-57.

—— (2001) 'The myths of coping with loss revisited', *Handbook of Bereavement Research: Consequences, Coping, and Care*, eds M. Stroebe, R. Hansson, W. Stroebe and H. Schut, American Psychological Association, Washington DC.

Yeatman, A. (1993) 'Voice and the representation of difference', *Feminism and the Politics of Differences*, eds A. Yeatman and S. Gunew, Allen & Unwin, Sydney.

—— (1994) *Postmodern Revisionings of the Political*, Routledge, London.

—— (1998) 'Introduction', *Activism and the Policy Proces*, ed. A. Yeatman, Allen & Unwin, Sydney.

Yellowly, M. (1990) *Social Work Theory and Psychoanalysis*, Von Nostrand, London.

Young, I. (1990) *Justice and the Politics of Difference*, Princeton University Press, Princeton, New Jersey.

—— (1994) 'Polity and group difference: A critique of the ideal of universal citizenship', *Citizenship: Critical Concepts*, eds B. S. Turner and P. Hamilton, Routledge, London.

INDEX